AF753835

IRAN

ARMED FORCES WEAPON SYSTEMS HANDBOOK

VOLUME 1

STRATEGIC INFORMATION AND WEAPON SYSTEMS

International Business Publications, USA
Washington DC, USA

IRAN

ARMED FORCES WEAPON SYSTEMS HANDBOOK

VOLUME 1 STRATEGIC INFORMATION AND WEAPON SYSTEMS

UPDATED ANNUALLY

We express our sincere appreciation to all government agencies and international organizations which provided information and other materials for this handbook

Cover Design: **International Business Publications, USA**

International Business Publications, USA. ***has used its best efforts in collecting, analyzing and preparing data, information and materials for this unique handbook. Due to the dynamic nature and fast development of the economy and business environment, we cannot warrant that all information herein is complete and accurate. IBP does not assume and hereby disclaim any liability to any person for any loss or damage caused by possible errors or omissions in the handbook.***

This handbook is for individual use only. Use this handbook for any other purpose, included but not limited to reproducing and storing in a retrieval system by any means, electronic, photocopying or using the addresses or other information contained in this handbook for any commercial purposes requires a special written permission from the publisher.

2018 Edition Updated Reprint International Business Publications, USA
ISBN 1-4387-2383-0

For additional analytical, business and investment opportunities information,
please contact Global Investment & Business Center, USA
at (703) 370-8082. Fax: (703) 370-8083. E-mail: ibpusa3@gmail.com
Global Business and Investment Info Databank - www.ibpus.com

Printed in the USA

For additional analytical, business and investment opportunities information,
please contact Global Investment & Business Center, USA
at (703) 370-8082. Fax: (703) 370-8083. E-mail: ibpusa3@gmail.com
Global Business and Investment Info Databank - www.ibpus.com

IRAN
ARMED FORCES WEAPON SYSTEMS HANDBOOK
VOLUME 1
STRATEGIC INFORMATION AND WEAPON SYSTEMS

TABLE OF CONTENTS

For additional analytical, business and investment opportunities information, please contact Global Investment & Business Center, USA at (703) 370-8082. Fax: (703) 370-8083. E-mail: ibpusa3@gmail.com Global Business and Investment Info Databank - www.ibpus.com

For additional analytical, business and investment opportunities information, please contact Global Investment & Business Center, USA at (703) 370-8082. Fax: (703) 370-8083. E-mail: ibpusa3@gmail.com
Global Business and Investment Info Databank - www.ibpus.com

STRATEGIC AND DEVELOPEMENT PROFILES

BASIC PROFILE

Capital and largest city	Tehran 35°41′N 51°25′E
Official languages	Persian
Spoken languages	Persian Azerbaijani Kurdish Lurish Gilaki Balochi Mazandarani Arabic Turkmen Armenian Georgian
Religion	Shia Islam(official)
Demonym	Iranian
Government	Islamic republic
- Supreme Leader	Ali Khamenei
- President	Hassan Rouhani
Legislature	Islamic Consultative Assembly
Unification	
- Median Empire	625 BCE
- Achaemenid Empire	550 BCE
- Sassanid Empire	224
- Safavid Empire	1501
- Islamic Republic	1 April 1979
- Current constitution	24 October 1979
- Constitution amendment	28 July 1989
Area	
- Total	1,648,195 km^2 (18th) 636,372 sq mi
- Water (%)	0.7
Population	

For additional analytical, business and investment opportunities information,
please contact Global Investment & Business Center, USA
at (703) 370-8082. Fax: (703) 370-8083. E-mail: ibpusa3@gmail.com
Global Business and Investment Info Databank - www.ibpus.com

- 2013 census	77,176,930 (17th)
- Density	48/km^2 (162rd) 124/sq mi
GDP (PPP)	2013 estimate
- Total	▼ $999.199 billion(18th)
- Per capita	$12,803
GDP (nominal)	2013 estimate
- Total	▲ $548.895 billion
- Per capita	$5,039
Gini	0.38 low
HDI (2013)	▲ 0.742 high · 76th
Currency	Rial (ریال) (IRR)
Time zone	IRST (UTC+3:30)
- Summer (DST)	IRDT (UTC+4:30)
Date format	yyyy/mm/dd (SH)
Drives on the	right
Calling code	+98
ISO 3166 code	IR
Internet TLD	.ir

IRAN: STRATEGIC INFORMATION

Iran officially the **Islamic Republic of Iran** is a country in Western Asia. The name *Iran* has been in use natively since antiquity and came into international use in 1935, before which the country was widely known as **Persia**. Both *Persia* and *Iran* are used interchangeably in cultural contexts; however, *Iran* is the name used officially in political contexts. The name *Iran* is a cognate of *Aryan*, and means "Land of the Aryans".

The 18th largest country in the world in terms of area at 1,648,195 km², Iran has a population of over 70 million. It is a country of particular geostrategic significance owing to its location in the Middle East and central Eurasia. Iran is bordered on the north by Armenia, Azerbaijan and Turkmenistan. As Iran is a littoral state of the Caspian Sea, which is an inland sea and condominium, Kazakhstan and Russia are also Iran's direct neighbors to the north. Iran is bordered on the east by Afghanistan and Pakistan, on the south by the Persian Gulf and the Gulf of Oman, on the west by Iraq and on the northwest by Turkey. Tehran is the capital, the country's largest city and the political, cultural, commercial and industrial center of the nation. Iran is a regional power, and holds an important position in international energy security and world economy as a result of its large reserves of petroleum and natural gas.

Iran is home to one of the world's oldest continuous major civilizations. The first Iranian dynasty formed during the Elamite kingdom in 2800 BCE. The Iranian Medes unified Iran into an empire in 625 BCE. They were succeeded by the Iranian Achaemenid Empire, the Hellenic Seleucid Empire and two subsequent Iranian empires, the Parthians and the Sassanids, before the Muslim conquest in 651 CE. Iranian post-Islamic dynasties and empires expanded the Persian language and culture throughout the Iranian plateau. Early Iranian dynasties which re-asserted Iranian independence included the Tahirids, Saffarids, Samanids and Buyids.

The blossoming of Persian literature, philosophy, medicine, astronomy, mathematics and art became major elements of Muslim civilization and started with the Saffarids and Samanids. Iran was once again reunified as an independent state in 1501 by the Safavid dynasty—who promoted Twelver Shi'a Islam as the official religion of their empire, marking one of the most important turning points in the history of Islam. "Persia's Constitutional Revolution" established the nation's first parliament in 1906, within a constitutional monarchy. Iran officially became an Islamic republic on 1 April 1979, following the Iranian Revolution.

Iran is a founding member of the UN, NAM, OIC and OPEC. The political system of Iran, based on the 1979 constitution, comprises several intricately connected governing bodies. The highest state authority is the Supreme Leader. Shia Islam is the official religion and Persian is the official language

COUNTRY OVERVIEW

Islamic Republic Proclaimed: April 1, 1979
Population : 66.5 million
Location/Size: Middle East - between the Persian Gulf and the Caspian Sea/636,296 square miles
Major Cities: Tehran (capital), Meshed, Isfahan, Tabriz, Shiraz, Ahwaz, Kermanshah, Qom, Ardebil, Qazvin
Languages: Persian and Persian dialects (58%), Turkic and Turkic dialects (26%), Kurdish (9%), Luri (2%), Baluch (1%), Arabic (1%), Turkish (1%), other (2%)
Ethnic Groups: Persian (51%), Azerbaijani (24%), Gilaki and Mazandarani (8%), Kurd (7%), Arab (3%), Lur (2%), Baluch (2%), Turkmen (2%), other (1%)
Religion: Shi'a Muslim (89%), Sunni Muslim (10%), Zoroastrian, Jewish, Christian, and Baha'i (1%)
Defense: Army (350,000), Revolutionary Guard (120,000), Navy (18,000), Air Force (30,000), army reserves (350,000)

The Iranian government has made debt reduction one of its top priorities. Iran was forced to reschedule much of its foreign debt in 1 992. Since then, it has been diligently paying off what it owes, in an effort to improve access to longer-term financing. As a result, Iranian letters of credit are much better received now than they were two years ago.

The economy is centrally planned, relying heavily on five-year plans. However, the government is taking measured steps toward its espoused goals of economic liberalization and inflation-fighting. Iran's chief source of foreign currency is the sale of oil and gas; as a result, the health of its economy depends upon prices for those commodities and on the size of its oil quotas under OPEC.

Currency: Rial (R)
Exchange Rates: rials per US dollar - 8,964 (2005), 8,614 (2004), 8,193.9 (2003), 6,907 (2002), 1,753.6 (2001)
note: Iran has been using a managed floating exchange rate regime since unifying multiple exchange rates in March 2002
Real Gross Domestic Product (GDP): $200.5 billion
Real GDP Growth Rate : -1%
Inflation Rate : 14.2%
Current Account Balance : $0.91 billion
Major Trading Partners: Germany, Italy, Japan, France, Turkey, United Kingdom, Netherlands,
Spain
Merchandise Exports : $15.14 billion
Merchandise Imports : $12.71 billion
Major Export Products: Petroleum and related products, carpets, pistachios
Major Import Products: Machinery, military equipment, metals, foodstuffs, pharmaceuticals, refined
oil products, technical services
Oil Export Revenues: $10.2 billion
Oil Export Revenues/Total Export Revenues: 80%-85%
Total External Debt (1998E): $18.8 billion

GEOGRAPHY

Location: Middle East, bordering the Gulf of Oman, the Persian Gulf, and the Caspian Sea, between Iraq and Pakistan
Geographic coordinates: 32 00 N, 53 00 E
Map references: Middle East

Area:
total: 1.648 million sq km
land: 1.636 million sq km
water: 12,000 sq km

Area—comparative: slightly larger than Alaska

Land boundaries:
total: 5,440 km
border countries: Afghanistan 936 km, Armenia 35 km, Azerbaijan-proper 432 km, Azerbaijan-Naxcivan exclave 179 km, Iraq 1,458 km, Pakistan 909 km, Turkey 499 km, Turkmenistan 992 km

For additional analytical, business and investment opportunities information, please contact Global Investment & Business Center, USA at (703) 370-8082. Fax: (703) 370-8083. E-mail: ibpusa3@gmail.com Global Business and Investment Info Databank - www.ibpus.com

Base 802511 (R01078) 9-96

Coastline: 2,440 km
note: Iran also borders the Caspian Sea (740 km)

Maritime claims:
contiguous zone: 24 nm
continental shelf: natural prolongation
exclusive economic zone: bilateral agreements, or median lines in the Persian Gulf
territorial sea: 12 nm

Climate: mostly arid or semiarid, subtropical along Caspian coast

Terrain: rugged, mountainous rim; high, central basin with deserts, mountains; small, discontinuous plains along both coasts

Elevation extremes:
lowest point: Caspian Sea -28 m
highest point: Qolleh-ye Damavand 5,671 m

Natural resources: petroleum, natural gas, coal, chromium, copper, iron ore, lead, manganese, zinc, sulfur

Land use:
arable land: 10%
permanent crops: 1%
permanent pastures: 27%
forests and woodland: 7%
other: 55%

Irrigated land: 94,000 sq km

Natural hazards: periodic droughts, floods; dust storms, sandstorms; earthquakes along western border and in the northeast

Environment—current issues: air pollution, especially in urban areas, from vehicle emissions, refinery operations, and industrial effluents; deforestation; overgrazing; desertification; oil pollution in the Persian Gulf; inadequate supplies of potable water

Environment—international agreements:
party to: Biodiversity, Climate Change, Desertification, Endangered Species, Hazardous Wastes, Marine Dumping, Nuclear Test Ban, Ozone Layer Protection, Wetlands
signed, but not ratified: Environmental Modification, Law of the Sea, Marine Life Conservation

PEOPLE

Population: 65,179,752

For additional analytical, business and investment opportunities information, please contact Global Investment & Business Center, USA at (703) 370-8082. Fax: (703) 370-8083. E-mail: ibpusa3@gmail.com
Global Business and Investment Info Databank - www.ibpus.com

Age structure:
0-14 years: 36% (male 11,963,438; female 11,447,191)
15-64 years: 60% (male 19,549,935; female 19,276,784)
65 years and over: 4% (male 1,561,877; female 1,380,527)

Population growth rate: 1.07%
Birth rate: 20.71 births/1,000 population
Death rate: 5.39 deaths/1,000 population

Net migration rate: -4.6 migrant(s)/1,000 population

Sex ratio:
at birth: 1.05 male(s)/female
under 15 years: 1.05 male(s)/female
15-64 years: 1.01 male(s)/female
65 years and over: 1.13 male(s)/female
total population: 1.03 male(s)/female

Infant mortality rate: 29.73 deaths/1,000 live births

Life expectancy at birth:
total population: 69.76 years
male: 68.43 years
female: 71.16 years

Total fertility rate: 2.45 children born/woman

Nationality:
noun: Iranian(s)
adjective: Iranian

Ethnic groups: Persian 51%, Azerbaijani 24%, Gilaki and Mazandarani 8%, Kurd 7%, Arab 3%, Lur 2%, Baloch 2%, Turkmen 2%, other 1%
Religions: Shi'a Muslim 89%, Sunni Muslim 10%, Zoroastrian, Jewish, Christian, and Baha'i 1%
Languages: Persian and Persian dialects 58%, Turkic and Turkic dialects 26%, Kurdish 9%, Luri 2%, Balochi 1%, Arabic 1%, Turkish 1%, other 2%

Literacy:
definition: age 15 and over can read and write
total population: 72.1%
male: 78.4%
female: 65.8% (1994 est.)

GOVERNMENT

Government ::Iran
Country name:

For additional analytical, business and investment opportunities information, please contact Global Investment & Business Center, USA at (703) 370-8082. Fax: (703) 370-8083. E-mail: ibpusa3@gmail.com Global Business and Investment Info Databank - www.ibpus.com

conventional long form: Islamic Republic of Iran
conventional short form: Iran
local long form: Jomhuri-ye Eslami-ye Iran
local short form: Iran
former: Persia

Government type:
theocratic republic

Capital:
name: Tehran
geographic coordinates: 35 40 N, 51 25 E
time difference: UTC+3.5 (8.5 hours ahead of Washington, DC during Standard Time)

Administrative divisions:
30 provinces (ostanha, singular - ostan); Ardabil, Azarbayjan-e Gharbi, Azarbayjan-e Sharqi, Bushehr, Chahar Mahal va Bakhtiari, Esfahan, Fars, Gilan, Golestan, Hamadan, Hormozgan, Ilam, Kerman, Kermanshah, Khorasan-e Jonubi, Khorasan-e Razavi, Khorasan-e Shomali, Khuzestan, Kohgiluyeh va Bowyer Ahmad, Kordestan, Lorestan, Markazi, Mazandaran, Qazvin, Qom, Semnan, Sistan va Baluchestan, Tehran, Yazd, Zanjan

Independence:
1 April 1979 (Islamic Republic of Iran proclaimed)

National holiday:
Republic Day, 1 April (1979)

Constitution:
2-3 December 1979; revised in 1989
note: the revision in 1989 expanded powers of the presidency and eliminated the prime ministership

Legal system:
based on sharia law system; has not accepted compulsory ICJ jurisdiction

Suffrage:
18 years of age; universal

Executive branch:

chief of state: Supreme Leader Ali Hoseini-KHAMENEI (since 4 June 1989)

head of government: President Hasan Fereidun RUHANI (since 3 August 2013); First Vice President Mohammad Reza RAHIMI (since 13 September 2009)

cabinet: Council of Ministers selected by the president with legislative approval; the Supreme Leader has some control over appointments to the more sensitive ministries

For additional analytical, business and investment opportunities information, please contact Global Investment & Business Center, USA at (703) 370-8082. Fax: (703) 370-8083. E-mail: ibpusa3@gmail.com Global Business and Investment Info Databank - www.ibpus.com

note:also considered part of the Executive branch of government are three oversight bodies: 1) Assembly of Experts (Majles-e Khoebregan), a popularly elected body charged with determining the succession of the Supreme Leader, reviewing his performance, and deposing him if deemed necessary; 2) Expediency Council or the Council for the Discernment of Expediency (Majma-ye- Tashkhis-e -Maslahat-e- Nezam) exerts supervisory authority over the executive, judicial, and legislative branches and resolves legislative issues when the Majles and the Council of Guardians disagree and since 1989 has been used to advise national religious leaders on matters of national policy; in 2005 the Council's powers were expanded to act as a supervisory body for the government; 3) Council of Guardians of the Constitution or Council of Guardians or Guardians Council (Shora-ye Negban-e Qanon-e Asasi) determines whether proposed legislation is both constitutional and faithful to Islamic law, vets candidates in popular elections for suitability, and supervises national elections

elections: supreme leader appointed for life by the Assembly of Experts; president elected by popular vote for a four-year term (eligible for a second term and additional nonconsecutive term); election last held on 14 June 2013 (next presidential election to be held in June 2017)

election results: Hasan Fereidun RUHANI 50.7%, Mohammad Baqer QALIBAF 16.6%, Saeed JALILI 11.4%, Mohsen REZAI 10.6%, Ali Akber VELAYATI 6.2%, other 4.5%

Legislative branch:
unicameral Islamic Consultative Assembly or Majles-e Shura-ye Eslami or Majles (290 seats; members elected by popular vote from single and multimember districts to serve four-year terms)

elections: last held on 2 March 2012 (first round); second round held on 4 May 2012; (next election to be held in 2016)

election results: percent of vote by party - NA; seats by party - NA

Judicial branch:
The Supreme Court (Qeveh Qazaieh) and the four-member High Council of the Judiciary have a single head and overlapping responsibilities; together they supervise the enforcement of all laws and establish judicial and legal policies; lower courts include a special clerical court, a revolutionary court, and a special administrative court

Political parties and leaders:
formal political parties are a relatively new phenomenon in Iran and most conservatives still prefer to work through political pressure groups rather than parties; often political parties or coalitions are formed prior to elections and disbanded soon thereafter; a loose pro-reform coalition called the 2nd Khordad Front, which includes political parties as well as less formal groups and organizations, achieved considerable success in elections for the sixth Majles in early 2000; groups in the coalition included the Islamic Iran Participation Front (IIPF), Executives of Construction Party (Kargozaran), Solidarity Party, Islamic Labor Party, Mardom Salari, Mojahedin of the Islamic Revolution Organization (MIRO), and Militant Clerics Society (Ruhaniyun); the coalition participated

in the seventh Majles elections in early 2004; following his defeat in the 2005 presidential elections, former MCS Secretary General and sixth Majles Speaker Mehdi KARUBI formed the National Trust Party; a new conservative group, Islamic Iran Developers Coalition (Abadgaran), took a leading position in the new Majles after winning a majority of the seats in February 2004; following the 2004 Majles elections, traditional and hardline conservatives have attempted to close ranks under the United Front of Principlists and the Broad Popular Coalition of Principlists; several reformist groups, such as the Mujahadin of the Islamic Revolution, came together as a reformist coalition in advance of the 2008 Majles elections; the IIPF has repeatedly complained that the overwhelming majority of its candidates have been unfairly disqualified from the 2008 elections

Political pressure groups and leaders:
groups that generally support the Islamic Republic: Ansar-e Hizballah-Islamic Coalition Party (Motalefeh); Followers of the Line of the Imam and the Leader; Islamic Engineers Society; Tehran Militant Clergy Association (Ruhaniyat); active pro-reform student group: Office of Strengthening Unity (OSU); opposition groups: Baluchistan People's Party (BPP); Freedom Movement of Iran; Green Path Movement [Mehdi KARUBI, Mir-Hosein MUSAVI]; Marz-e Por Gohar; National Front; and various ethnic and Monarchist organizations; armed political groups that have been repressed by the government: Democratic Party of Iranian Kurdistan (KDPI); Jundallah; Komala; Mujahedin-e Khalq Organization (MEK or MKO); People's Fedayeen; People's Free Life Party of Kurdistan (PJAK)

International organization participation:
CICA, CP, ECO, FAO, G-15, G-24, G-77, IAEA, IBRD, ICAO, ICC, ICCt (signatory), ICRM, IDA, IDB, IFAD, IFC, IFRCS, IHO, ILO, IMF, IMO, IMSO, Interpol, IOC, IOM, IPU, ISO, ITSO, ITU, MIGA, NAM, OIC, OPCW, OPEC, PCA, SAARC (observer), SCO (observer), UN, UNCTAD, UNESCO, UNHCR, UNIDO, UNITAR, UNMIS, UNWTO, UPU, WCL, WCO, WFTU, WHO, WIPO, WMO, WTO (observer)

Diplomatic representation in the US:
none; note - Iran has an Interests Section in the Pakistani Embassy; address: Iranian Interests Section, Pakistani Embassy, 2209 Wisconsin Avenue NW, Washington, DC 20007; telephone: (202) 965-4990; FAX (202) 965-1073

Diplomatic representation from the US:
none; note - the US Interests Section is located in the Embassy of Switzerland No. 39 Shahid Mousavi (Golestan 5th), Pasdaran Ave., Tehran, Iran; telephone [98] 21 2254 2178/2256 5273; FAX [98] 21 2258 0432

Flag description:
three equal horizontal bands of green (top), white, and red; the national emblem (a stylized representation of the word Allah in the shape of a tulip, a symbol of martyrdom) in red is centered in the white band; ALLAH AKBAR (God is Great) in white Arabic script is repeated 11 times along the bottom edge of the green band and 11 times along the top edge of the red band

ECONOMY

For additional analytical, business and investment opportunities information, please contact Global Investment & Business Center, USA at (703) 370-8082. Fax: (703) 370-8083. E-mail: ibpusa3@gmail.com Global Business and Investment Info Databank - www.ibpus.com

Economy - overview:
Iran's economy is marked by an inefficient state sector, reliance on the oil sector, which provides the majority of government revenues, and statist policies, which create major distortions throughout the system. Most economic activity is controlled by the state. Private sector activity is typically limited to small-scale workshops, farming, and services. Price controls, subsidies, and other rigidities weigh down the economy, undermining the potential for private-sector-led growth. Significant informal market activity flourishes. The legislature recently passed President Mahmud AHMADI-NEJAD's bill to reduce subsidies, particularly on food and energy. The bill would phase out subsidies - which benefit Iran's upper and middle classes the most - over three to five years and replace them with cash payments to Iran's lower classes. This is the most extensive economic reform since the government reduced gasoline subsidies in 2007. However, previous government-led efforts to reform subsidies - such as in the 1990s under former president Hashemi RAFSANJANI - were met with stiff resistance and violent protests. High oil prices in recent years allowed Iran to greatly increase its export earnings and amass nearly $100 billion in foreign exchange reserves.

But with Iran's oil export price from March to December 2009 averaging just $55 per barrel, the Iranian government is facing difficulties. Tehran formulated its 2009 budget to anticipate lower oil prices and has reduced some spending. Although inflation has fallen substantially because of lower oil prices, Iran continues to suffer from double-digit unemployment and underemployment. Underemployment among Iran's educated youth has convinced many to seek jobs overseas, resulting in a significant "brain drain."

GDP (purchasing power parity):
$876 billion (est.)
country comparison to the world: 17
note: data are in 2009 US dollars

GDP (official exchange rate):
$331.8 billion (est.)

GDP - real growth rate:
2.6% (est.)
country comparison to the world: 72
3.5% (est.)
6.5% (est.)

GDP - per capita (PPP):
$12,900 (est.)
country comparison to the world: 85
$13,000 (est.)
$12,300 (est.)
note: data are in 2009 US dollars

GDP - composition by sector:
agriculture: 10.9%
industry: 45.2%

services: 43.9% (est.)

Labor force:
25.02 million
country comparison to the world: 22
note: shortage of skilled labor (est.)

Labor force - by occupation:
agriculture: 25%
industry: 31%
services: 45% (June 2007)

11.8% (est.)
country comparison to the world: 128
10.3% (est.)
note: data are according to the Iranian Government

Population below poverty line:
18% (est.)

Household income or consumption by percentage share:
lowest 10%: 2.6%
highest 10%: 29.6% (2005)

Distribution of family income - Gini index:
44.5 (2006)
country comparison to the world: 46

Investment (gross fixed):
27.7% of GDP (est.)
country comparison to the world: 32

Budget:
revenues: $97.71 billion
expenditures: $84.78 billion (est.)

Public debt:
19.4% of GDP (est.)
country comparison to the world: 104
19.4% of GDP (est.)

Inflation rate (consumer prices):
16.8% (est.)
country comparison to the world: 215
25.6% (est.)
note: official Iranian estimate

Commercial bank prime lending rate:

NA% (31 December 2008)
country comparison to the world: 69
12% (31 December 2007)

Stock of money:
$NA (31 December 2008)
$46.13 billion (31 December 2007)

Stock of quasi money:
$NA (31 December 2008)
$68.71 billion (31 December 2007)

Stock of domestic credit:
$NA (31 December 2008)
$109.7 billion (31 December 2007)

Market value of publicly traded shares:
$NA (31 December 2008)
country comparison to the world: 58
$45.57 billion (31 December 2007)
$37.94 billion (31 December 2006)

Agriculture - products:
wheat, rice, other grains, sugar beets, sugar cane, fruits, nuts, cotton; dairy products, wool; caviar

Industries:
petroleum, petrochemicals, fertilizers, caustic soda, textiles, cement and other construction materials, food processing (particularly sugar refining and vegetable oil production), ferrous and non-ferrous metal fabrication, armaments

Industrial production growth rate:
4% excluding oil (est.)
country comparison to the world: 28

Electricity - production:
192.6 billion kWh (est.)
country comparison to the world: 19

Electricity - consumption:
153.8 billion kWh (est.)
country comparison to the world: 20

Electricity - exports:
2.52 billion kWh (est.)

Electricity - imports:
1.842 billion kWh (est.)

For additional analytical, business and investment opportunities information, please contact Global Investment & Business Center, USA at (703) 370-8082. Fax: (703) 370-8083. E-mail: ibpusa3@gmail.com Global Business and Investment Info Databank - www.ibpus.com

Oil - production:
4.174 million bbl/day (est.)
country comparison to the world: 4

Oil - consumption:
1.755 million bbl/day (est.)
country comparison to the world: 14

Oil - exports:
2.719 million bbl/day (est.)
country comparison to the world: 3

Oil - imports:
212,200 bbl/day (est.)
country comparison to the world: 47

Oil - proved reserves:
136.2 billion bbl based on Iranian claims (1 January 2009 est.)
country comparison to the world: 3

Natural gas - production:
116.3 billion cu m (est.)
country comparison to the world: 5

Natural gas - consumption:
119 billion cu m (est.)
country comparison to the world: 4

Natural gas - exports:
4.246 billion cu m (est.)
country comparison to the world: 28

Natural gas - imports:
6.9 billion cu m (est.)
country comparison to the world: 28

Natural gas - proved reserves:
28.08 trillion cu m (1 January 2009 est.)
country comparison to the world: 2

Current account balance:
$2.249 billion (est.)
country comparison to the world: 35
$20.19 billion (est.)

Exports:
$70.16 billion (est.)

country comparison to the world: 37
$98.42 billion (est.)

Exports - commodities:
petroleum 80%, chemical and petrochemical products, fruits and nuts, carpets

Exports - partners:
China 15.3%, Japan 14.3%, India 10.4%, South Korea 6.4%, Turkey 6.4%, Italy 4.5% (2008)

Imports:
$57.16 billion (est.)
country comparison to the world: 41
$67.25 billion (est.)

Imports - commodities:
industrial raw materials and intermediate goods, capital goods, foodstuffs and other consumer goods, technical services

Imports - partners:
UAE 19.3%, China 13%, Germany 9.2%, South Korea 7%, Italy 5.1%, France 4.3%, Russia 4.2% (2008)

Reserves of foreign exchange and gold:
$81.31 billion (31 December 2009 est.)
country comparison to the world: 14
$96.56 billion (31 December 2008 est.)

Debt - external:
$18.73 billion (31 December 2009 est.)
country comparison to the world: 69
$21.06 billion (31 December 2008 est.)

Stock of direct foreign investment - at home:
$7.854 billion (31 December 2009 est.)
country comparison to the world: 77
$6.954 billion (31 December 2008 est.)

Stock of direct foreign investment - abroad:
$793 million (31 December 2009 est.)
country comparison to the world: 69
$993 million (31 December 2008 est.)

Exchange rates:
Iranian rials (IRR) per US dollar - 9,900 (2009), 9,142.8 (2008), 9,407.5 (2007), 9,227.1 (2006), 8,964 (2005)
note: Iran has been using a managed floating exchange rate regime since unifying multiple exchange rates in March 2002

COMMUNICATIONS

Telephones - main lines in use:	18.986 million
Telephones - mobile cellular:	7.222 million
Telephone system:	*general assessment:* inadequate, but currently being modernized and expanded with the goal of not only improving the efficiency and increasing the volume of the urban service but also bringing telephone service to several thousand villages, not presently connected *domestic:* as a result of heavy investing in the telephone system since 1994, the number of long-distance channels in the microwave radio relay trunk has grown substantially; many villages have been brought into the net; the number of main lines in the urban systems has approximately doubled; thousands of mobile cellular subscribers are being served; moreover, the technical level of the system has been raised by the installation of thousands of digital switches *international:* country code - 98; HF radio and microwave radio relay to Turkey, Azerbaijan, Pakistan, Afghanistan, Turkmenistan, Syria, Kuwait, Tajikistan, and Uzbekistan; submarine fiber-optic cable to UAE with access to Fiber-Optic Link Around the Globe (FLAG); Trans-Asia-Europe (TAE) fiber-optic line runs from Azerbaijan through the northern portion of Iran to Turkmenistan with expansion to Georgia and Azerbaijan; satellite earth stations - 9 Intelsat and 4 Inmarsat
Radio broadcast stations:	AM 72, FM 5, shortwave 5
Television broadcast stations:	28 (plus 450 low-power repeaters)
Internet country code:	.ir
Internet hosts:	5,242
Internet users:	7.5 million

TRANSPORTATION

Railways:
total: 7,286 km
broad gauge: 94 km 1.676-m gauge
standard gauge: 7,192 km 1.435-m gauge (146 km electrified)

Highways:
total: 162,000 km

For additional analytical, business and investment opportunities information, please contact Global Investment & Business Center, USA at (703) 370-8082. Fax: (703) 370-8083. E-mail: ibpusa3@gmail.com Global Business and Investment Info Databank - www.ibpus.com

paved: 81,000 km (including 470 km of expressways)
unpaved: 81,000 km

Waterways: 904 km; the Shatt al Arab is usually navigable by maritime traffic for about 130 km; channel has been dredged to 3 m and is in use

Pipelines: crude oil 5,900 km; petroleum products 3,900 km; natural gas 4,550 km

Ports and harbors: Abadan (largely destroyed in fighting during 1980-88 war), Ahvaz, Bandar 'Abbas, Bandar-e Anzali, Bushehr, Bandar-e Imam Khomeyni, Bandar-e Lengeh, Bandar-e Mahshahr, Bandar-e Torkaman, Chabahar (Bandar Beheshti), Jazireh-ye Khark, Jazireh-ye Lavan, Jazireh-ye Sirri, Khorramshahr (limited operation since November 1992), Now Shahr

Merchant marine:
total: 132 ships (1,000 GRT or over) totaling 3,238,293 GRT/5,658,259 DWT
ships by type: bulk 46, cargo 35, chemical tanker 4, combination bulk 1, container 5, liquefied gas tanker 1, multifunction large-load carrier 6, oil tanker 21, refrigerated cargo 2, roll-on/roll-off cargo 10, short-sea passenger 1

Airports: 288

Airports—with paved runways:
total: 110
over 3,047 m: 38
2,438 to 3,047 m: 18
1,524 to 2,437 m: 25
914 to 1,523 m: 23
under 914 m: 6

Airports—with unpaved runways:
total: 178
over 3,047 m: 1
2,438 to 3,047 m: 5
1,524 to 2,437 m: 14
914 to 1,523 m: 126
under 914 m: 32

Heliports: 11

MILITARY

Military branches:
Islamic Republic of Iran Regular Forces (Artesh): Ground Forces, Navy, Air Force of the Military of the Islamic Republic of Iran (Niru-ye Hava'i-ye Artesh-e Jomhuri-ye Eslami-ye Iran, IRIAF; Islamic Revolutionary Guard Corps (Sepah-e Pasdaran-e Enqelab-e Eslami, IRGC): Ground Forces, Navy, Air Force, Qods Force (special operations), Basij Force (Popular Mobilization Army); Law Enforcement Forces (2008)

For additional analytical, business and investment opportunities information, please contact Global Investment & Business Center, USA at (703) 370-8082. Fax: (703) 370-8083. E-mail: ibpusa3@gmail.com Global Business and Investment Info Databank - www.ibpus.com

Military service age and obligation:
19 years of age for compulsory military service; 16 years of age for volunteers; 17 years of age for Law Enforcement Forces; 15 years of age for Basij Forces (Popular Mobilization Army); conscript military service obligation - 18 months; women exempt from military service (2008)

Manpower available for military service:
males age 16-49: 20,212,275
females age 16-49: 19,638,751 (est.)

Manpower fit for military service:
males age 16-49: 17,658,573
females age 16-49: 17,148,290 (est.)

Manpower reaching militarily significant age annually:
male: 700,213
female: 664,846 (est.)

Military expenditures:
2.5% of GDP (2006)
country comparison to the world: 67

TRANSNATIONAL ISSUES

Disputes—international: Iran and Iraq restored diplomatic relations in 1990 but are still trying to work out written agreements settling outstanding disputes from their eight-year war concerning border demarcation, prisoners-of-war, and freedom of navigation and sovereignty over the Shatt al Arab waterway; Iran occupies two islands in the Persian Gulf claimed by the UAE: Lesser Tunb (called Tunb as Sughra in Arabic by UAE and Jazireh-ye Tonb-e Kuchek in Persian by Iran) and Greater Tunb (called Tunb al Kubra in Arabic by UAE and Jazireh-ye Tonb-e Bozorg in Persian by Iran); it jointly administers with the UAE an island in the Persian Gulf claimed by the UAE (called Abu Musa in Arabic by UAE and Jazireh-ye Abu Musa in Persian by Iran)—over which Iran has taken steps to exert unilateral control since 1992, including access restrictions and a military build-up on the island; the UAE has garnered significant diplomatic support in the region in protesting these Iranian actions; Caspian Sea boundaries are not yet determined among Azerbaijan, Iran, Kazakhstan, Russia, and Turkmenistan

Illicit drugs: despite substantial interdiction efforts, Iran remains a key transshipment point for Southwest Asian heroin to Europe; domestic consumption of narcotics remains a persistent problem and Iranian press reports estimate that there are at least 1.2 million drug users in the country

GEOGRAPHY & LOCATION

Iran is one of the world's most mountainous countries. Its mountains have helped to shape both the political and the economic history of the country for several centuries. The mountains enclose several broad basins, or plateaus, on which major agricultural and urban settlements are located. Until the twentieth century, when major highways and railroads were constructed through the mountains to connect the population centers, these basins tended to be relatively isolated from one another. Typically, one major town dominated each basin, and there were complex economic relationships between the town and the hundreds of villages that surrounded it. In the higher elevations of the mountains rimming the basins, tribally organized groups practiced transhumance, moving with their herds of sheep and goats between traditionally established summer and winter pastures. There are no major river systems in the country, and historically transportation was by means of caravans that followed routes traversing gaps and passes in the mountains. The mountains also impeded easy access to the Persian Gulf and the Caspian Sea.

With an area of 1,648,000 square kilometers, Iran ranks sixteenth in size among the countries of the world. Iran is about one-fifth the size of the continental United States, or slightly larger than the combined area of the contiguous states of California, Arizona, Nevada, Oregon, Washington, and Idaho.

Located in southwestern Asia, Iran shares its entire northern border with the Soviet Union. This border extends for more then 2,000 kilometers, including nearly 650 kilometers of water along the southern shore of the Caspian Sea. Iran's western borders are with Turkey in the north and Iraq in the south, terminating at the Shatt al Arab (which Iranians call the Arvand Rud). The Persian Gulf and Gulf of Oman littorals form the entire 1,770-kilometer southern border. To the east lie Afghanistan on the north and Pakistan on the south. Iran's diagonal distance from Azarbaijan in the northwest to Baluchestan va Sistan in the southeast is approximately 2,333 kilometers.

TOPOGRAPHY

Iran consists of rugged, mountainous rims surrounding high interior basins. The main mountain chain is the Zagros Mountains, a series of parallel ridges interspersed with plains that bisect the country from northwest to southeast. Many peaks in the Zagros exceed 3,000 meters above sea level, and in the south-central region of the country there are at least five peaks that are over 4,000 meters. As the Zagros continue into southeastern Iran, the average elevation of the peaks declines dramatically to under 1,500 meters. Rimming the Caspian Sea littoral is another chain of mountains, the narrow but high Alborz Mountains. Volcanic Mount Damavand (5,600 meters), located in the center of the Alborz, is not only the country's highest peak but also the highest mountain on the Eurasian landmass west of the Hindu Kush

The center of Iran consists of several closed basins that collectively are referred to as the Central Plateau. The average elevation of this plateau is about 900 meters, but several of the mountains that tower over the plateau exceed 3,000 meters. The eastern part of the plateau is covered by two salt deserts, the Dasht-e Kavir and the Dasht-e Lut. Except for some scattered oases, these deserts are uninhabited.

Iran has only two expanses of lowlands: the Khuzestan plain in the southwest and the Caspian Sea coastal plain in the north. The former is a roughly triangular-shaped extension of the Mesopotamia plain and averages about 160 kilometers in width. It extends for about 120 kilometers inland, barely rising a few meters above sea level, then meets abruptly with the first foothills of the Zagros. Much of the Khuzestan plain is covered with marshes. The Caspian plain is both longer and narrower. It extends for some 640 kilometers along the Caspian shore, but its widest point is less than 50 kilometers, while at some places less than 2 kilometers separate the shore from the Alborz foothills. The Persian Gulf coast south of Khuzestan and the Gulf of Oman coast have no real plains because the Zagros in these areas come right down to the shore.

There are no major rivers in the country. Of the small rivers and streams, the only one that is navigable is the Karun, which shallow- draft boats can negotiate from Khorramshahr to Ahvaz, a distance of about 180 kilometers. Several other permanent rivers and streams also drain into the Persian Gulf, while a number of small rivers that originate in the northwestern Zagros or Alborz drain into the Caspian Sea. On the Central Plateau, numerous rivers, most of which have dry beds for the greater part of the year, form from snow melting in the mountains during the spring and flow through permanent channels, draining eventually into salt lakes that also tend to dry up during the summer months. There is a permanent salt lake, Lake Urmia (the traditional name, also cited as Lake Urmiyeh, to which it has reverted after being called Lake Rezaiyeh under Mohammad Reza Shah), in the northwest, whose brine content is too high to support fish or most other forms of aquatic life. There are also several connected salt lakes along the Iran-Afghanistan border in the province of Baluchestan va Sistan.

CLIMATE

Iran has a variable climate. In the northwest, winters are cold with heavy snowfall and subfreezing temperatures during December and January. Spring and fall are relatively mild, while summers are dry and hot. In the south, winters are mild and the summers are very hot, having average daily temperatures in July exceeding 38° C. On the Khuzestan plain, summer heat is accompanied by high humidity.

In general, Iran has an arid climate in which most of the relatively scant annual precipitation falls from October through April. In most of the country, yearly precipitation averages 25 centimeters or less. The major exceptions are the higher mountain valleys of the Zagros and the Caspian coastal plain, where precipitation averages at least 50 centimeters annually. In the western part of the Caspian, rainfall exceeds 100 centimeters annually and is distributed relatively evenly throughout the year. This contrasts with some basins of the Central Plateau that receive ten centimeters or less of precipitation annually.

ADMINISTRATIVE STRUCTURE

On the first level of country subdivisions of Iran are the provinces.

For additional analytical, business and investment opportunities information, please contact Global Investment & Business Center, USA at (703) 370-8082. Fax: (703) 370-8083. E-mail: ibpusa3@gmail.com
Global Business and Investment Info Databank - www.ibpus.com

Each province is further subdivided into counties called shahrestan and each shahrestan is subdivided into districts called bakhsh There are usually a few cities and rural agglomerations in each county. Rural agglomerations are a collection of a number of villages. One of the cities of the county is appointed as the capital of the county.

According to the Statistical Center of Iran, the figures are as follows

English	Persian sing.	Persian pl.	number
Provinces	ostān	ostānhā	30
Counties	shahrestān		324
Districts	bakhsh		865
Townships	shahr		982
rural agglomerations	dehestān		2378

Iran is divided into thirty one provinces (*ostān*), each governed by an appointed governor (استاندار, ostāndār). The provinces are divided into counties (*shahrestān*), and subdivided into districts (*bakhsh*) and sub-districts (*dehestān*).

Iran has one of the highest urban growth rates in the world. From 1950 to 2002, the urban proportion of the population increased from 27% to 60%.The United Nations predicts that by 2030, 80% of the population will be urban.

Most internal migrants have settled near the cities of Tehran, Isfahan, Ahvaz, and Qom. The listed populations are from the 2006/07 (1385 AP) census. Tehran, with a population of 7,705,036, is the largest city in Iran and is the capital. Tehran, like many big cities, suffers from severe air pollution. It is the hub of the country's communication and transport network.

Mashhad, with a population of 2,410,800, is the second largest Iranian city and the centre of the Razavi Khorasan Province. Mashhad is one of the holiest Shia cities in the world as it is the site of the Imam Reza shrine. It is the centre of tourism in Iran, and between 15 and 20 million pilgrims go to the Imam Reza's shrine every year.

Another major Iranian city is Isfahan (population 1,583,609), which is the capital of Isfahan Province. The Naqsh-e Jahan Square in Isfahan has been designated by UNESCO as a World Heritage Site. The city contains a wide variety of Islamic architectural sites ranging from the 11th to the 19th century. The growth of the suburban area around the city has turned Isfahan into Iran's second most populous metropolitan area (3,430,353).

The fourth major city of Iran is Tabriz (population 1,378,935), the capital of the East Azerbaijan Province. It is also the second industrial city of Iran after Tehran. Tabriz had been the second largest city in Iran until the late 1960s and one of its former capitals and

For additional analytical, business and investment opportunities information, please contact Global Investment & Business Center, USA at (703) 370-8082. Fax: (703) 370-8083. E-mail: ibpusa3@gmail.com Global Business and Investment Info Databank - www.ibpus.com

residence of the crown prince under the Qajar dynasty. The city has proven extremely influential in the country's recent history.

The fifth major city is Karaj (population 1,377,450), located in Alborz Province and situated 20 km west of Tehran, at the foot of the Alborz mountains; however, the city is increasingly becoming an extension of metropolitan Tehran.

The sixth major Iranian city is Shiraz (population 1,214,808); it is the capital of Fars Province. The Elamite civilization to the west greatly influenced the area, which soon came to be known as Persis. The ancient Persians were present in the region from about the 9th century BC, and became rulers of a large empire under the Achaemenid dynasty in the 6th century BC. The ruins of Persepolis and Pasargadae, two of the four capitals of the Achaemenid Empire, are located in or near Shiraz. Persepolis was the ceremonial capital of the Achaemenid Empire and is situated 70 kilometres (43 mi) northeast of modern Shiraz. UNESCO declared the citadel of Persepolis a World Heritage Site in 1979.

Largest cities or towns of Iran

Rank	City name	Province	Pop.	Rank	City name	Province	Pop.
1	Tehran	Tehran	8,778,535	11	Urmia	West Azerbaijan	662,734
2	Mashhad	Razavi Khorasan	3,069,941	12	Kerman	Kerman	621,374
3	Karaj	Alborz	2,024,765	13	Zahedan	Sistan and Baluchestan	594,683
4	Isfahan	Esfahan	1,755,382	14	Arak	Markazi	480,560
5	Tabriz	East Azerbaijan	1,657,967	15	Hamadan	Hamadan	479,640
6	Shiraz	Fars	1,287,423	16	Qazvin	Qazvin	446,760
7	Qom	Qom	1,071,503	17	Yazd	Yazd	432,194
8	Ahwaz	Khuzestan	1,068,908	18	Ardabil	Ardabil	418,262
9	Rasht	Gilan	1,010,193	19	Bandar Abbas	Hormozgan	379,301
10	Kermanshah	Kermanshah	828,313	20	Zanjan	Zanjan	376,284

IMPORTANT INFORMATION FOR UNDERSTANDING IRAN

PROFILE

OFFICIAL NAME: Islamic Republic of Iran

Geography
Area: 1.6 million sq. km. (636,295 sq. mi., slightly larger than Alaska).
Arable land: 9.78% of the country.
Cities: *Capital*--Tehran. *Other cities*--Isfahan, Tabriz, Mashhad, Shiraz, Yazd, Qom.
Terrain: Desert and mountains.
Climate: Semiarid; subtropical along the Caspian coast.

People
Nationality: *Noun and adjective*--Iranian(s).
Population (July 2008 est.): 65.8 million.
Population growth rate (est.): 0.79%.
Ethnic groups: Persians 51%, Azeri 24%, Gilaki and Mazandarani 8%, Kurd 7%, Arab 3%, Lur 2%, Baloch 2%, Turkmen 2%, other 1%.
Religions: Shi'a Muslim 89%; Sunni Muslim 9%; Zoroastrian, Jewish, Christian, and Baha'i 2%.
Languages: Persian and Persian dialects 58%, Turkic languages (besides Turkish) 26%, Kurdish 9%, Luri 2%, Balochi 1%, Arabic 1%, Turkish 1%, other 2%.
Education: *Literacy* (total population age 15 and over who can read and write, 2003)--79% (male: 86%, female: 73%).
Health (est.): *Infant mortality rate*--36.93 deaths/1,000 live births. *Life expectancy at birth* (2008)--total population: 70.86 yrs.

Government
Type: Islamic republic.
Constitution: Ratified in December 1979, revised 1989.
Branches: *Executive*--Supreme Leader (head of state), President (head of government), Council of Ministers, Assembly of Experts, Expediency Council, Council of Guardians. *Legislative*--290-member Majles (National Assembly, or Islamic Consultative Assembly). *Judicial*--Supreme Judiciary.
Political parties: Several conservative groups have come together under two separate coalitions, the United Front of Principlists and the Broad and Popular Coalition of Principlists. Some conservative groups remain outside either coalition. Similarly, several reformist groups, such as the Islamic Iran Participation Front (IIFP, also known as Mosharekat) and the Mojahideen of the Islamic Revolution (MIRO) came together as a reformist coalition in advance of the 2008 Majles elections. Another influential reformist group is the National Trust Party.
Administrative subdivisions: 30 provinces.
Suffrage: Universal suffrage; 18 years of age.

Economy
GDP (purchasing power parity, 2008 est.): $859.7 billion.
GDP (official exchange rate, 2008 est.): $222.4 billion.

For additional analytical, business and investment opportunities information, please contact Global Investment & Business Center, USA at (703) 370-8082. Fax: (703) 370-8083. E-mail: ibpusa3@gmail.com Global Business and Investment Info Databank - www.ibpus.com

GDP real growth rate (est.): 6.4%.
GDP composition by sector (est.): Agriculture 10.8%, industry 44.3%, services 44.9%.
Per capita income (PPP, 2007 est.): $12,300.
Work force (est.): 24.35 million.
Work force - by occupation (June 2007): Agriculture 25%, industry 31%, services 45%.
Unemployment rate (according to the Iranian Government): 12.5%.
Natural resources: Petroleum, natural gas, coal, chromium, copper, iron ore, lead manganese, zinc, sulfur.
Agriculture: *Principal products*--wheat, rice, other grains, sugar beets, fruits, nuts, cotton, dairy products, wool, caviar.
Industry: *Types*--petroleum, petrochemicals, textiles, cement and building materials, food processing (particularly sugar refining and vegetable oil production), metal fabricating (particularly steel and copper), armaments.
Trade (est.): *Exports*--$106.4 billion (f.o.b.): petroleum 80%, chemical and petrochemical products, carpets, fruits, nuts. *Major export partners* (2007)--U.A.E. (17.1%), Germany (13.6%), Italy (6.7%), Turkey (5.3%), India (4.8%), Azerbaijan (4%), Turkmenistan (2.4%), China (3%), Singapore (2.5%). *Imports*--$67.79 billion (f.o.b.): industrial raw materials and intermediate goods, capital goods, foodstuffs and other consumer goods, technical services, military supplies. *Major import partners*--Germany (12%), China (10.5%), U.A.E. (9.4%), France (5.6%), Italy (5.4%), South Korea (5.4%), Russia (4.5%).

PEOPLE

Iran is a pluralistic society. Persians are the largest ethnic group in Iran, though many are actually of mixed ancestry. The population of the country has important Turkic elements (e.g., Azeris) and Arabs predominate in the southwest. In addition, Iran's population includes Kurds, Balochi, Bakhtyari, Lurs, and other smaller minorities, such as Armenians, Assyrians, Jews, and Brahuis (or Brohi).

The 1979 Islamic Revolution and the 1980-88 Iran-Iraq war transformed Iran's class structure politically, socially, and economically. During this period, Shi'a clerics took a more dominant position in politics and nearly all aspects of Iranian life, both urban and rural. After the fall of the Pahlavi dynasty in 1979, much of the urban upper class of prominent merchants, industrialists, and professionals, favored by the former monarch, Shah Mohammad Reza Pahlavi, lost standing and influence to the senior clergy and their supporters. However, Bazaar merchants, who were allied with the clergy against the Shah, gained significant political and economic power after the revolution. The urban working class has enjoyed a somewhat enhanced status and economic mobility, spurred in part by opportunities provided by revolutionary organizations and the government bureaucracy. Though the number of clergy holding senior positions in the Majles and elsewhere in government has declined since the 1979 revolution, Iran has nevertheless witnessed the rise of a post-revolutionary elite among clerics who are strongly committed to the preservation of the Islamic Republic.

Most Iranians are Muslims; 89% belong to the Shi'a branch of Islam, the official state religion, while about 9% belong to the Sunni branch. Non-Muslim minorities include Zoroastrians, Jews, Baha'is, and Christians.

HISTORY

The ancient nation of Iran, historically known as Persia, has traditionally been a major power in the region. Despite invasions by Arabs, Seljuk Turks, and Mongols, Iran has always reasserted its national identity and taken pride in its unique cultural and political heritage.

Archeological findings indicate that human activity in Iran dates back to the middle Paleolithic era, about 100,000 years ago. The sixth millennium B.C. saw the emergence of a fairly sophisticated agricultural society and the rise of proto-urban population centers. Many dynasties have ruled Iran, beginning with the Achaemenid (559-330 B.C.), which was founded by Cyrus the Great. After the conquest of Persia by Alexander the Great ushered in the Hellenistic period (300-250 B.C.), ancient Iran was ruled by the Parthian (250 B.C.-226 A.D.) and the Sassanian (226-651) dynasties.

The seventh century Arab conquest of Iran, which introduced Islam to the population, was followed by invasions by the Seljuk Turks and the Mongols. Iran experienced a political and cultural revival under the Safavid dynasty (1502-1736), during which Shah Abbas expelled the Uzbeks and Ottomans from Persia. The conqueror Nadir Shah and his Afsharid dynasty (1736-1749) were succeeded by the Zand dynasty (1750-1794), which was founded by Karim Khan, and later the Qajar (1795-1925) and the Pahlavi (1925-1979) dynasties.

Many date the beginning of modern Iranian history to the nationalist uprisings against the Shah in 1905 and the establishment of a limited constitutional monarchy in 1906. The discovery of oil in 1908 would later become a key factor in Iranian history and development.

In 1921, Reza Khan, an Iranian officer of the Persian Cossack Brigade, seized control of the government. In 1925, after finally ousting the Qajar dynasty, he declared himself Shah and established the Pahlavi dynasty.

Reza Shah forcibly enacted policies of modernization and secularization in Iran and reasserted government authority over the country's tribes and provinces. In 1935, Reza Shah Pahlavi changed the country's name to Iran to accentuate Persia's Aryan roots. During World War Two, the Allies feared that the Shah's close relations with Nazi Germany would jeopardize Iran as a source of oil and a vital supply link to the Soviet Union. In September 1941, following the occupation of western Iran by the Soviet Union and the United Kingdom, Reza Shah was forced to abdicate. His son, Mohammad Reza Pahlavi, ascended to the throne.

After the war, Soviet troops stationed in northwestern Iran refused to withdraw across the border and, instead, supported short-lived, pro-Soviet separatist regimes in the northern provinces of Azerbaijan and Kurdistan. In 1946, under U.S. and United Nations pressure, the Soviets were forced to withdraw their troops. The Shah's forces then moved in to suppress the Azerbaijani and Kurdish revolts.

In 1951, the government of nationalist Prime Minister Mohammed Mossadegh (alternatively spelled Mossadeq) nationalized the British-owned Anglo-Iranian Oil

For additional analytical, business and investment opportunities information, please contact Global Investment & Business Center, USA at (703) 370-8082. Fax: (703) 370-8083. E-mail: ibpusa3@gmail.com Global Business and Investment Info Databank - www.ibpus.com

Company. In the face of strong public support for Mossadegh, the Shah fled to Rome. Although Mossadegh was not a communist, the U.S. and U.K. feared that he had links to the communist Tudeh Party. Consequently, in August 1953, the U.S. and U.K. engineered a coup against the democratically elected Mossadegh, during which pro-Shah army forces arrested the Prime Minister. The Shah returned to Iran soon thereafter and, fearing further opposition, began to govern Iran in an increasingly authoritarian manner.

In 1961, Iran administered a series of economic, social, and administrative reforms--pushed by the Kennedy administration--that became known as the White Revolution. As a result of this program, which was driven by reform, modernization and economic growth proceeded at an unprecedented rate. This tremendous growth was fueled by Iran's vast petroleum reserves, which were then the third-largest in the world. However, while Iran's economy prospered, democratic reform and civil liberties deteriorated. The Shah's autocratic method of rule and the abusive practices of SAVAK (his internal security and intelligence service) alienated large sectors of the population, including the Shi'a clergy.

In 1978, domestic turmoil turned to revolution driven by several disparate groups--nationalists, Islamists, Marxists, and students--who joined together in opposition to the Shah. In January 1979, the Shah left Iran for Egypt and later traveled to the U.S. to seek medical treatment for cancer; he died in exile in Egypt one year later.

On February 1, 1979, exiled religious leader Ayatollah Ruhollah Khomeini returned from France to assume control of the revolution and establish himself as Supreme Leader of a new, theocratic republic guided by Islamic principles. Following Khomeini's death on June 3, 1989, the Assembly of Experts chose the outgoing president of the republic, Ali Khamenei, to succeed him as Supreme Leader. Although the transition appeared smooth externally, there was debate amongst senior clerics regarding Khamenei's relative lack of religious credentials.

In August 1989, Akbar Hashemi-Rafsanjani, Speaker of the Majles, was elected President by an overwhelming majority. He was re-elected June 1993, albeit with a more modest majority. Some Western observers attributed the reduced support for Rafsanjani in 1993 to popular disenchantment with Iran's deteriorating economy. In August 1997, an overwhelming majority of Iranians elected reformist cleric Mohammad Khatami as President, hoping he would usher in a new era of freedom and reform. Khatami had modest successes in broadening the participation of Iranians in government by holding popular elections for local government councils and encouraging the development of civil society. Although many liberal-minded Iranians were disappointed that Khatami did not support student protesters in 1999, he retained enough popular support to secure re-election in June 2001.

In February 2004, elections were held for the Seventh Majles, in which many reformists were prohibited from running, resulting in a more conservative group of parliamentarians in control of the Majles. In March 2008, the Iranian Government again interfered in parliamentary elections. Although reformist candidates managed to hold onto their positions, the Eighth Majles remained under the control of conservative blocs.

None of the seven presidential candidates on the ballot for the June 17, 2005 elections received a majority, resulting in a two-candidate runoff on June 24 between Tehran mayor Mahmoud Ahmadi-Nejad and former president Akbar Hashemi Rafsanjani. Some Iranian politicians alleged voter fraud and electoral interference by the Basij militia forces during the first round of voting. Ahmadi-Nejad, who won in the second round with nearly 62% of the vote according to Iranian Government figures, assumed office in August 2005. Ahmadi-Nejad was re-elected as Iran's president in June 2009, amid a contested poll result. According to the Iranian Government's official results, Ahmadi-Nejad won 62.6% of the vote, while his closest challenger, Mir Hossein Mousavi, received 33.8%.

GOVERNMENT

The December 1979 Iranian constitution defines the political, economic, and social order of the Islamic Republic. The document establishes Shi'a Islam of the Twelver (Jaafari) sect as Iran's official religion. Sunni Islam, Zoroastrianism, Judaism, and Christianity are the only other recognized, legal minority religions. The country is governed by secular and religious leaders through governing bodies, whose duties often overlap.

The Supreme Leader holds power for life unless removed by the Assembly of Experts. He has final say on all domestic, foreign, and security policies for Iran, though he establishes and supervises those policies in consultation with other bodies, including the National Security Council and the Expediency Council. The Supreme Leader is the final arbiter on nearly all disputes among the various branches of government, although the Expediency Council is charged with resolving disputes between the Majles and the Guardian Council. The Supreme Leader appoints officials to key positions including the head of judiciary and the Council of Guardians. He has the power to remove the president and is commander-in-chief of the armed forces.

The constitution stipulates that the Assembly of Experts, which consists of 86 popularly-elected clerics elected to 8-year terms, chooses the Supreme Leader based on jurisprudent qualifications and commitment to the principles of the revolution. The Assembly of Experts reviews his performance periodically and has the power to depose and replace him. Pragmatic conservative candidates generally polled better than their hardline conservative opponents during the December 15, 2006 elections for the Assembly of Experts. (This vote coincided with municipal council elections, and turnout, according to unverified Iranian Government statistics, was reportedly 60%.) Citizens will not vote for representatives for the Assembly again until 2014.

The Council of Guardians consists of 12 persons. The Supreme Leader appoints the six religious members of the Council, while the Majles selects the six lay members from candidates recommended by the judiciary (which is, in turn, selected by the Supreme Leader). The non-clerics play a role only in determining whether legislation before the Majles conforms to Iran's constitution. The religious members, on the other hand, take part in all deliberations, considering all bills for conformity to Islamic principles. The Council of Guardians can veto any law. This body also certifies the competence of candidates for the presidency, the Assembly of Experts, and the Majles, and it has the power of approbatory supervision over elections.

For additional analytical, business and investment opportunities information, please contact Global Investment & Business Center, USA at (703) 370-8082. Fax: (703) 370-8083. E-mail: ibpusa3@gmail.com Global Business and Investment Info Databank - www.ibpus.com

The president of the Islamic Republic of Iran is elected by universal suffrage to a 4-year term. The president supervises the affairs of the executive branch, appointing and supervising the Council of Ministers (members of the cabinet), coordinating government decisions, and selecting government policies to be placed before the Majles.

The Majles, or National Assembly, consists of 290 members elected to 4-year terms. Elections are held by secret ballot from amongst the candidates approved by the Council of Guardians.

In 1988, Ayatollah Khomeini created the Council for Expediency, which resolves legislative issues on which the Majles and the Council of Guardians fail to reach an agreement. Since 1989, it has been used to advise the Supreme Leader on matters of national policy as well. The Expediency Council is composed of the president, the speaker of the Majles, the judiciary chief, the clerical members of the Council of Guardians, and other members appointed by the Supreme Leader for 3-year terms. Cabinet members and Majles committee chairs also serve as temporary members when issues under their jurisdiction are considered. In 2005, it was announced that the Expediency Council, which now has over 40 members, would have supervisory powers over all branches of government, though that has not resulted in any noticeable change in this institution's day-to-day authority or operations.

Judicial authority is constitutionally vested in the Supreme Court and the four-member High Council of the Judiciary; although these are two separate groups, they have overlapping responsibilities and one head. Together, they are responsible for supervising the enforcement of all laws and establishing judicial and legal policies.

Iran has two military forces. The national military is charged with defending Iran's borders, while the Islamic Revolutionary Guard Corps (IRGC) is charged with protecting the revolution and its achievements. The Qods Force, a fifth branch of the IRGC, is the regime's primary mechanism for cultivating and supporting terrorists abroad. The Qods Force provides aid in the form of weapons, training, and funding to Hamas and other Palestinian terrorist groups, Lebanese Hizballah, Iraq-based militants, and Taliban fighters in Afghanistan.

Iran has 30 provinces managed by an appointed governor general. The provinces are further divided into counties, districts, and villages. Sixty percent of eligible voters took part in the first-ever municipal and local council elections in 1999, although a lower percentage went to the polls in the second round in 2003. Turnout for the December 15, 2006 elections, during which citizens also elected Assembly of Expert representatives, was reportedly over 60%. The local councils select mayors.

Principal Government Officials

Supreme Leader-Ali Hoseini-KHAMENEI, *Ayatollah*
Pres.-Hasan Fereidun RUHANI, *Hojjat ol-Eslam*
Sec. of the Cabinet-Mohsen HAJI-MIRZAIE
Head, Presidential Office-Mohammad NAHAVANDIAN
First Vice Pres.-Eshaq JAHANGIRI

Vice Pres. for Economic Affairs-
Vice Pres. for Executive Affairs-
Vice Pres. for Implementation of the Constitution-
Vice Pres. for Intl. Affairs-
Vice Pres. for Legal Affairs-Elham AMINZADEH
Vice Pres. for Management, Development, & Human Resources (Acting)-Mohammad Baqer NOBAKHT
Vice Pres. for Parliamentary Affairs-Majid ANSARI, *Hojjat ol-Eslam*
Vice Pres. for Planning & Strategic Supervision-Mohammad Baqer NOBAKHT
Vice Pres. for Science & Technology-
Vice Pres. & Head, Atomic Energy Organization of Iran-Ali Akbar SALEHI
Vice Pres. & Head, Cultural Heritage, Handicrafts, & Tourism Organization-Mohammad Ali NAJAFI
Vice Pres. & Head, Environmental Protection Organization-
Vice Pres. & Head, Martyrs & War Veterans Affairs Foundation-
Presidential Adviser & Head, Organizations Coordination Center-
Presidential Adviser & Head, Women's Affairs & Family Center-
Min. of Agricultural Jihad-Mohammad HOJJATI
Min. of Communication & Information Technology-Mahmud VAEZI
Min. of Culture & Islamic Guidance-Ali JANATI
Min. of Defense & Armed Forces Logistics-Hosein DEHQAN
Min. of Economic Affairs & Finance-Ali TAYEBNIA
Min. of Education (Acting)-Ali Asqar FANI
Min. of Energy-Hamid CHITCHIAN
Min. of Foreign Affairs-Mohammad Javad ZARIF-Khonsari
Min. of Health, Treatment, & Medical Education-Seyed Hasan QAZIZADEH-Hashemi
Min. of Industry, Mining, & Trade-Mohammad Reza NEMATZADEH
Min. of Intelligence & Security-Mahmud ALAVI, *Hojjat ol-Eslam*
Min. of Interior-Abdolreza Rahmani-FAZLI
Min. of Justice-Mostafa PUR-MOHAMMADI, *Hojjat ol-Eslam*
Min. of Labor, Cooperatives, & Social Welfare-Ali RABIEI
Min. of Petroleum-Bijan Namdar-ZANGANEH
Min. of Roads & Urban Development-Abbas Ahmad AKHUNDI
Min. of Science, Research, & Technology (Acting)-Jafar TOWFIQI-Darian
Min. of Sports & Youth (Acting)-Seyed Reza AMIRI-SALEHI
Governor, Central Bank of Iran-Valiollah SEIF
Permanent Representative to the UN, New York-Mohammad KHAZAI-Torshizi

POLITICAL CONDITIONS

For additional analytical, business and investment opportunities information, please contact Global Investment & Business Center, USA at (703) 370-8082. Fax: (703) 370-8083. E-mail: ibpusa3@gmail.com Global Business and Investment Info Databank - www.ibpus.com

The Islamic Republic of Iran's post-Revolution difficulties have included an 8-year war with Iraq, internal political struggles and unrest, and economic disorder. The early days of the regime were characterized by severe human rights violations and political turmoil, including the seizure of the U.S. Embassy compound and its occupants on November 4, 1979, by Iranian students. Iranian authorities released the 52 hostages only after 444 days of captivity.

By mid-1982, the clergy had won a succession of post-revolution power struggles that first eliminated the center of the political spectrum and then the leftists, including the communist Tudeh Party and the Mujahedin-e Khalq (MEK or MKO). Assassinations, acid attacks on uncovered women, and other acts of political violence punctuated this period. Although the Islamic Republic of Iran experienced a partial expansion of political and social freedoms during the tenure of former president Khatami, serious problems remained. Since taking office in 2005, President Ahmadi-Nejad's administration has cracked down on civil society, continued to violate human rights, tightened constraints on press freedom and harassed activists, including Nobel Prize laureate Shirin Ebadi.

The Islamic Republican Party (IRP) was Iran's sole political party until its dissolution in 1987. Iran now has a variety of groups engaged in political activity; some are oriented along ideological or ethnic lines, while others are more akin to professional political parties seeking members and recommending candidates for office. Conservatives consistently thwarted the efforts of reformists during the Khatami era and have consolidated their control on power since the 2004 Seventh Majles elections and President Ahmadi-Nejad's 2005 victory.

The Islamic Republic of Iran has faced armed opposition from a number of groups, including the Mujahideen-e Khalq (added to the U.S. Government's Foreign Terrorist Organizations list in 1999), the People's Fedayeen, the Kurdish Democratic Party of Iran, the Party for a Free Life in Kurdistan (added the to the U.S. Government's Foreign Terrorist Organizations list in 2009), and the Baluchi group Jundallah.

ECONOMY

Pre-revolutionary Iran's economic development was rapid. Traditionally an agricultural society, by the 1970s Iran had achieved significant industrialization and economic modernization, largely helped by the growing worldwide demand for oil. However, the pace of growth had slowed dramatically by 1978, just before the Islamic Revolution. Since the fall of the Shah, economic recovery has proven elusive due to a combination of factors, including state interference in the economy and fluctuations in the global energy market. Economic activity was further disrupted by years of domestic political upheaval immediately following the revolution. These conditions were worsened by the war with Iraq and the decline in world oil prices beginning in late 1985. After the Iran-Iraq war, Iran's economic situation began to improve: GDP grew for two consecutive years, partly from an oil windfall in 1990, and there was a substantial increase in imports. Iran's social policies during the Iran-Iraq war additionally resulted in a baby boom, which has left Iran with a large, underemployed youth population today. As a result, Iran suffers from a "brain drain" as its educated youth leave the country to pursue better economic opportunities abroad.

For additional analytical, business and investment opportunities information, please contact Global Investment & Business Center, USA at (703) 370-8082. Fax: (703) 370-8083. E-mail: ibpusa3@gmail.com
Global Business and Investment Info Databank - www.ibpus.com

In March 1989, the government instituted a new 5-year plan for economic development, which loosened state control and allowed Iranians greater latitude in accessing foreign capital. However, mismanagement and inefficient bureaucracy, as well as political and ideological infighting, hampered the formulation and execution of a consolidated economic policy, and Iran fell short of the plan's goals. Economic growth was further hindered by a decrease in oil revenues in 1991 and growing external debt. Former president Khatami followed the market reform plans of his predecessor, President Rafsanjani, and indicated that he would pursue diversification of Iran's oil-reliant economy, although he made little progress; high inflation and expansive public transfer programs, as well as powerful economic and political vested interests, posed obstacles for rapid reform during the Khatami era.

Unemployment, a major problem even before the revolution, has continued to plague Iran. However, unemployment statistics only tell part of the story--underemployment continues to affect a large portion of Iran's young, educated workforce. Although Iran's poorer, rural population initially enjoyed a psychological boost from the attention given them by the new Islamic government, they are only marginally better off in economic terms. The government has made some progress on rural development, including electrification, road building, and increased access to education, but Iran still suffers from inefficiencies related to agricultural land usage that are politically difficult to reconcile. The agriculture sector still suffers from shortages of capital, raw materials, and equipment- problems that date back to the 1980-1988 Iran-Iraq war.

Although Islam guarantees the right to private ownership, banks and some industries--including the petroleum, transportation, utilities, and mining sectors--were nationalized after the revolution. Under President Rafsanjani, Iran first began to pursue some privatization through its nascent equities markets. However, the industrial sector, plagued by low labor productivity and shortages of raw materials and spare parts, remains uncompetitive against foreign imports.

Today, Iran's economy is struggling as a result of a bloated and inefficient state sector and an overdependence on the oil sector (which provides over 85% of government revenues). Although the Supreme Leader issued a decree in July 2006 to privatize 80% of the shares of most government-owned companies, private sector activity is typically limited to small-scale workshops, farming, and the service industry. As a result of inefficiencies in the economy, significant informal market activity flourishes and shortages of goods are common. President Ahmadi-Nejad has failed to make any notable progress in fulfilling the goals of the nation's latest 5-year plan. A combination of price controls and subsidies continues to weigh down the economy, while administrative controls and widespread corruption undermine the potential for private-sector-led growth. President Ahmadi-Nejad has made known his plan to eliminate Iran's inefficient subsidies on food and petroleum imports; however, whether this plan will be actually implemented is unclear. Previous government-led efforts at economic reform--such as fuel rationing in July 2007 and the imposition of the value added tax (VAT) in October 2008--were met with stiff resistance and violent protests.

High oil prices in recent years allowed Iran to greatly increase its export earnings and amass over $70 billion in foreign exchange reserves. However, with oil prices currently

For additional analytical, business and investment opportunities information, please contact Global Investment & Business Center, USA at (703) 370-8082. Fax: (703) 370-8083. E-mail: ibpusa3@gmail.com Global Business and Investment Info Databank - www.ibpus.com

below $40 per barrel, the Iranian Government is facing a particularly worrisome economic situation. The government has heavily withdrawn from the country's Oil Stabilization Fund and there have even been reports that President Ahmadi-Nejad's administration has illegally dipped into the foreign exchange reserves. Inflation is approaching 30%, while the unemployment rate continues to be in the double digits. Widespread underemployment amongst Iran's educated youths has convinced many to seek employment overseas. While Iran's economic quandary may look grim, the Islamic Republic has fared worse--notably during the Iran-Iraq war. With the government's 2009 budget formulated to anticipate lower oil prices, it is very possible that Iran will be able weather adverse economic circumstances once again.

FOREIGN RELATIONS

Following the revolution, Ayatollah Khomeini steered Iran's foreign policy sharply away from that of the Shah, who was once the U.S.'s strongest ally in the region. In September 1980, during the U.S. hostage crisis, Iraq invaded Iran to prevent the spread of the Islamic Revolution to Iraq's Shi'a, seize the heavily-Arab province of Khuzestan, and gain control of the Shatt al-Arab, the waterway between the two countries. With the remnants of the Shah's strong (and U.S.-supplied) military infrastructure and thousands of willing youth volunteers, the Islamic Republic of Iran surprised Iraq with its ability to defend itself. In 1982, Ayatollah Khomeini turned down an Iraqi cease-fire proposal and demanded that Saddam Hussein be removed. After eight punishing years of war, in July 1988 the Islamic Republic of Iran at last agreed to the cease-fire implemented in UN Security Council Resolution 598. Neither nation made any significant territorial gains in the war, although both suffered massive casualties.

Iran's relations with many of its Arab neighbors were strained during the early years of the Islamic Republic because of fears that the Islamic Revolution would spread abroad.

In 1981, Iran supported a plot to overthrow the Bahrain Government and, in 1983, Ayatollah Khomeini expressed support for Shi'a who bombed Western embassies in Kuwait. In 1987, Iranian pilgrims rioted during the hajj (pilgrimage) in Mecca, Saudi Arabia. Iranian officials were involved in both training and assisting Saudi Hizballah operatives in executing the 1996 terrorist bombing of the U.S. military housing facility at Khobar Towers near Dhahran, Saudi Arabia, which killed 19 and wounded more than 500 other persons, including 240 U.S. military personnel. Senior IRGC and Qods Force officials were indicted by the Government of Argentina for their alleged roles in the 1994 terrorist bombing of the Asociación Mutual Israelita Argentina (the Argentine Israelite Mutual Association or AMIA), which killed 85 people and wounded scores of others.

Since September 2002, the International Atomic Energy Agency (IAEA) has been working to clarify the true nature of Iran's nuclear program. The November 2004 Director General's report indicated that Iran failed to report, declare, and provide design (or updated design) information on many issues. This includes:

- Six failures to report the import of nuclear material, activities to process/use this material, testing of centrifuges, laser enrichment activities, production of specific nuclear materials, and the irradiation of nuclear materials and subsequent separation of plutonium.

For additional analytical, business and investment opportunities information, please contact Global Investment & Business Center, USA at (703) 370-8082. Fax: (703) 370-8083. E-mail: ibpusa3@gmail.com Global Business and Investment Info Databank - www.ibpus.com

- Two failures to declare nuclear facilities, including a pilot centrifuge enrichment facility at Kalaye Electric Company, the laser enrichment plant at the Tehran Nuclear Research Center, and a pilot uranium laser enrichment plant at Lashkar Ab'ad.
- Six failures to provide design information or updated design information for facilities in which nuclear material processing and storage took place.
- The report also indicated a frequent failure to cooperate to facilitate the implementation of safeguards as evidenced by the extensive concealment activities.

Under international pressure, on November 10, 2003 Iran agreed to suspend all uranium-enrichment and reprocessing activities voluntarily, as well as cooperate fully with the IAEA. Iran then signed the Additional Protocol to the Safeguards Agreement on December 18, 2003, and agreed to implement it voluntarily pending ratification, granting IAEA inspectors greater access in verifying the correctness and completeness of Iran's revised declaration to the IAEA on its nuclear program. Iran terminated its first suspension following inconclusive negotiations with the EU-3 and disagreements as to the scope of the required suspension, leading to additional negotiations and a second suspension that began in November 2004. This second suspension ended with Iran's restart of its uranium conversion activities at its facility in Esfahan in August 2005. The IAEA Board found Iran in noncompliance with its Safeguards Agreement in September 2005 and, after Iran restarted uranium enrichment activities at Natanz in January 2006, reported Iran to the UN Security Council for its noncompliance. In February 2006, Iran ended its voluntary implementation of the Additional Protocol.

In response to the IAEA Board's report of noncompliance, the UNSC has adopted a Presidential Statement (S/PRST/2006, March 2006) and five resolutions (UNSCRs) on Iran: UNSCR 1696 (July 2006), UNSCR 1737 (December 2006), UNSCR 1747 (March 2007), UNSCR 1803 (March 2008), and UNSCR 1835 (September 2008). Three of the five resolutions (UNSCRs 1737, 1747, and 1803) impose Chapter VII (legally binding) sanctions on Iran.

In June 2006, China, France, Germany, Russia, the United States, and United Kingdom--the P5+1, also known as the EU 3+3--offered Iran a substantial incentives package of economic cooperation and assistance in return for Tehran's full cooperation with the IAEA and suspension of its uranium enrichment-related and reprocessing activities. The P5+1 presented Iran with a refreshed package of incentives in June 2008, but Iran has yet to respond clearly and positively to this offer, or comply with its UNSC and IAEA obligations. On April 8, 2009, the P5+1 invited Iran to meet with the group to resolve international concerns and rebuild the confidence of the international community.

Both Iran and Russia believe they have important national interests at stake in developments in Central Asia and the Transcaucasus, particularly regarding energy resources in the Caspian Sea. The U.S. has expressed concern about Russia's sales of military equipment and technology to Iran and Russian assistance in building a nuclear facility at Bushehr.

Iran spends about 3.3% of its GDP on its military. Iran's armed forces consist of both a

For additional analytical, business and investment opportunities information, please contact Global Investment & Business Center, USA at (703) 370-8082. Fax: (703) 370-8083. E-mail: ibpusa3@gmail.com Global Business and Investment Info Databank - www.ibpus.com

national military, which was held over from the Shah's government, and the Islamic Revolutionary Guard Corps, each with its own ground, naval, and air braches. The Iran-Iraq war took a heavy toll on Iran's military, which was once the strongest in the region during the Shah's reign. Iran has since worked to modernize its military, both conventionally and through the development of its ballistic missile and nuclear programs.

U.S.-IRANIAN RELATIONS

On November 4, 1979, Iranian students seized the American Embassy in Tehran, where they held 52 Americans hostage for 444 days. Although it has been claimed that Ayatollah Khomeini did not have prior knowledge of the students' plans, he gave his full support to them throughout the seizure. The students claimed that they occupied the American Embassy to avert another U.S.-orchestrated coup to restore the Shah to power; suspicions arose after the U.S. admitted the Shah for medical treatment in October 1979.

On April 7, 1980, the United States broke diplomatic relations with Iran, and on April 24, 1981, the Swiss Government assumed representation of U.S. interests in Tehran. Iranian affairs in the United States are represented by the Embassy of Pakistan, in the Iranian Interests Section, in Washington, DC. The Islamic Republic of Iran also has a permanent mission to the United Nations in New York City.

In accordance with the Algiers declaration of January 20, 1981, the Iran-U.S. Claims Tribunal (located in The Hague, Netherlands) was established for the purpose of handling claims of U.S. nationals against Iran and of Iranian nationals against the U.S. However, U.S. interaction with Iran at The Hague solely covers legal matters.

The U.S. Government, by executive orders issued by the President as well as by congressional legislation, prohibits nearly all trade with Iran. Sanctions have been imposed on Iran because of its sponsorship of terrorism, its refusal to comply with IAEA regulations regarding its nuclear program, and its human rights violations. However, these sanctions are meant to target the Iranian Government, not the people of Iran. As a result, there are a number of exemptions allowed by the U.S. Government intended to benefit the Iranian people. The following trade is permitted: licensed exports of U.S. agricultural and medical products to Iran, U.S. donations of articles intended to relieve human suffering in Iran (food, clothing, etc.), gifts valued at $100 or less, trade in "informational" materials (films, publications, etc.), U.S. imports of Iranian carpets, and U.S. imports of Iranian foodstuffs intended for human consumption (dried fruit, nuts, etc.). Trade restrictions have been temporarily lifted in the past during humanitarian crises, such as the 2003 Bam earthquake, to allow for donations from American citizens and permit U.S.-based non-governmental organizations to assist with the relief and reconstruction efforts. For a comprehensive overview of legally permitted trade with Iran, please visit the website of the Office of Foreign Assets Control at the Department of Treasury (http://www.treas.gov/offices/enforcement/ofac/programs/iran/iran.pdf).

Obstacles to improved relations between the U.S. and the Islamic Republic of Iran remain. The U.S. objects to Iran's sponsorship of terrorism, its nuclear weapons ambitions, and its violations of human rights. The Islamic Republic of Iran still has not recognized Israel's right to exist and has hindered the Middle East peace process by arming militants, including Hamas, Hizballah, and Palestinian Islamic Jihad. Although the Islamic Republic of Iran has contributed to positive reconstruction efforts in Iraq and Afghanistan, Tehran has also pursued policies to undermine stability in both countries. Additionally the U.S. Government is concerned with the Islamic Republic of Iran's recent crackdown on human rights and detainment of civil society actors. The U.S. continues to call on Iran to cooperate more fully in the investigation into the case of Robert Levinson, an American citizen, who went missing on Kish Island, Iran, between March 8 and 9, 2007.

Despite these obstacles, U.S. and Iranian representatives have discussed a number of issues of concern over the years. U.S. and Iranian envoys cooperated during operations against the Taliban in 2001 and during the Bonn Conference in 2002, which established a broad-based government for the Afghan people under President Karzai. Former Secretary of State Condoleezza Rice and her Iranian counterpart attended talks on Iraq in Sharm El Sheikh, Egypt, on May 3, 2007. The U.S. and Iranian ambassadors to Iraq further took part in face-to-face discussions in Baghdad, with Iraqi officials in attendance, on May 28, 2007. Representatives from the three countries engaged in a second round of talks on July 24, 2007, and the ambassadors met for a third discussion on August 6, 2007. On July 19, 2008, Under Secretary of State for Political Affairs William Burns joined the P5+1, a group of representatives from Russia, China, France, Germany, and the United Kingdom that met with Iran's top nuclear negotiator in Geneva, Switzerland. On March 31, 2009 Secretary of State Hillary Clinton headed the U.S. delegation to the UN conference on Afghanistan at The Hague, where Iran was one of the 70 nations represented. On April 8, 2009, Under Secretary Burns participated in the P5+1 meeting in London, where the U.S. announced plans to participate fully in the P5+1 process and join in any future meetings with representatives of the Islamic Republic of Iran.

TRAVEL AND BUSINESS INFORMATION

The U.S. Department of State's Consular Information Program advises Americans traveling and residing abroad through Country Specific Information, Travel Alerts, and Travel Warnings. **Country Specific Information** exists for all countries and includes information on entry and exit requirements, currency regulations, health conditions, safety and security, crime, political disturbances, and the addresses of the U.S. embassies and consulates abroad. **Travel Alerts** are issued to disseminate information quickly about terrorist threats and other relatively short-term conditions overseas that pose significant risks to the security of American travelers. **Travel Warnings** are issued when the State Department recommends that Americans avoid travel to a certain country because the situation is dangerous or unstable.

For the latest security information, Americans living and traveling abroad should regularly monitor the Department's Bureau of Consular Affairs Internet web site at http://www.travel.state.gov, where the current Worldwide Caution, Travel Alerts, and Travel Warnings can be found. Consular Affairs Publications, which contain information on obtaining passports and planning a safe trip abroad, are also available at http://www.travel.state.gov. For additional information on international travel, see http://www.usa.gov/Citizen/Topics/Travel/International.shtml.

The Department of State encourages all U.S. citizens traveling or residing abroad to register via the State Department's travel registration website or at the nearest U.S. embassy or consulate abroad. Registration will make your presence and whereabouts

For additional analytical, business and investment opportunities information, please contact Global Investment & Business Center, USA at (703) 370-8082. Fax: (703) 370-8083. E-mail: ibpusa3@gmail.com Global Business and Investment Info Databank - www.ibpus.com

known in case it is necessary to contact you in an emergency and will enable you to receive up-to-date information on security conditions.

Emergency information concerning Americans traveling abroad may be obtained by calling 1-888-407-4747 toll free in the U.S. and Canada or the regular toll line 1-202-501-4444 for callers outside the U.S. and Canada.

The National Passport Information Center (NPIC) is the U.S. Department of State's single, centralized public contact center for U.S. passport information. Telephone: 1-877-4-USA-PPT (1-877-487-2778); TDD/TTY: 1-888-874-7793. Passport information is available 24 hours, 7 days a week. You may speak with a representative Monday-Friday, 8 a.m. to 10 p.m., Eastern Time, excluding federal holidays.

Travelers can check the latest health information with the U.S. Centers for Disease Control and Prevention in Atlanta, Georgia. A hotline at 800-CDC-INFO (800-232-4636) and a web site at http://wwwn.cdc.gov/travel/default.aspx give the most recent health advisories, immunization recommendations or requirements, and advice on food and drinking water safety for regions and countries. The CDC publication "Health Information for International Travel" can be found at http://wwwn.cdc.gov/travel/contentYellowBook.aspx.

IRAN MILITARY FORCES: STRATEGIC INFORMATION

Founded	1923 (as modern military)
Current form	1980
Service branches	Army Air Force Navy Air Defense Force IRGC
Headquarters	Tehran
Leadership	
Commander-in-chief	Sayyid Ali Khamenei
Commander of IAF Commander of IRIA Commander of IRIAF Commander of IRIN Commander of IRIADF Commander of IRGC	Hassan Firuzabadi Ataollah Salehi Hassan Shah-Safi Habibollah Sayyari Farzad Esmaili Mohammad Ali Jafari
Manpower	
Active personnel	545,000 (ranked 8th)
Reserve personnel	1,800,000 (ranked 6th)
Expenditures	
Budget	$9.041 billion (25th by total expenditure)
Percent of GDP	1.8%
Industry	
Domestic suppliers	Defense Industries Organization Iran Aviation Industries Organization Aerospace Industries Organization Iran Electronics Industries Marine Industries Organization
Foreign suppliers	Russia China Cuba Belarus North Korea Syria Ukraine Armenia

The **Armed Forces of the Islamic Republic of Iran** include the IRIA and the IRGC and the Police Force These forces total about 545,000 active personnel (not including the Police Force and the Army of the Guardians of the Islamic Revolution). All branches of armed forces fall under the command of General Headquarters of Armed Forces The Ministry of Defense and Armed Forces Logistics is responsible for planning logistics and funding of the armed forces and is not involved in in-the-field military operational command.

- The Iranian Military consists of the Islamic Republic of Iran Army, Islamic Republic of Iran Navy, Islamic Republic of Iran Air Force, and the Iranian Air Defense Force. The regular armed forces have an estimated 545,000 personnel: the Islamic Republic of Iran Army, 465,000 personnel; the Islamic Republic of Iran Navy, 28,000 personnel; and the Islamic Republic of Iran Air Force, 52,000 airmen. Iranian Air Defense Force is a branch split off from the IRIAF.

- The Army of the Guardians of the Islamic Revolution, or Revolutionary Guards, has an estimated 120,000 personnel in five branches: Its own Navy, Air Force, and Ground Forces; and the Quds Force (Special Forces).

- The Basij is a paramilitary volunteer force controlled by the Islamic Revolutionary Guards. Its membership is a matter of controversy. Iranian sources claim a membership of 12.6 million, including women, of which perhaps 3 million are combat capable. There are a claimed 2,500 battalions of which some are full-time personnel. Globalsecurity.org quotes a 2005 study by the Center for Strategic and International Studies estimating 90,000 active-duty full-time uniformed members, 300,000 reservists, and a total of 11 million men that can be mobilized if need be.

Iran's military was called the Middle East's most powerful by General John Abizaid chief of United States Central Command (U.S. forces' commander in the region). However General Abizaid said he did not include the Israel Defense Forces as they did not fall into his area of operations.

MODERN HISTORY

When the Pahlavi dynasty took power in 1925, following years of war with Russia, the standing Persian army was almost non-existent. The new king Reza Shah Pahlavi, was quick to develop a new military. In part, this involved sending hundreds of officers to European and American military academies. It also involved having foreigners re-train the existing army within Iran. In this period the Iranian Air Force was established and the foundation for a new Navy was laid.

The British and Russians invaded Iran in 1941. Following World War II, 1500 Iranian troops supported the Sultan of Oman against the Dhofar Rebellion from 1962-1975. In 1971, Iranian forces besieged Abu Musa and the Tunb islands. Before the Islamic revolution of 1979, Iran contributed to United Nations peacekeeping operations. Iran joined ONUC in the Congo in the 1960s, and ten years later, Iranian troops joined UNDOF on the Golan Heights.

Several years later Revolutionary Iran was taken by surprise by the Iraqi invasion that began the Iran–Iraq War of 1980-1988. During this conflict, there were several confrontations with the United States. From 1987, the United States Central Command sought to stop Iranian mine-laying vessels from blocking the international sea lanes

For additional analytical, business and investment opportunities information, please contact Global Investment & Business Center, USA at (703) 370-8082. Fax: (703) 370-8083. E-mail: ibpusa3@gmail.com Global Business and Investment Info Databank - www.ibpus.com

through the Persian Gulf in Operation Prime Chance. The operation lasted until 1989. On April 18, 1988, the U.S. retaliated for the Iranian mining of the USS Samuel B. Roberts (FFG-58) in Operation Praying Mantis. A former military-associated police force, the Iranian Gendarmerie, disbanded in 1990.

In 1991, the Iranian armed forces received a number of fleeing Iraqi aircraft which were incorporated into the Air Force. From 2003, there have been repeated U.S. and British allegations that Iranian forces have been covertly involved in the Iraq War. In 2007, Iranian Revolutionary Guard forces also took prisoner Royal Navy personnel when a boat's party from HMS Cornwall was seized in Iran waters.

Iran has launched no wars of choice in modern history, and its leadership adheres to a doctrine of "no first strike." The country's military budget is the lowest per capita in the Persian Gulf region besides the UAE.

COMMANDERS

The Iranian Air Force is equipped with a fleet of F-4 and F-14 aircraft provided by the United States before the Iranian Revolution. Iran also produces its own fighter jets, such as HESA Saeqeh.

Iran has 3 Russian-built Kilo class submarines patrolling the Persian Gulf. Iran is also producing its own submarines.

- Ayatollah Ali Khamenei (Supreme Leader and the Commander-in-Chief of the Armed Forces, in Persian: فرمانده کل قوا)

- General Ahmad Vahidi (Minister of Defense)
- General Hassan Firouzabadi (Head of the Armed Forces General Command Headquarters, in Persian: مسلح یروهایس ستاد کل نیری)
- Major General Yahya Rahim Safavi (Senior Advisor to the Leader of the Islamic Revolution)
- General Mohammad Hejazi (Deputy Chief of the Armed Forces)

- Islamic Republic of Iran Army (Artesh)
  - General Ataollah Salehi (Commander-in-Chief of the Army, in Persian: فرمانده کل ارتش)
  - General Abdolrahim Mousavi (Chief of the Joint Staff of the Army)
  - General Ahmad Reza Pourdastan (Commander of the Ground Force)
  - General Hassan Shah-Safi (Commander of the Air Force)
  - Major General Ahmad Mighani (Commander of Air Defense)
  - Admiral Habibollah Sayyari (Commander of the Navy)
- IRGC
  - Major General Mohammad Ali Jafari (Commander-in-Chief of the IRGC, in Persian: فرمانده کل سپاه پاسداران)
  - Brigadier General Hossein Salami (Chief of the Joint Staff of the IRGC)
  - Brigadier General Mohammad-Reza Zahedi (Commander of IRGC Ground Force)

For additional analytical, business and investment opportunities information, please contact Global Investment & Business Center, USA at (703) 370-8082. Fax: (703) 370-8083. E-mail: ibpusa3@gmail.com Global Business and Investment Info Databank - www.ibpus.com

  - Brigadier General Amir Ali Hajizadeh (Commander of IRGC Air Force)
  - Rear Admiral Morteza Saffari (Commander of IRGC Navy)
  - Brigadier General Qassem Soleimani (Commander of Quds Force)
  - Brigadier General Mohammad Reza Naghdi (Commander of Basij forces)

- Iranian Police
  - Brigadier General Esmaeil Ahmadi-Moghaddam (Commander-in-Chief of the Police,

BUDGET

Iran's 2007 defense budget was estimated to be $7.31 billion by London's International Institute for Strategic Studies This was $102 per capita, a lower figure than other Persian Gulf nations and lower as a percentage of gross national product than all other Persian Gulf states (2.6% of GDP in 2007). This makes Iran's ranking the 25th largest defense expenditure globally.In 2010 the Iranian government put the security and defence budget at $18 billion.

DEFENSE INDUSTRY

Under the last Shah of Iran, Mohammad Reza Pahlavi, Iran's military industry was limited to assembly of foreign weapons. In the assembly lines that were put up by American firms, such as Bell, Litton and Northrop, Iranian workers put together a variety of helicopters, aircraft, guided missiles, electronic components and tanks. In 1973 the Iran Electronics Industries (IEI) was established. The company was set up in a first attempt to organize the assembly and repair of foreign-delivered weapons. The Iranian Defense Industries Organization was the first to succeed in taking a step into what could be called a military industry by reverse engineering Soviet RPG-7, BM21, and SAM-7 missiles in 1979.

Nevertheless, most of Iran's weapons before the Islamic revolution were imported from the United States and Europe. Between 1971 and 1975, the Shah went on a buying spree, ordering $8 billion in weapons from the United States alone. This alarmed the United States Congress, which strengthened a 1968 law on arms exports in 1976 and renamed it the Arms Export Control Act. Still, the United States continued to sell large amounts of weapons to Iran until the 1979 Islamic Revolution.

After the Islamic revolution, Iran found itself severely isolated and lacking technological expertise. Because of economic sanctions and a weapons embargo put on Iran by the United States, Iran was forced to rely on its domestic arms industry for weapons and spare parts since there were very few countries willing to do business with Iran.

The Islamic Revolutionary Guards were put in charge of creating what is today known as the Iranian military industry. Under their command Iran's military industry was enormously expanded, and with the Ministry of Defense pouring investment into the missile industry, Iran soon accumulated a vast arsenal of missiles. Since 1992, it also has produced its own tanks, armored personnel carriers, radar systems, guided missiles, submarines, military vessels and fighter planes.

For additional analytical, business and investment opportunities information, please contact Global Investment & Business Center, USA at (703) 370-8082. Fax: (703) 370-8083. E-mail: ibpusa3@gmail.com Global Business and Investment Info Databank - www.ibpus.com

In recent years, official announcements have highlighted the development of weapons such as the Fajr-3 (MIRV), Hoot, Kowsar, Fateh-110, Shahab-3 missile systems and a variety of unmanned aerial vehicles, at least one of which Israel claims has been used to spy on its territory. In 2006, an Iranian UAV acquired and allegedly tracked the American aircraft carrier USS Ronald Reagan for 25 minutes without being detected before returning safely to its base.

BALLISTIC PROGRAM

On November 2, 2006, Iran fired unarmed missiles to begin 10 days of military simulations. Iranian state television reported "dozens of missiles were fired including Shahab-2 and Shahab-3 missiles. The missiles had ranges from 300 km to up to 1300 km. Iranian experts have made some changes to Shahab-3 missiles installing cluster warheads in them with the capacity to carry 1,400 bombs." These launches come after some United States-led military exercises in the Persian Gulf on October 30, 2006, meant to train for blocking the transport of weapons of mass destruction Iran is also believed to have started the development of an ICBM/IRBM missile project, known as Ghadr-110 with a range of 3000 km; the program is paralleled with advancement of a satellite launcher named IRIS.

WEAPONS OF MASS DESTRUCTION

Although Iran is a signatory to the Nuclear Non-Proliferation Treaty, Israel has alleged that Iran is developing nuclear weapons. The United Nations' International Atomic Energy Agency, in its February 2006 report on Iran's nuclear program (Israel itself accused had developing nuclear weapon since 1980s), said it had no evidence of this. Recently, the United States of America released an intelligence report that the Islamic Republic of Iran is not developing a nuclear detonation device. Iran is currently attempting to create the radioactive fuel for energy purposes that could potentially be used in a nuclear weapon; however, as long as Iran's centrifuge plants are being actively inspected, they cannot be used to make a bomb.

Iran ratified the Chemical Weapons Convention in 1997. Iranian troops and civilians suffered tens of thousands of casualties from Iraqi chemical weapons during the 1980-88 Iran–Iraq War. As a result, Iran has publicly stood against the use of chemical weapons, making numerous vitriolic comments against Iraq's use of such weapons in international forums.

Even today, more than eighteen years after the end of the Iran–Iraq War, about 30,000 Iranians are still suffering and dying from the effects of chemical weapons employed by Iraq during the war. The need to manage the treatment of such a large number of casualties has placed Iran's medical specialists in the forefront of the development of effective treatment regimes for chemical weapons victims, and particularly for those suffering from exposure to mustard gas.

Iran ratified the Biological weapons Convention in 1973. Iran has advanced biological and genetic engineering research programs supporting an industry that produces world-class vaccines for both domestic use and export

For additional analytical, business and investment opportunities information, please contact Global Investment & Business Center, USA at (703) 370-8082. Fax: (703) 370-8083. E-mail: ibpusa3@gmail.com Global Business and Investment Info Databank - www.ibpus.com

IRAN'S MILITARY DOCTRINE[1]

* The Iran-Iraq War (1980-1988) was a defining moment for the Iranian military and it continues to underpin many aspects of Iranian military doctrine.

* Iranian military planners are adept at incorporating lessons from other conflicts, such as the U.S.-led invasion of Iraq and the 2006 war between Israel and Hezbollah, to refine their own doctrines and strategies.

* To challenge a technologically superior adversary, such as the United States, Iranian doctrine emphasizes aspects of asymmetric warfare that play to Iran's strengths, including geography, strategic depth and public willingness to accept casualties.

* The Islamic Revolutionary Guard Corps (IRGC), the branch of the Iranian military tasked with protecting the Islamic revolution, is undergoing a major restructuring to enhance its survivability and give regional commanders more flexibility to respond to potential threats.

Iranian military doctrine constitutes a unique hybrid of western (especially U.S.) military concepts coupled with ideological tenets, including martyrdom and revolutionary zeal. Since the 1979 revolution, Iranian military doctrine has continued to evolve and adapt with the regime's shifting threat perceptions and regional political developments.

Iran's armed forces have tailored their war-fighting strategies to counter technologically superior adversaries, such as the United States. Tacitly acknowledging it has little chance of winning a conventional force-on-force conflict, Iran has opted for deterrence-based model of attrition warfare that raises an opponent's risks and costs, rather than reducing its own. The goal is to inflict a psychological defeat that inhibits an enemy's willingness to fight.

Asymmetric warfare plays a central role in Iranian military theory. Iran's armed forces appear to be focusing on the development of niche capabilities that play to Iranian strengths—manpower, strategic depth and a willingness to accept casualties—while exploiting the weaknesses of Iran's adversaries, who are regarded as risk averse, casualty sensitive and heavily dependent on technology and regional basing facilities for access.

DOCTRINE EVOLUTION

The basis of Iranian military doctrine was developed during Iran's long and traumatic war with Iraq (1980-1988). Most senior officers are veterans of the "imposed war," which has had a major influence on Iranian strategic thinking. Concepts such as self-reliance, "holy defense," and export of the revolution first entered the military lexicon during the Iran-Iraq War and were codified as doctrine in the early 1990s. These ideas mingled with concepts from pre-revolutionary doctrine, which was heavily influenced by the United States, to form a unique hybrid that distinguished modern Iranian military doctrine from its largely Soviet-inspired counterparts in the Arab world.

---

[1] **by Michael Connell** is director of Iranian Studies at the Center for Naval Analyses, a non-profit institution that conducts research and analysis in Washington D.C.

After the war, Tehran gradually scaled back its efforts to export its revolution. As its foreign policy goals shifted, Iran's national security strategy also became more defensive. Iranian military strategists began to pay more attention to the principles of modern maneuver warfare, such as combined and joint operations. In the mid-1990s, there was even talk about merging the IRGC with the regular military, the Artesh, to alleviate the command and control-related problems of having two parallel military services operating in tandem. Iran's military capabilities still lagged behind its doctrine, but by the end of the decade, its forces were gradually evolving into professional, Western-style militaries.

The 9/11 attacks and U.S. invasions of Iraq and Afghanistan led Tehran to reconsider the trajectory of its armed forces. The regional security environment had changed drastically. Ba'athist Iraq and Taliban Afghanistan—two of Iran's main rivals—were no longer a threat. But the United States suddenly had troops positioned along both its western and eastern flanks. This confluence of events, coupled with rumblings in Washington about opportunities for regime change, led Tehran to reassess its national security strategy. Iran's armed forces began to tailor their strategies specifically to counter the perceived U.S. threat.

LAND WARFARE DOCTRINE

In 2005, the IRGC announced that it was incorporating a flexible, layered defense —referred to as a mosaic defense—into its doctrine. The lead author of this plan was General Mohammad Jafari, then director of the IRGC's Center for Strategy, who was later appointed commander of the IRGC.

As part of the mosaic defense, the IRGC has restructured its command and control architecture into a system of 31 separate commands—one for the city of Tehran and 30 for each of Iran's provinces. The primary goal of restructuring has been to strengthen unit cohesion at the local level and give commanders more latitude to respond to potential threats—both foreign and domestic. But the new structure would also make it difficult for hostile forces to degrade Iranian

command and control, a lesson the Iranian military has learned by analyzing U.S. operations in Iraq, Afghanistan and the Balkans.

The mosaic defense plan allows Iran to take advantage of its strategic depth and formidable geography to mount an insurgency against invading forces. Most of Iran's population centers and major lines of communication are spread out within the interior of the country. Iran's borders are ringed by rugged mountain ranges that serve as natural barriers to invasion. As enemy supply lines stretched into Iran's interior, they would be vulnerable to interdiction by special stay-behind cells, which the IRGC has formed to harass enemy rear operations.

The Artesh, a mix of armored, infantry and mechanized units, would constitute Iran's initial line of defense against invading forces. IRGC troops would support this effort, but they would also form the core of popular resistance, the bulk of which would be supplied by the Basij, the IRGC's paramilitary volunteer force. The IRGC has developed a wartime mobilization plan for the Basij, called the Mo'in Plan, according to which Basij personnel would augment regular IRGC units in an invasion scenario.

IRGC and Basij exercises have featured simulated ambushes on enemy armored columns and helicopters. Much of this training has been conducted in an urban environment, suggesting that Iran intends to lure enemy forces into cities where they would be deprived of mobility and close air support. Iran has emphasized passive defense measures—techniques used to enhance the battlefield survivability —including camouflage, concealment and deception.

NAVAL DOCTRINE

Tehran views maritime combat operations much the same way as it views land-based operations. Iranian naval doctrine is geared toward confronting a technologically superior adversary—often assumed to be the U.S. Navy—with a form of guerrilla warfare at sea. The bases of this doctrine were developed during the Tanker War (1984-1988), during which Iran used aircraft, speedboats, sea mines and land-based anti-ship cruise missiles to attack civilian tanker shipping in the Persian Gulf. After a U.S. frigate, the *Samuel B. Roberts*, was badly damaged by an Iranian mine, the U.S. Navy retaliated with Operation Praying Mantis (1988), destroying two Iranian oil platforms and sinking several Iranian surface vessels, including a corvette, a guided missile patrol craft and smaller gunboats.

After Operation Praying Mantis, Iran apparently determined that its maritime forces would not be as effective in a conventional force-on-force naval conflict with adversaries such as the United States. Incorporating lessons learned

from the Tanker War, the IRGC Navy (IRGCN) and, to a lesser degree, the regular Navy (IRIN) developed an asymmetric strategy based on avoiding direct or sustained confrontations at sea. It instead relies on surprise attacks, ambushes and hit-and-run operations. Rather than inflict a decisive defeat, Iran's maritime forces would seek to inflict enough causalities to raise the cost of victory to an unpalatable level.

Iran's naval doctrine relies on a layered defense and massing of firepower, integrating multiple sea, land and air-based weapons simultaneously to overwhelm and confuse adversaries. As Iran's naval doctrine has matured, the Iranians have acquired a large inventory of naval materiel suitable for asymmetric warfare. This includes naval mines, which can be covertly deployed using small boats or commercial vessels; land and sea-based anti-ship cruise missiles; small fast-attack craft, which can engage in swarming operations or suicide attacks; and submarines, including three Russian-supplied KILO-class diesel-electric submarines and numerous North Korean and domestically produced midget submarines, which can be used in the Gulf's shallow areas.

Geography is a key element in Iranian naval planning. The Gulf's confined space, which is less than 100 nautical miles wide in many places, limits the maneuverability of large surface assets, such as aircraft carriers. But it plays to the strengths of Iran's naval forces, especially the IRGCN. The Gulf's northern coast is dotted with rocky coves ideally suited for terrain masking and small boat operations. The Iranians have also fortified numerous islands in the Gulf that sit astride major shipping lanes.

Iran has developed a strategy to deny hostile navies access to the Persian Gulf that focuses on the strategically sensitive Strait of Hormuz. This strategic maritime chokepoint is only 29 nautical miles wide at its narrowest point. Iranian officials have hinted that they might close the strait during a conflict, thereby temporarily cutting off as much as 30 percent of the world's oil supply. But closing the strait would also cause tremendous economic damage for the Iranians, so they are not likely to undertake such a measure lightly. Given the strait's importance, however, disrupting maritime traffic in it or even threatening to do so would be an effective tool for Iran to pressure neighbors and intimidate foes.

AIR AND AIR DEFENSE DOCTRINE

Iranian air and air defense doctrine is focused on defending Iranian airspace and deterring aggression, although certain Iranian aircraft, such as the Su-24 fighter-bomber, can be used in an

For additional analytical, business and investment opportunities information, please contact Global Investment & Business Center, USA at (703) 370-8082. Fax: (703) 370-8083. E-mail: ibpusa3@gmail.com Global Business and Investment Info Databank - www.ibpus.com

offensive capacity. Surface-to-air missiles (SAMs) and interceptor aircraft—most of which belong to the regular Islamic Republic of Iran Air Force (IRIAF)—both play an important role in this effort.

Iran's pilots are among the best trained in the region. They continue to use U.S. training manuals and employ U.S. tactics—a legacy of U.S.-Iranian military exchanges during the shah's rule.

The IRIAF and the Air Defense Force, a separate command within the Artesh, face numerous challenges in defending Iranian air space. In this case, geography is a limiting factor, given the size of Iran and its mountainous terrain, which tend to produce gaps in radar coverage. For the IRIAF, aging and outdated equipment remains another problem. Many aircraft in the IRIAF's inventory, including mainstays such as the F-14A and the F-4D, were supplied by the United States before the 1979 revolution. Some of these platforms have been kept running, either by cannibalizing parts from other aircraft or procuring spare parts on the black market, but IRIAF readiness levels are assumed to be low due to maintenance issues.

Iran has managed to acquire several batteries of the advanced Tor-M1 medium altitude SAM system from the Russians, but its air defense capabilities remain limited. As of mid-2010, efforts to buy the advanced long-range SA-300 SAM from the Russians had failed. Iran also lacks an integrated air defense network or the ability to engage air-to-air targets beyond visual range.

As a result of these challenges, Iran's military has opted to use its limited air and air defense assets to protect high-value point targets, including Tehran and the country's nuclear facilities. Iranian pilots have been trained to compensate for the limitations of their aircraft, avionics and weapons systems by using advanced tactics, such as terrain masking, to ambush enemy aircraft without being detected. Iran's air and air defense forces have also attempted to augment the survivability of their units with passive defense measures, including asset dispersion and the use of forward operating bases, hardened shelters and hidden installations.

BALLISTIC MISSILE DOCTRINE

Iran's ballistic missile program dates back to the middle of the 1980s, during the Iran-Iraq War. For Tehran, Iraq's use of ballistic missiles against Iranian strategic targets highlighted a critical vulnerability in Iran's defenses; it also demoralized Iran's civilian population. To deter Iraq from attacking its population centers and strategic industries, Iran initiated its own ballistic missile program, beginning with the initial shipment of a limited number of SCUD-B missiles from Libya. By the end of the war, Iran had launched over 100 ballistic missiles at Iraqi targets in what would become known as the "War of the Cities."

Iran's strategic missile forces are now key to its deterrence strategy, in part because they are implicitly linked to Iran's weapons of mass destruction

programs. In 2010, Iran had the largest inventory of ballistic missiles in the Middle East. The IRGC, which has operational control over Iran's missile forces, continues to extend the range and improve the performance of its ballistic missiles, several classes of which can range Israel and the Gulf countries. Their limited accuracy suggests they would not be useful in a conventional counter-force role. Instead, they are probably intended for strategic targets such as cities, oil production and export facilities, ports and water desalinization plants.

THE FUTURE

For additional analytical, business and investment opportunities information, please contact Global Investment & Business Center, USA at (703) 370-8082. Fax: (703) 370-8083. E-mail: ibpusa3@gmail.com Global Business and Investment Info Databank - www.ibpus.com

* Iranian military doctrine is primarily defensive in nature and based on deterring perceived adversaries. Iran is therefore unlikely to seek a direct, force-on-force confrontation with the United States.

* However, there is ample room for miscommunication between Iranian and U.S. forces at the tactical and operational levels. The recent push to decentralize command and control within the IRGC could have unintended consequences in terms of escalation, especially in the Persian Gulf.

* For the foreseeable future, lack of coordination between the IRGC and the Artesh is likely to remain a key weak point in terms of Iranian military planning, due to underlying structural issues and institutional rivalries.

For additional analytical, business and investment opportunities information, please contact Global Investment & Business Center, USA at (703) 370-8082. Fax: (703) 370-8083. E-mail: ibpusa3@gmail.com
Global Business and Investment Info Databank - www.ibpus.com

IRAN'S STRATEGIC CAPABILITIES AND WEAPONS OF MASS DESTRUCTION PROGRAMS

Many in the Obama Administration view Iran, as the Bush Administration did, as one of the key national security challenges facing the United States. [10] This assessment is based largely on Iran's weapons of mass destruction (WMD) programs—and particularly in light of revelations in September 2009 that Iran is building at least one more nuclear site than it had previously declared—and its ability to exert influence in the region counter to U.S. objectives.[11] Many experts agree that Iran's core national security goals are to protect itself from foreign, primarily U.S., interference or attack, and to exert regional influence that Iran believes is commensurate with its size and concept of nationhood. On the other hand, some see the internal unrest as distracting Iranian leaders from exerting influence outside Iran and from making key decisions that might be needed to further accelerate WMD programs.

[10] A March 16, 2006 "National Security Strategy" document stated that the United States "may face no greater challenge from a single country than from Iran."

[11] See http://www.whitehouse.gov/nsc/nss/2006/.

CONVENTIONAL MILITARY/REVOLUTIONARY GUARD/QODS FORCE

Iran's armed forces are extensive but they are widely considered relatively combat ineffective against a well-trained, sophisticated military such as that of the United States or a regional power such as Turkey, and Iran lacks the logistical ability to project power much beyond its borders. Still, Iranian forces could still cause damage to U.S. forces and allies in the Gulf region, and they are sufficiently effective to deter or fend off conventional threats from Iran's weaker neighbors such as post-war Iraq, Turkmenistan, Azerbaijan, and Afghanistan. Iran's armed forces have few formal relationships with foreign militaries, but Iran and India have a "strategic dialogue" and some Iranian naval officers reportedly have undergone some training in India. Iran and Turkey agreed in principle in April 2008 to jointly fight terrorism along their border. Most of Iran's other military-to-military relationships, such as with Russia, Ukraine, Belarus, North Korea, and a few others, generally center on Iranian arms purchases or upgrades.

Iran's armed forces are divided organizationally. The Islamic Revolutionary Guard Corps (IRGC, known in Persian as the *Pasdaran*)[12] controls the *Basij* (Mobilization of the Oppressed) volunteer militia that enforces adherence to Islamic customs and has been the main instrument to repress the postelection protests in Iran. The IRGC and the regular military report to a Joint Headquarters, headed by Hassan Firuzabadi. In line with some congressional and Administration ideas to try to weaken the IRGC by addressing its vulnerabilities, a provision of the National Defense Authorization Act for FY2010 (Section 1224, P.L. 111-84) calls for a report on Iran's conventional military strategy and power, in particular the capabilities of the IRGC.

[12] For a more extensive discussion of the IRGC, see Katzman, Kenneth. "The Warriors of Islam: Iran's Revolutionary Guard," *Westview Press*, 1993.

The Revolutionary Guard

The IRGC is generally loyal to Iran's hardliners politically and is clearly more politically influential than is Iran's regular military, which is numerically larger but was held over from the Shah's era. Its influence has, by all accounts, grown sharply over the past few years as the regime has relied on it to suppress dissent. As described in a 2009 Rand Corporation study, " Founded by a decree from Ayatollah Khomeini shortly after the victory of the 1978-1979 Islamic Revolution, Iran's Islamic Revolutionary Guards Corps (IRGC) has evolved well beyond its original foundations as an ideological guard for the nascent revolutionary regime. Today the IRGC functions as an expansive sociopolitical-economic conglomerate whose influence extends into virtually every corner of Iranian political life and society. Bound together by the shared experience of war and the socialization of military service, the Pasdaran have articulated a populist, authoritarian, and assertive vision for the Islamic Republic of Iran that they maintain is a more faithful reflection of the revolution's early ideals. The IRGC's presence is particularly powerful in Iran's highly factionalized political system, in which [many senior figures] hail from the ranks of the IRGC. Outside the political realm, the IRGC oversees a robust apparatus of media resources, training activities, education programs designed to bolster loyalty to the regime, prepare the citizenry for homeland defense, and burnish its own institutional credibility vis-a-vis other factional actors. It is in the economic sphere, however, that the IRGC has seen the greatest growth and diversification—strategic industries and commercial services ranging from dam and pipeline construction to automobile manufacturing and laser eye surgery have fallen under its sway, along with a number of illicit smuggling and black market enterprises."

Through its Qods (Jerusalem) Force, the IRGC has a foreign policy role in exerting influence throughout the region by supporting pro-Iranian movements, as discussed further below. The Qods Force numbers approximately 10,00015,000 personnel who provide advice, support, and arrange weapons deliveries to pro-Iranian factions in Lebanon, Iraq, Persian Gulf states, Gaza/West Bank, Afghanistan, and Central Asia. It also operates a worldwide intelligence network to give Iran possible terrorist option and to assist in procurement of WMD-related technology. The Qods Force commander, Brig. Gen. Qassem Soleimani, is said to have his own independent channel to Supreme Leader Khamene'i, bypassing the IRGC and Joint Staff command structure. The Qods Force commander during 1988-1995 was Brig. Gen. Ahmad Vahidi, confirmed as Defense Minister on September 3, 2009. He led the unit during several major initiatives such as its alleged assistance to two bombings of Israeli and Jewish targets in Buenos Aires (the 1994 bombing he is wanted by Interpol for a role in it; the buildup of Lebanese Hezbollah's rocket capabilities; the recruitment of Saudi Hezbollah activists later accused of the June 1996 Khobar Towers bombing; and the assassination of Iranian dissident leaders in Europe in the early 1990s.

IRGC leadership developments are significant because of the political influence of the IRGC. On September 2, 2007, Khamene'i replaced Rahim Safavi with Mohammad Ali Jafari as Commander In Chief of the Guard; Jafari is considered a hardliner against political dissent and is reputedly close to the Supreme Leader and less so to Ahmadinejad. The Basij reports to the IRGC Commander in Chief; its leadership was changed in October 2009, to Brig. Gen. Mohammad Reza Naqdi (replacing Hossein

For additional analytical, business and investment opportunities information, please contact Global Investment & Business Center, USA at (703) 370-8082. Fax: (703) 370-8083. E-mail: ibpusa3@gmail.com Global Business and Investment Info Databank - www.ibpus.com

Taeb). It operates from thousands of positions in Iran's institutions. Command reshuffles in July 2008 that integrated the Basij more closely with provincially-based IRGC units furthered the view that the Basij is playing a more active role in uncovering suspected plotting by Iran's minorities and others. In November 2009, the regime gave the IRGC's intelligence units greater authority, perhaps surpassing those of the Ministry of Intelligence, in monitoring dissent. More information on how the Iranian military might perform against the United States is discussed later. The IRGC Navy now has responsibility to patrol the entire Persian Gulf, and that the regular Navy is patrolling the Strait of Hormuz and Gulf of Oman.

As noted, the IRGC is also increasingly involved in Iran's economy, acting through a network of contracting businesses it has set up, most notably Ghorb (also called Khatem ol-Anbiya, Persian for "Seal of the Prophet"). Active duty IRGC senior commanders reportedly serve on Ghorb's board of directors. In late September 2009, the Guard bouht a 50% stake in Iran Telecommunication Company at a cost of $7.8 billion. In the past five years, Guard affiliated firms have won 750 oil and gas and construction contracts, and the Guard has its own civilian port facilities (New York Times, September 29, 2009). On October 21, 2007, the Treasury Department designated several IRGC companies as proliferation entities under Executive Order 13382. Also that day, the IRGC as a whole, the Ministry of Defense, several IRGC commanders, and several Iranian banks were sanctioned under that same executive order. Simultaneously, the Qods Force was named as a terrorism supporting entity under Executive Order 13224. Both orders freeze the U.S.-based assets and prevent U.S. transactions with the named entities, but these entities are believed to have virtually no U.S.-based assets that could be frozen. The designations stopped short of concurring with provisions of bills in the 110th Congress—H.R. 1400 (passed by the House on September 25), S. 970, and the FY2008 defense authorization bill (P.L. 110-181, Senate amendment adopted September 6, 2007, by vote of 76-22)— for the Revolutionary Guard to be designated a foreign terrorist organization, or FTO. **Sources:** Frederic Wehrey et al. "The Rise of the Pasdaran." Rand Corporation. 2009. Katzman, Kenneth. "The Warriors of Islam: Iran's Revolutionary Guard." Westview Press, 1993.

Iran's Conventional Military Arsenal

Military Personnel	Tanks	Surface-Air Missiles Combat Aircraft Ships Defense Budget (billions U.S. $)
545,000 (regular military and Revolutionary Guard Corps (IRGC). IRGC is about one-third of total force.	1,693 (incl. 480 T72)	150 I-Hawk plus some Stinger 280 (incl. 25 MiG29 and 30 Su24) 200 (incl. 10 Chinese-made Hudong, 40 Boghammer, 3 frigates) Also has 3 Kilo subs 6.6

Ship-launched cruise missiles. Iran is able to arm its patrol boats with Chinese-made C-802 cruise missiles. Iran also has Chinese-supplied HY-2 Seerseekers emplaced along Iran's coast.

Midget Subs. Iran is said to possess several, possibly purchased assembled or in kit form from North Korea. Iran claimed on November 29, 2007, to have produced a new small sub equipped with sonar-evading technology.

Anti-aircraft missile systems. Russia has sold and now delivered to Iran (January 2007) 30 anti-aircraft missile systems (Tor M1), worth over $1 billion. In September 2006, Ukraine agreed to sell Iran the Kolchuga radar system that can improve Iran's detection of combat aircraft. In December 2007, Russia agreed to sell the even more capable S-300 (also known as SA-20 "Gargoyle") air defense system, purportedly modeled after the U.S. Patriot system, which

U.S. officials say would greatly enhance Iran's air defense capability. The value of the deal is estimated at $800 million. Amid unclear or weak denials by Iranian and Russian officials, U.S. officials told journalists on December 11, 2008, that Iran has indeed contracted for the missile. It is reportedly was due for delivery by March 2009 and to be operational by June 2009, but Russian press reports in February 2009 about the visit of Iran's Defense Minister to Moscow indicate that Russia has placed delivery on hold due to "political considerations"—expectations of possible adverse reaction by the Obama Administration. Delivery has not taken place to date, by all accounts, and Israel said in August 2009 that Russia had agreed not to deliver any equipment to Iran that would upset the regional balance of power.

NUCLEAR PROGRAM AND RELATED INTERNATIONAL DIPLOMACY

Since 2005, Iran and the international community have been seeking to limit Iran's nuclear program. U.S. officials say they are operating under the assumption that Iran intends to develop a nuclear weapon from that program. Then International Atomic Energy Agency (IAEA) Director Mohammad El Baradei[13] said in a press interview on June 17, 2009, that "My gut feeling is that Iran definitely would like to have the technology ... that would enable it to have nuclear weapons if they decided to do so." In February 2009, the Director of National Intelligence (DNI) Dennis Blair reiterated previous assessments that it is likely that Iran will eventually try to develop a nuclear weapon. These assessments were given additional weight on September 25, 2009, when President Obama and French and British leaders revealed purported longstanding intelligence that Iran is developing a uranium enrichment site on a Revolutionary Guard base near Qom that appears unsuitable for purely civilian use. Iran had formally notified the IAEA of the site in prior days and asserted that, because the site was not operational, the site was not a violation of its Safeguards Agreement with the IAEA, although IAEA and U.S. officials maintain this violates agreed reporting requirements of Iran.

The Obama Administration faces policy choices in light of IAEA reports (February 19, 2009) that Iran has now enriched enough uranium for a nuclear weapon, although only if enriched to 90%. An IAEA report of June 5, 2009, reiterated that Iran's enrichment thus far has been 5%, which is a level that would permit only civilian uses, but added that Iran has now installed over 7,000 centrifuges, of which over 5,000 are being fed with uranium feedstock. There continues to be no evidence that Iran has diverted any nuclear material for a nuclear weapons program, but the IAEA asserts that it cannot verify that Iran's

For additional analytical, business and investment opportunities information, please contact Global Investment & Business Center, USA at (703) 370-8082. Fax: (703) 370-8083. E-mail: ibpusa3@gmail.com Global Business and Investment Info Databank - www.ibpus.com

current program is purely peaceful. Several of its reports (January 31, 2006, February 27, 2006, May 26, 2008, and September 15, 2008) describe Iranian documents that show a possible involvement of Iran's military in the program.

Some U.S. officials, including Secretary of Defense Gates, have signaled less urgency, saying on March 1, 2009, that Iran is "not close" to a nuclear weapon. The George W. Bush Administration's December 2007 NIE assessed that Iran will likely be technically capable of producing enough highly enriched uranium for a nuclear weapon some time during 2010-2015. This time frame was reiterated in February 12, 2009, testimony by Director of National Intelligence Dennis Blair and by him again since then.[14] Because of the Qom site revelation, it is no longer clear that Iran's weaponization efforts are on hold, as the 2007 NIE had said they have been (since 2003). On the other hand, some experts say that there has been some slowdown in Iran's program in recent months, possibly due to the turmoil resulting from the domestic unrest, and/or technical difficulties.

[13] A new IAEA Director, Japanese official Yukiya Amano, took office December 2009.

IRAN'S ARGUMENTS AND THE INTERNATIONAL RESPONSE

International scrutiny of Iran's nuclear program intensified in 2002, when Iran confirmed PMOI allegations that Iran was building two facilities that could potentially be used to produce fissile material useful for a nuclear weapon: a uranium enrichment facility at Natanz and a heavy water production plant at Arak,[15]considered ideal for the production of plutonium. It was revealed in 2003 that the founder of Pakistan's nuclear weapons program, A.Q. Khan, sold Iran nuclear technology and designs.[16]

Iranian leaders have addressed the scrutiny by saying that Iran's nuclear program is for electricity generation and that enrichment is its "right" as a party to the NPT. Iran professes that WMD is inconsistent with its ideology and says that its leaders, including the late Ayatollah Khomeini, have issued formal pronouncements (*fatwas*) that nuclear weapons are un-Islamic. Iran says its oil resources are finite and that enriching uranium to make nuclear fuel is allowed under the 1968 Nuclear Non-Proliferation Treaty,[17] to which Iran is a party. An analysis was published by the National Academy of Sciences challenging the U.S. view that Iran is petroleum rich and therefore has no need for a nuclear power program. According to the analysis, the relative lack of investment could cause Iran to have negligible exports of oil by 2015.[18] The United States and its partners now accept Iran's right to purely peaceful uses of nuclear energy. In the past, U.S. officials have said that Iran's gas resources make nuclear energy unnecessary.

[14] Text at http://www.dni.gov/press_releases/20071203_release.pdf.

[15] In November 2006, the IAEA, at U.S. urging, declined to provide technical assistance to the Arak facility on the grounds that it was likely for proliferation purposes. [16] Lancaster, John and Kamran Khan. "Pakistanis Say Nuclear Scientists Aided Iran." *Washington Post*, January 24, 2004.

[17] For Iran's arguments about its program, see Iranian paid advertisement "An Unnecessary Crisis—Setting the Record Straight About Iran's Nuclear Program," in the *New York Times*, November 18, 2005. P. A11.

[18] Stern, Roger. "The Iranian Petroleum Crisis and United States National Security," P*roceedings of the National Academy of Sciences of the United States of America*. December 26, 2006.

There is widespread belief among experts that Iran's governing factions perceive a nuclear weapons capability as a means of ending Iran's perceived historic vulnerability to invasion and domination by great powers, and as a symbol of Iran as a major nation. Others believe a nuclear weapon represents the instrument with which Iran intends to intimidate its neighbors and dominate the Persian Gulf region. There are also fears Iran might transfer WMD to extremist groups or countries. On the other hand, some Iranian strategists maintain that a nuclear weapons will bring Iran only further sanctions, military containment, U.S. attempted interference in Iran, and efforts by neighbors to develop countervailing capabilities. Some members of the domestic opposition, such as Musavi, have positions on the nuclear issue similar to those of regime leaders, but some opposition factions see the nuclear program as an impediment to eventual re-integration with the West and might be willing to significantly limit the program.

U.S. officials have generally been less concerned with Russia's work, under a January 1995 contract, on an $800 million nuclear power plant at Bushehr. Russia insisted that Iran sign an agreement under which Russia would provide reprocess the plant's spent nuclear material; that agreement was signed on February 28, 2005. The plant was expected to become operational in 2007, but Russia had insisted (including during President Putin's visit to Iran in October 2007) that Iran first comply with the U.N. resolutions discussed below. In December 2007, Russia began fueling the reactor, and Iran says it expects the plant to become operational in 2009. Some preliminary tests of the plant began in February 2009, but, possibly as a sign of Russian cooperation with international pressure on Iran, Russia has not brought the plant to operational status to date. As part of this work, Russia has trained 1,500 Iranian nuclear engineers.

DIPLOMATIC EFFORTS IN 2003 AND 2004/PARIS AGREEMENT

In 2003, France, Britain, and Germany (the "EU-3") opened a separate diplomatic track to curb Iran's program. On October 21, 2003, Iran pledged, in return for peaceful nuclear technology, to

(1) fully disclose its past nuclear activities, (2) to sign and ratify the "Additional Protocol" to the NPT (allowing for enhanced inspections), and (3) to suspend uranium enrichment activities. Iran signed the Additional Protocol on December 18, 2003, although the *Majles* has not ratified it. Iran discontinued abiding by the Protocol after the IAEA reports of November 10, 2003, and February 24, 2004, stated that Iran had violated its NPT reporting obligations over an 18-year period.

In the face of the U.S. threat to push for Security Council action, the EU-3 and Iran reached a more specific November 14, 2004, "Paris Agreement," committing Iran to

For additional analytical, business and investment opportunities information, please contact Global Investment & Business Center, USA at (703) 370-8082. Fax: (703) 370-8083. E-mail: ibpusa3@gmail.com Global Business and Investment Info Databank - www.ibpus.com

suspend uranium enrichment (which it did as of November 22, 2004) in exchange for renewed trade talks and other aid.[19] The Bush Administration did not openly support the track until March 11, 2005, when it announced it would drop U.S. objections to Iran applying to join the World Trade Organization (it applied in May 2005) and to selling civilian aircraft parts to Iran. The Bush Administration did not participate directly in the talks.

[19] For text of the agreement, see http://www.iaea.org/NewsCenter/Focus/IaeaIran/eu_iran14112004.shtml. EU-3—Iran negotiations on a permanent nuclear pact began on December 13, 2004, and related talks on a trade and cooperation accord (TCA) began in January 2005.

Reference to the Security Council

The Paris Agreement broke down just after Ahmadinejad's election; Iran rejected as insufficient an EU-3 offer to assist Iran with peaceful uses of nuclear energy and provide limited security guarantees in exchange for Iran's (1) permanently ending uranium enrichment; (2) dismantling the Arak heavy-water reactor;[20] (3) no-notice nuclear inspections; and (4) a pledge not to leave the NPT (it has a legal exit clause). On August 8, 2005, Iran broke the IAEA seals and began uranium "conversion" (one step before enrichment) at its Esfahan facility. On September 24, 2005, the IAEA Board declared Iran in non-compliance with the NPT and decided to refer the issue to the Security Council,[21] but no time frame was set for the referral. After Iran resumed enrichment activities, on February 4, 2006, the IAEA board voted 27-3[22] to refer the case to the Security Council. On March 29, 2006, the Council agreed on a presidency "statement" setting a 30-day time limit (April 28, 2006) for ceasing enrichment.[23]

Establishment of "P5+1" Contact Group/June 2006 Incentive Package

Taking a multilateral approach, the George W. Bush Administration offered on May 31, 2006, to join the nuclear talks with Iran if Iran first suspends its uranium enrichment. Such talks would center on a package of incentives and possible sanctions—formally agreed on June 1, 2006—by a newly formed group of nations, the so-called "Permanent Five Plus 1" (P5+1: United States, Russia, China, France, Britain, and Germany). EU representative Javier Solana formally presented the P5+1 offer to Iran on June 6, 2006. (The package is Annex I to Resolution 1747.)

Incentives:

- Negotiations on an EU-Iran trade agreements and acceptance of Iran into the World Trade Organization.
- Easing of U.S. sanctions to permit sales to Iran of commercial aircraft/parts.
- Sale to Iran of a light-water nuclear reactor and guarantees of nuclear fuel (including a five year buffer stock of fuel), and possible sales of light-water research reactors for medicine and agriculture applications.
- An "energy partnership" between Iran and the EU, including help for Iran to modernize its oil and gas sector and to build export pipelines.
- Support for a regional security forum for the Persian Gulf, and support for the objective of a WMD free zone for the Middle East.

For additional analytical, business and investment opportunities information, please contact Global Investment & Business Center, USA at (703) 370-8082. Fax: (703) 370-8083. E-mail: ibpusa3@gmail.com Global Business and Investment Info Databank - www.ibpus.com

- The possibility of eventually allowing Iran to resume uranium enrichment if it complies with all outstanding IAEA requirements.

[20] In November 2006, the IAEA, at U.S. urging, declined to provide technical assistance to the Arak facility. [21]Voting in favor: United States, Australia, Britain, France, Germany, Canada, Argentina, Belgium, Ghana, Ecuador, Hungary, Italy, Netherlands, Poland, Portugal, Sweden, Slovakia, Japan, Peru, Singapore, South Korea, India. Against:

Venezuela. Abstaining: Pakistan, Algeria, Yemen, Brazil, China, Mexico, Nigeria, Russia, South Africa, Sri Lanka, Tunisia, and Vietnam. [22] Voting no: Cuba, Syria, Venezuela. Abstaining: Algeria, Belarus, Indonesia, Libya, South Africa. [23] See http://daccessdds.un.org/doc/UNDOC/GEN/N06/290/88/PDF/N0629088.pdf?OpenElement.

Sanctions:[24]

- Denial of visas for Iranians involved in Iran's nuclear program and for high-ranking Iranian officials.
- A freeze of assets of Iranian officials and institutions; a freeze of Iran's assets abroad; and a ban on some financial transactions.
- A ban on sales of advanced technology and of arms to Iran; and a ban on sales to Iran of gasoline and other refined oil products.
- An end to support for Iran's application to the WTO.

Resolution 1696

Iran did not immediately respond to the offer. On July 31, 2006, the Security Council voted 14-1 (Qatar voting no) for U.N. Security Council Resolution 1696, giving Iran until August 31, 2006, to fulfill the longstanding IAEA nuclear demands (enrichment suspension, etc). Purportedly in deference to Russia and China, it was passed under Article 40 of the U.N. Charter, which makes compliance mandatory, but not under Article 41, which refers to economic sanctions, or Article 42, which would authorize military action. It called on U.N. member states not to sell Iran WMD-useful technology. On August 22, 2006, Iran responded, but Iran did not offer enrichment suspension, instead offering vague proposals of engagement with the West.

Resolution 1737

With the backing of the P5+1, chief EU negotiator Javier Solana negotiated with Iran to try arrange a temporary enrichment suspension, but talks ended on September 28, 2006, without agreement. The Security Council adopted U.N. Security Council Resolution 1737 unanimously on December 23, 2006, under Chapter 7, Article 41 of the U.N. Charter. It prohibits sale to Iran— or financing of such sale—of technology that could contribute to Iran's uranium enrichment or heavy-water reprocessing activities. It also required U.N. member states to freeze the financial assets of 10 named Iranian nuclear and missile firms and 12 persons related to those programs. It called on—but did not mandate—member states not to permit travel by these persons. In deference to Russia, the Resolution did not apply to the Bushehr reactor.

For additional analytical, business and investment opportunities information, please contact Global Investment & Business Center, USA at (703) 370-8082. Fax: (703) 370-8083. E-mail: ibpusa3@gmail.com Global Business and Investment Info Databank - www.ibpus.com

RESOLUTION 1747 AND RESULTS

Resolution 1737 demanded enrichment suspension by February 21, 2007. With no Iranian compliance, on March 24, 2007, after only three weeks of P5+1 negotiations, Resolution 1747 was adopted unanimously, which

- added 10 military/WMD-related entities; 3 Revolutionary Guard entities; 8 persons, and 7 Revolutionary Guard commanders. Bank Sepah is among the entities sanctioned.
- banned arms transfers by Iran, a provision targeted at Iran's alleged arms supplies to Lebanese Hezbollah and to Shiite militias in Iraq.
- required all countries to report to the United Nations when sanctioned Iranian persons travel to their territories.
- called for (but did not require) countries to avoid selling arms or dual use items to Iran and to avoid any new lending or grants to Iran.

[24] One source purports to have obtained the contents of the package from ABC News: http://www.basicint.org/pubs/ Notes/BN060609.htm.

Resolution 1747 demanded Iran suspend enrichment by May 24, 2007. Iran did not comply, but, suggesting it wanted to avoid further isolation, in August 2007, Iran agreed to sign with the IAEA an agreement to clear up outstanding questions on Iran's past nuclear activities by the end of 2007. On September 28, 2007, the P5+1 grouping—along with the EU itself—agreed to a joint statement pledging to negotiate another sanctions resolution if there is no progress reported by the IAEA in implementing the August 2007 agreement or in negotiations with EU representative Javier Solana. The IAEA and Solana indicated that Iran's responses fell short; Solana described a November 30, 2007, meeting with Iranian negotiator Sayid Jallili as "disappointing."

RESOLUTION 1803 AND ADDITIONAL INCENTIVES

After several months of negotiations, Resolution 1803 was adopted by a vote of 14-0 (Indonesia abstaining) on March 3, 2008. It (1) bans sales of dual use items to Iran; (2) authorizes, but does not require, inspections of cargo, carried by Iran Air Cargo and Islamic Republic of Iran Shipping Line, suspected of shipping WMD-related goods; (3) imposes a firm travel ban on five Iranians named in Annex II to the Resolution and requires reports on international travel by 13 individuals named in Annex I; (4) calls for, but does not impose, a prohibition on financial transactions with Iran's Bank Melli and Bank Saderat; and (5) adds 12 entities to those sanctioned under Resolution 1737. (On June 23, 2008, the EU, acting under Resolution 1803, froze the assets of Bank Melli and several IRGC entities and commanders.)

Resolution 1803 also stated the willingness of the P5+1 to consider additional incentives to resolve the Iranian nuclear issue through negotiation "on the basis of their June 2006 proposals." The Bush Administration agreed to expand the June 2006 incentive package at a meeting in London on May 2, 2008, resulting in an offer to Iran to add political cooperation and enhanced energy cooperation to prior incentive packages. EU envoy

Solana presented the package (which included a signature by Secretary of State Rice) on June 14, 2008, but Iran was non-committal.

Sensing increasing pressure, in July 2008, Iran indicated it might be ready to first accept a six week "freeze for freeze," i.e., the P5+1 would freeze further sanctions efforts and Iran would freeze any expansion of uranium enrichment (though not suspend outright). To try to take advantage of what appeared to be an Iranian willingness to compromise, the Bush Administration sent Undersecretary of State for Political Affairs William Burns to join Solana and the other P5+1 representatives at a meeting in Geneva on July 19, 2008. Iran did not accept the "freeze for freeze" idea by an extended deadline of August 2, 2008.

Resolution 1835

As a result of the lack of progress, the P5+1 began discussing another sanctions resolution. Ideas reportedly considered included adding more Iranian banks to those sanctioned, or banning insurance for Iran's tanker fleet. On August 7, 2008, the EU implemented the sanctions specified in Resolution 1803, including asserting the authority to inspect suspect shipments, and called on its members to refrain from providing new credit guarantees on exports to Iran. However, the August 2008 crisis between Russia and Georgia set back U.S.-Russia relations, and Russia opposed new U.N. sanctions on Iran. In an effort to demonstrate to Iran continued unity, the Council did adopt (September 27, 2008) Resolution 1835, calling on Iran to comply with previous resolutions, but restating a willingness to negotiate and imposing no new sanctions.

With Iran still not complying, the P5+1 met again in October and in November of 2008. However, with U.S. partner officials uncertain about what U.S. policy toward Iran might be under a new U.S. Administration, there was no consensus on new sanctions.

THE P5+1 PROCESS UNDER PRESIDENT OBAMA

After President Obama was inaugurated, the P5+1 met in Germany (February 4, 2009), reportedly focusing on the new U.S. Administration's approach on Iran. It recommitted to the "two track" strategy of incentives and sanctions.[25] Another P5+1 meeting was held in London on April 8, 2009, during which Undersecretary Burns told the other members of the group that, henceforth, a

U.S. diplomat would attend all of the group's meetings with Iran. Iran put off new meetings until after the Iranian June 12, 2009, election.[26] In order to try to show good faith to Iran, the Obama Administration did not press for new sanctions.

As far as a time frame for an Iranian response, on May 18, 2009, in the context of a meeting with visiting Israeli Prime Minister Benjamin Netanyahu, President Obama said he expect a positive response by Iran to the U.S. outreach "by the end of [2009]," but that the United States would not entertain the idea of endless talks that yield no result. The July 9, 2009, G-8 summit statement, which included Russian concurrence, mentioned late September 2009 (G-20 summit on September 24) as a time by which the

P5+1 would expect Iran to come to new talks and offer constructive proposals for a settlement, lest the P5+1 consider "crippling sanctions" on Iran's economy.

OCTOBER 1 TENTATIVE AGREEMENT AND SUBSEQUENT DEVELOPMENTS

Perhaps sensing the pressure, on September 1, 2009, Iran's senior negotiator, Sayed Jallili, said Iran would come to new talks. On September 9, 2009, Iran distributed its long anticipated proposals to settle the nuclear issue. To P5+1 representatives in Iran (Swiss Ambassador represented the United States).[27] The Iranian proposals were criticized by many as vague but the United States and its partners considered it a sufficient basis to schedule a meeting with Iran for October 1, 2009, in Geneva.

In light of September 25 revelations about the previously unreported Iranian nuclear site—and despite Iran's insistence that it would allow the facility to be inspected—little progress was expected at the meeting. However, the seven hour session, in which U.S. Under Secretary of State William Burns, representing the United States, also met privately with Iranian negotiator Sayed

[25] Dempsey, Judy. "U.S. Urged to Talk With Iran." *International Herald Tribune*, February 5, 2009. [26] CRS conversations with European diplomats in July 2009.

[27] "Cooperation for Peace, Justice, and Progress." Text of Iranian proposals. http://enduringamerica.com/2009/09/11/ irans-nukes-full-text-of-irans-proposal-to-51-powers/

Jallili, resulted in tentative agreements to (1) meet again later in October; (2) allow the IAEA to inspect the newly revealed Iranian facility near Qom; and (3) allow Russia and France, subject to technical talks to begin by mid-October, to re-process about 75% of Iran's low-enriched uranium for medical use.

The technical talks were held October 19-21, 2009, at IAEA headquarters in Vienna, Austria, and chaired on the U.S. side by Deputy Energy Secretary Daniel Poneman. A draft agreement was approved by the P5+1 countries and the IAEA. Iran has not accepted the draft, instead offering tentative counter-proposals to ship its enriched uranium to France and Russia in increments. On the other hand, some Iranian officials have floated the concept of having the uranium sent to Turkey for enrichment, a proposal that U.S. officials reportedly offered a substitute for Russian or French enrichment. All of Iran's proposals were deemed insufficiently specific or responsive to meet P5+1 demands by the end of 2009. Some attribute the Iranian refusal to agree to the October 1 terms as due to the internal political pressure from reformist leaders, such as Musavi, who are trying to paint Ahmadinejad as so politically weak that he is forced to accept a deal that disadvantages Iran. The Qom facility was inspected during October 25-29, 2009, as agreed.

Because Iran did not accept the October 1 terms by the end of 2009, the P5+1 countries have returned to considering sanctions against Iran. The P5+1 met in Brussels on November 21, 2009, issuing a statement calling on Iran to accept the October 1 proposal. Later, with reported help from China, which had received an NSC briefing on the likely adverse implications for the oil market if Iran's nuclear program proceeds apace, the IAEA Board adopted a resolution on November 27, 2009. China and Russia voted for the Resolution.[28] The Resolution (Gov/2009/82) urged Iran to suspend construction at the Qom site; and called on Iran to confirm it had not decided to construct any other undeclared nuclear facility. As a response to the Resolution, which Iran viewed as contrary to the spirit of negotiated resolution of the nuclear disputes, Iranian officials announced they would construct 10 new uranium enrichment sites, and Ahmadinejad, in early December, declared Iran would enrich uranium to 20% purity for medical uses (but which could be taken as an intent to later make weapons grade uranium).

Some of the specific sanctions ideas under consideration before the latest phase of the dispute included those previously considered: cutting Iran's banks off from the international banking system; banning insurance or re-insurance to carry gasoline products to Iran; and a ban on arms sales to Iran. In light of the unrest in Iran, several December 2009 and January 2010 press reports say the Administration is focusing on sanctioning the Revolutionary Guard and other security organs that are suppressing the Iranian protesters. (See further in "Further International and Multilateral Sanctions" section below.) However, the support of Russia and China for any new sanctions remains uncertain. Despite comments by Secretary Clinton on January 4, 2010, that new sanctions are needed, China's Ambassador to the United Nations said on January 6, 2010, that diplomacy is still possible and that, therefore, "some more time and patience" are needed before new sanctions should be enacted. The reluctance of the two countries to sanction Iran has increased discussion of a group of "like-minded" countries enacting additional sanctions on Iran.

[28] Three countries voted no: Malaysia, Cuba, and Venezuela. Six abstained: Afghanistan, Pakistan, Turkey, Brazil, Egypt, and South Africa. Azerbaijan left the meeting before voting.

Require Iran to suspend uranium enrichment

Prohibit transfer to Iran of nuclear, missile, and dual use items to Iran, except for use in light-water reactors Prohibit Iran from exporting arms or WMD-useful technology Freeze the assets of 40 named Iranian persons and entities, including Bank Sepah. Require that countries exercise restraint with respect to travel of 35 named Iranians and ban the travel of 5 others Calls on states not to export arms to Iran or support new business with Iran Calls for "vigilance" (a non-binding call to cut off business) with respect to all Iranian banks, particularly Bank Melli and

Bank Saderat Calls on countries to inspect cargoes carried by Iran Air Cargo and Islamic Republic of Iran Shipping Lines if there are indications they carry cargo banned for carriage to Iran.

CHEMICAL WEAPONS, BIOLOGICAL WEAPONS, AND MISSILES

Official U.S. reports and testimony continue to state that Iran is seeking a self-sufficient chemical weapons (CW) infrastructure, and that it "may have already" stockpiled blister, blood, choking, and nerve agents—and the bombs and shells to deliver them. This

For additional analytical, business and investment opportunities information, please contact Global Investment & Business Center, USA at (703) 370-8082. Fax: (703) 370-8083. E-mail: ibpusa3@gmail.com Global Business and Investment Info Databank - www.ibpus.com

raises questions about Iran's compliance with its obligations under the Chemical Weapons Convention (CWC), which Iran signed on January 13, 1993, and ratified on June 8, 1997. These officials and reports also say that Iran "probably maintain[s] an offensive [biological weapons] BW program ... and probably has the capability to produce at least small quantities of BW agents."

BALLISTIC MISSILES/WARHEADS

At the February 2009 Annual Threat Assessment of the Intelligence Community, Director of National Intelligence, Dennis Blair, testified "although many of their statements are exaggerations, Iranian officials throughout the past year have repeatedly claimed greater ballistic missile capabilities that could threaten U.S. and allied interests."[29] Tehran appears to view its ballistic missiles as an integral part of its strategy to deter or retaliate against forces in the region, including U.S. forces. However, Iran's technical capabilities are a matter of some debate among experts, and Iran appears to be focus more on missiles capable of hitting regional targets rather than those of intercontinental range. The chart below contains some details on Iran's missile programs and recent tests.

In August 2008, the George W. Bush Administration reached agreements with Poland and the Czech Republic to establish a missile defense system to counter Iranian ballistic missiles. These agreements were reached over Russia's opposition, which was based on the belief that the missile defense system would be used to neutralize Russian capabilities. However, reportedly based on assessments of Iran's focus on missiles of regional range, on September 17, 2009, the Obama Administration reoriented this missile defense program to focus, at least initially, on ship-based

[29] Annual Threat Assessment of the Intelligence for the Senate Select Committee on Intelligence, Dennis C. Blair, Director of National Intelligence, February 12, 2009.

systems, possibly later returning to the idea of Poland and Czech-based systems. Some saw this as an effort to win Russia's support for additional sanctions on Iran, and Russian statements did shift somewhat toward the U.S. position on Iran after the Obama missile defense announcement.

Table 7. Iran's Ballistic Missile Arsenal

Shahab-3 800-mile range. Two of first three tests (July 1998, July 2000, and September 2000) reportedly

("Meteor") unsuccessful. After successful test in June 2003, Iran called missile operational (capable of hitting Israel). Despite claims, some U.S. experts say the missile not completely reliable—some observers said Iran detonated in mid-flight a purportedly more accurate version on August 12, 2004. On May 31, 2005, Iran announced it had tested a solid-fuel version. Iran tested several of the missiles on September 28, 2009, in advance of the October 1 meeting with the P5+1.

Shahab-4 /Sijji 1,200-1,500-mile range. In October 2004, Iran announced it had extended range of the Shahab-3 to 1,200 miles, and it added in early November 2004

For additional analytical, business and investment opportunities information, please contact Global Investment & Business Center, USA at (703) 370-8082. Fax: (703) 370-8083. E-mail: ibpusa3@gmail.com Global Business and Investment Info Databank - www.ibpus.com

that it is capable of "mass production" of it. Agence France Presse report (February 6, 2006) said January 2006 test succeeded. Related missiles claimed by Iran to have 1,200 mile range, include the "Ashoura" (claimed in November 2007); the "Ghadr" (displayed at military parade in September 2007); and the "Sijil," tested on November 12, 2000 (solid fuel). "Sijil 2" tested successfully on May 20, 2009 and December 16, 2009, but Secretary Gates said the range is likely closer to 1,200 miles than to 1,500. Still, this test potentially puts large portions of the Near East and Southeastern Europe in range, including U.S. bases in Turkey.

BM-25 1,500-mile range. On April 27, 2006, Israel's military intelligence chief said that Iran had received a shipment of North Korean-supplied BM-25 missiles. Missile said to be capable of carrying nuclear warheads. The Washington Times appeared to corroborate this reporting in a July 6, 2006, story, which asserted that the North Korean-supplied missile is based on a Soviet-era "SS-N-6" missile.

ICBM U.S. officials believe Iran might be capable of developing an intercontinental ballistic missile (3,000 mile range) by 2015. In February 2008 Iran claimed to have launched a probe into space, suggesting its missile technology might be improving to the point where an Iranian ICBM is realistic.

Other On September 6, 2002, Iran said it successfully tested a 200 mile range "Fateh 110" missile (solid

Missiles propellent), and Iran said in late September 2002 that it had begun production. Iran also possesses a few hundred short-range ballistic missiles, including the Shahab-1 (Scud-b), the Shahab-2 (Scud-C), and the Tondar-69 (CSS-8). In January 2009, Iran claimed to have tested a new air-to-air missile.

Space Following an August 2008 failure, in early February 2009, Iran successfully launched a small, low-

Vehicle earth satellite on a Safir-2 rocket (range about 155 miles). The Pentagon said the launch was "clearly a concern of ours" because "there are dual-use capabilities here which could be applied toward the development of long-range missiles."

Warheads Wall Street Journal report of September 14, 2005, said that U.S. intelligence believes Iran is working to adapt the Shahab-3 to deliver a nuclear warhead. Subsequent press reports say that U.S. intelligence captured an Iranian computer in mid-2004 showing plans to construct a nuclear warhead for the Shahab.30 The IAEA is seeking additional information from Iran.

FOREIGN POLICY AND SUPPORT FOR TERRORIST GROUPS

Iran's foreign policy is a product of the ideology of Iran's Islamic revolution, blended with long-standing national interests. Some interpret Iran's objectives as the overturning of the power structure in the Middle East, which Iran believes favors the United States, Israel, and their "collaborators"—Sunni Muslim regimes such as Egypt, Jordan, and

Saudi Arabia. The State Department report on international terrorism for 2008 released April 30, 2009, again stated (as it has for more than a decade) that Iran "remained the most active state sponsor of terrorism" in 2008, and it again attributed the terrorist activity primarily to the Qods Force of the Revolutionary Guard.

[30] Broad, William and David Sanger. "Relying On Computer, U.S. Seeks to Prove Iran's Nuclear Aims." *New York Times*, November 13, 2005.

The report focused particular attention on Iran's lethal **support to Shiite militias in Iraq as well** as on shipments to and training of "selected" Taliban fighters in Afghanistan.[31] On October 27, 2008, the deputy commander of the Basij became the first top Guard leader to publicly acknowledge that Iran supplies weapons to "liberation armies" in the region, a reference to pro-Iranian movements discussed below. The appointment of Brig. Gen. Ahmad Vahidi, the former Qods Forces commander, as Defense Minister in September 2009 (who got the highest number of Majles votes for his confirmation) caused concern in some neighboring states.

Some experts believe that Iran has been ascendant in the region because of the installation of pro-Iranian regimes in Iraq and Afghanistan, and the strength of Hezbollah in Lebanon and Hamas in Gaza. Iran might, according to this view, seek to press its advantage to strengthen regional Shiite movements and possibly drive the United States out of the Gulf. During a visit to the Middle East in March 2009, Secretary of State Clinton said, after meeting with several Arab and Israeli leaders in the region, that "There is a great deal of concern about Iran from this whole region."

Others reach an opposite conclusion, stating that Iran now feels more encircled than ever by pro-

U.S. regimes. Elections in Lebanon in 2009 that boosted pro-U.S. factions, U.S. engagement with Syria, stability in Iraq, and an influx of U.S. troops to Afghanistan have rendered Iran weaker than it has been in recent years.

RELATIONS WITH THE PERSIAN GULF STATES

The Persian Gulf monarchy states (Gulf Cooperation Council, GCC: Saudi Arabia, Kuwait, Bahrain, Qatar, Oman, and the United Arab Emirates) fear the strategic influence of Iran but they do not openly support U.S. conflict with Iran that might cause Iran to retaliate against Gulf state targets. The Gulf states privately welcome Iran's postelection turmoil because it means that Iran might be strategically weakened and consumed by internal infighting. However, there is concern in the Gulf that Iran might assert itself in the region to focus public attention outside Iran. Commercial relations between the Gulf states and Iran are normal, and several of the Gulf states, particularly Kuwait and UAE, have excess oil refining capacity and sell gasoline to Iran.

Since the mid-1990s, Iran has tried to blunt Gulf state fears of Iran by curtailing activity, conducted during the 1980s and early 1990s, to sponsor Shiite Muslim extremist groups in these states, all of which are run by Sunni governments. Iran found, to its detriment, that such activity caused the Gulf states to ally closely with the United States. In part to counter Iran's perceived growing influence in the Gulf, in December 2006 the summit of the GCC leaders announced that the GCC states might jointly study their own development of "peaceful nuclear technology." On the other hand, seeking to avoid further tensions with Iran, the GCC leaders invited Ahmadinejad to speak at the December 2007 summit of the GCC leaders in Doha, Qatar, marking the first time an Iranian president had been invited since the GCC was formed in 1981. His speech reiterated a consistent Iranian theme that the Gulf countries, including Iran, should set up their own security structure without the help of "outside powers" but also called for a "new chapter" in Iran-GCC relations.

[31] U.S. Department of State. *Country Reports on Terrorism 2008.* Released April 30, 2009. http://www.state.gov/s/ct/ rls/crt/2008/index.htm

- *Saudi Arabia.* Many observers closely watch the relationship between Iran and Saudi Arabia because of Saudi alarm over the emergence of a pro-Iranian government in Iraq and Iran's nuclear program. Saudi Arabia sees itself as leader of the Sunni Muslim world and views Shiite Muslims as heretical and disloyal internally. However, the Saudis, who do not want a repeat of Iran's sponsorship of disruptive and sometimes violent demonstrations at annual Hajj pilgrimages in Mecca in the 1980s and 1990s—or an increase in Iranian support for Saudi Shiite dissidents—are receptive to easing tensions with Iran. The Saudis continue to blame a pro-Iranian movement in the Kingdom, Saudi Hezbollah, for the June 25, 1996, Khobar Towers housing complex bombing, which killed 19 U.S. airmen.[32] After restoring relations in December 1991 (after a four-year break), Saudi-Iran ties progressed to high-level contacts during Khatemi's presidency, including Khatemi visits in 1999 and 2002, and Ahmadinejad has visited on several occasions.
- *United Arab Emirates* (UAE) concerns about Iran never fully recovered from the April 1992 Iranian expulsion of UAE security forces from the Persian Gulf island of Abu Musa, which it and the UAE shared under a 1971 bilateral agreement. (In 1971, Iran, then ruled by the U.S.-backed Shah, seized two other islands, Greater and Lesser Tunb, from the emirate of Ras al-Khaymah, as well as part of Abu Musa from the emirate of Sharjah.) In general, the UAE (particularly the federation capital, Abu Dhabi, backs U.S. efforts to dissuade Iran from developing its nuclear capability through international sanctions. Abu Dhabi generally takes a harder line against Iran than does the emirate of Dubai, which has an Iranian-origin resident community as large as 300,000 and business ties to Iran). On the islands dispute, the UAE wants to refer the dispute to the International Court of Justice (ICJ). Iran insists on resolving the issue bilaterally. The UAE formally protested Iran's setting up of a maritime and ship registration office on Abu Musa in July 2008. The United States supports UAE proposals but takes no formal position on sovereignty. Still seeking to avoid antagonizing Iran, in May 2007 the UAE received Ahmadinejad (the highest level Iranian visit since the 1979 revolution) and allowed him to lead an anti-U.S. rally of a reported several hundred Iranian-origin residents of Dubai at a soccer stadium there.

- *Qatar*, like most of the other Gulf states, does not seek confrontation and seeks to accommodate some of its interests, yet Qatar remains wary that Iran might eventually seek to encroach on its large North Field (natural gas). It shares that field with Iran (called South Pars on Iran's side) and Qatar earns large revenues from natural gas exports from it. Qatar's fears were heightened on April 26, 2004, when Iran's deputy Oil Minister said that Qatar is probably producing more gas than "her right share" from the field and that Iran "will not allow" its wealth to be used by others. Possibly to try to ease such implied threats, Qatar invited Ahmadinejad to the December 2007 GCC summit there.

[32] Walsh, Elsa. "Annals of Politics: Louis Freeh's Last Case." *The New Yorker*, May 14, 2001. The June 21, 2001, federal grand jury indictments of 14 suspects (13 Saudis and a Lebanese citizen) in the Khobar bombing indicate that Iranian agents may have been involved, but no indictments of any Iranians were announced. In June 2002, Saudi Arabia reportedly sentenced some of the eleven Saudi suspects held there. The 9/11 Commission final report asserts that Al Qaeda might have had some as yet undetermined involvement in the Khobar Towers attacks.

- *Bahrain* is about 60% Shiite, many of whom are of Persian origin, but its government is dominated by the Sunni Muslim Al Khalifa family. In 1981 and again in 1996, Bahrain publicly accused Iran of supporting Bahraini Shiite dissidents (the Islamic Front for the Liberation of Bahrain, Bahrain-Hezbollah, and other Bahraini dissident groups) in efforts to overthrow the ruling Al Khalifa family. Bahraini fears that Iran would try to interfere in Bahrain's November 25, 2006, parliamentary elections by providing support to Shiite candidates did not materialize, although the main Shiite opposition coalition won 18 out of the 40 seats of the elected body. Tensions have flared several times since July 2007 when Iranian editorialists asserted that Bahrain is part of Iran—that question was the subject of the 1970 U.N.-run referendum in which Bahrainis opted for independence. The issued flared again after a February 20, 2009, statement by Ali Akbar Nateq Nuri, an adviser to Khamene'i, that Bahrain was at one time an Iranian province. The statement caused major criticism of Iran throughout the region, and contributed to a decision by Morocco to break relations with Iran. Still, Bahrain has sought not to antagonize Iran and has apparently allowed Iran's banks to establish a presence in Bahrain's vibrant banking sector. On March 12, 2008, the Treasury Department sanctioned the Bahrain-based Future Bank under Executive order 13382 that sanctions proliferation entities. Future Bank purportedly is controlled by Bank Melli. The bank remains in operation.
- *Oman*. Of the GCC states, the Sultanate of Oman is closest politically to Iran and has refused to ostracize or even harshly criticize Iranian policies. Some press reports say local Omani officials routinely turn a blind eye to or even cooperate in the smuggling of western goods to Iran. Sultan Qaboos made a state visit to Iran in August 2009, coinciding with the inauguration of Ahmadinejad.

IRANIAN POLICY IN IRAQ

The U.S. military ousting of Saddam Hussein benefitted Iran strategically,[33] and during 20042008, U.S.-Iran differences in Iraq widened to the point where some were describing the competition as a U.S.-Iran "proxy war" inside Iraq. The acute source of tension was evidence, detailed on several occasions by U.S. commanders in Iraq, that the *Qods* Force was providing arms (including highly lethal "explosively forced projectiles," EFPs, which have killed U.S. soldiers), training, guidance, and financing to Shiite militias involved in sectarian violence.

However, recent Defense Department reports on Iraq stability—most recently in September 2009—corroborate a widespread perception that Iranian interference in Iraq has lessened, including fewer Iranian weapons shipments. In Iraq itself, the Shiite militias and political parties that benefit most from Iranian support fared poorly in the January 31, 2009, provincial elections in Iraq, and the results were viewed as a setback for Iran's influence in Iraq. One Shiite militia, Asa'ib al Haq (League of the Righteous) has reconciled with the government and its leaders (Khazali brothers) have been released from U.S. custody. Iran was unable to derail the U.S.-Iraq defense pact (which took effect January 1, 2009). In January 2009, Iraqi Prime Minister Nuri al

[33] This issue is covered in greater depth in CRS Report RS22323, *Iran's Activities and Influence in Iraq*, by Kenneth Katzman.

Maliki visited Iran for the fourth time since he became Prime Minister, reportedly to assure Iran that the pact did not threaten Iran.

Iran also has signed a number of agreements with Iraq on transportation, energy cooperation, free flow of Shiite pilgrims, border security, intelligence sharing, and other cooperation; several more agreements, including a $1 billion credit line for Iranian exports to Iraq, were signed during Ahmadinejad's March 2-3, 2008, visit to Iraq; implementing agreements were signed in April 2008. The two countries now do about $4 billion in bilateral trade.

After at first rejecting dialogue with Iran on the Iraq issue, the George W. Bush Administration supported and attended several regional conferences on Iraq, attended by Iran, and undertook bilateral talks with Iran on the Iraq issue. Several meetings were held in Baghdad in 2007, with no concrete results, according to former Ambassador to Iraq Crocker, who led the U.S. side at the talks. A round of talks was tentatively scheduled for December 18, 2007, but Iran repeatedly postponed them because of differences over the agenda and the level of talks (Iran wanted them to be at the ambassador level). On May 5, 2008, Iran indefinitely suspended this dialogue, and, in February 2009, Iran said there was no need to resume it.

A provision of the FY2008 defense authorization bill (P.L. 110-181) required a report to Congress on Iran's interference in Iraq. On several occasions since January 2008, the Treasury Department has taken action against suspected Iranian and pro-Iranian operatives in Iraq by designating individuals and organizations as a threat to stability in Iraq under the July 17, 2007, Executive Order 13438, which freezes the assets and bans transactions with named individuals. The named entities, which includes a senior Qods Forces leader, are in the tables on sanctioned entities in CRS Report RS20871, *Iran Sanctions*, by Kenneth Katzman. On July 2, 2009, a pro-Iranian militia offshoot, Khata'ib Hezbollah (Hezbollah Battalions) was named under the order, and was also designated

For additional analytical, business and investment opportunities information, please contact Global Investment & Business Center, USA at (703) 370-8082. Fax: (703) 370-8083. E-mail: ibpusa3@gmail.com Global Business and Investment Info Databank - www.ibpus.com

a Foreign Terrorist Organization (FTO) under the Immigration and Naturalization Act. On July 9, 2009, the United States military turned over to Iraqi custody five Iranian Qods Forces operatives (Iran claims they are diplomats) arrested in 2007 in Irbil, northern Iraq. The men returned to Iran.

SUPPORTING PALESTINIAN MILITANT GROUPS

Iran's support for Palestinian militant groups has long concerned U.S. Administrations, as part of an apparent effort by Tehran to obstruct an Israeli-Palestinian peace, which Iran believes would strengthen the United States and Israel. Ahmadinejad's various statements on Israel were discussed above, although Supreme Leader Khamene'i has repeatedly called Israel a "cancerous tumor." He used that term again during a March 4, 2009, press conference in Tehran. In December 2001, Rafsanjani said that it would take only one Iranian nuclear bomb to destroy Israel, whereas a similar strike against Iran by Israel would have far less impact because Iran's population is large.

Iran has hosted numerous conferences to which anti-peace process terrorist organizations were invited (for example: April 24, 2001, and June 2-3, 2002). During his presidency, Khatemi also issued sharp criticisms and recriminations against Israel, but he also conversed with Israel's president at the 2005 funeral of Pope John Paul II. The formal position of the Iranian Foreign Ministry, considered a bastion of moderates, is that Iran would not seek to block an Israeli-Palestinian settlement but that the peace process is too weighted toward Israel to result in a fair settlement.

IRAN AND HAMAS

The State Department report on terrorism for 2007 (mentioned above) again accused Iran of providing "extensive" funding, weapons, and training to Hamas, Palestinian Islamic Jihad (PIJ), the Al Aqsa Martyr's Brigades, and the Popular Front for the Liberation of Palestine-General Command (PFLP-GC). All are named as foreign terrorist organizations (FTO) by the State Department for their use of violence to undermine the Arab-Israeli peace process. Some saw Iran's regional policy further strengthened by Hamas's victory in the January 25, 2006, Palestinian legislative elections, and even more so by Hamas's June 2007 armed takeover of the Gaza Strip. The Hamas gains potentially positioned it to block any peace settlement with Israel. Hamas activists downplay Iranian influence on them, asserting that Iran is mostly Shiite, while Hamas members are Sunni Muslims.[34] Hamas was reputed to receive about 10% of its budget in the early 1990s from Iran, although since then Hamas has cultivated funding from wealthy Persian Gulf donors and supporters in Europe and elsewhere.

Still, it was evident from the December 27, 2008-January 17, 2009, Israel-Hamas war in Gaza, that Iran provides material support to Hamas. Joint Chiefs Chairman Adm. Mike Mullen said on January 27, 2009, that the United States boarded but did not seize a ship carrying light arms to Hamas from Iran; the ship (the Monchegorsk) later went to Cyprus. On March 11, 2009, a U.N. committee monitoring Iran's compliance with Resolution 1747, which bans Iranian arms exports, said Iran might have violated that resolution with the alleged shipment. Hamas appeared to corroborate allegations of Iranian weapons supplies when its exiled leader, Khaled Meshal, on February 1, 2009, publicly praised

For additional analytical, business and investment opportunities information, please contact Global Investment & Business Center, USA at (703) 370-8082. Fax: (703) 370-8083. E-mail: ibpusa3@gmail.com Global Business and Investment Info Databank - www.ibpus.com

Iran for helping Hamas achieve "victory" over Israel in the conflict.[35] On December 29, 2008, Khamene'i said that Muslims worldwide were "duty-bound" to defend Palestinians in the Gaza Strip against the Israeli offensive against the Hamas-run leadership there, but the Iranian leadership did not attempt to send Iranian volunteers to Gaza to fight on Hamas' behalf. Iranian weaponry might also have been the target of a January 2009 strike on a weapons delivery purportedly bound for Gaza in transit via Sudan (presumably via Egypt).

Sunni Arab leaders in Egypt, Jordan, Saudi Arabia, and throughout the region apparently fear Iran's reported attempts to discredit these leaders for what Iran considers insufficient support for Hamas in its recent war with Israel. Some Iranian efforts reportedly involve establishing Hezbollah cells in some of these countries, particularly Egypt, purportedly to stir up opposition to these governments and build public support for Hezbollah and Hamas. [36] These countries are also said to fear that President Obama's outreach to Iran might lead the United States to downplay their concerns about Iran—a sentiment that Secretary of Defense Gates tried to allay during his visit to the Middle East in May 2009.

LEBANESE HEZBOLLAH AND SYRIA

Iran has maintained a close relationship with Hezbollah since the group was formed in 1982 by Lebanese Shiite clerics who were sympathetic to Iran's Islamic revolution and belonged to the Lebanese Da'wa Party. Hezbollah was responsible for several acts of anti-U.S. and anti-Israel terrorism in the 1980s and 1990s.[37] Hezbollah's attacks on Israeli forces in southern Lebanon contributed to an Israeli withdrawal in May 2000, but, despite United Nations certification of Israel's withdrawal, Hezbollah maintained military forces along the border. Hezbollah continued to remain armed and outside Lebanese government control, despite U.N. Security Council Resolution 1559 (September 2, 2004) that required its dismantlement. In refusing to disarm, Hezbollah says it was resisting Israeli occupation **of some Lebanese territory (Shib'a Farms).**

[34] CNN "Late Edition" interview with Hamas co-founder Mahmoud Zahar, January 29, 2006. [35] Hamas Leader Praises Iran's Help in Gaza 'Victory.' CNN.com. February 1, 2009.

[36] Slackman, Michael. "Egypt Accuses Hezbollah of Plotting Attacks in Sinai and Arms Smuggling to Gaza." New York Times, April 14, 2009

Although Iran likely did not instigate Lebanese Hezbollah to provoke the July-August 2006 war, Iran has long been its major arms supplier. Hezbollah fired Iranian-supplied rockets on Israel's northern towns during the fighting. Reported Iranian shipments to Hezbollah prior to the conflict included the "Fajr" (dawn) and Khaybar series of rockets that were fired at the Israeli city of Haifa (30 miles from the border), and over 10,000 Katyusha rockets that were fired at cities within 20 miles of the Lebanese border.[38] Iran also supplied Hezbollah with an unmanned aerial vehicle (UAV), the *Mirsad*, which Hezbollah briefly flew over the Israel-Lebanon border on November 7, 2004, and April 11, 2005; at least three were shot down by Israel during the conflict. On July 14, 2006, Hezbollah apparently hit an Israeli warship with a C-802 sea-skimming missile probably provided by Iran. (See Table 5 above for information on Iran's acquisition of that weapon from China.) Iran also purportedly provided advice during the conflict; about 50 Revolutionary Guards Qods Force personnel were in Lebanon (down from about 2,000 when Hezbollah was formed, according to a *Washington Post* report of April 13, 2005) when the conflict began; that number might have increased during the conflict to help Hezbollah operate the Iran-supplied weaponry. In November 2009, Israel intercepted a ship that it asserted was carrying 500 tons of arms purportedly for Hezbollah.

Even though Hezbollah reduced its overt military presence in southern Lebanon in accordance with the conflict-related U.N. Security Council Resolution 1701 (July 31, 2006), Hezbollah was perceived as a victor in the war for holding out against heavy Israeli air-strikes and some ground action. Iran supported Hezbollah's demands and provided it with leverage by resupplying it, after the hostilities, with 27,000 rockets, more than double what Hezbollah had at the start of the 2006 war.[39] Among the post-war deliveries were 500 Iranian-made "Zelzal" (Earthquake) missiles with a range of 186 miles, enough to reach Tel Aviv from south Lebanon. Iran also made at least $150 million available for Hezbollah to distribute to Lebanese citizens (mostly Shiite supporters of Hezbollah) whose homes were damaged in the Israeli military campaign.[40] The State Department terrorism report for 2008, referenced above, specifies Iranian aid to Hezbollah as exceeding $200 million in 2008, and says that Iran trained over 3,000 Hezbollah fighters in Iran during the year.

Neither Israel nor the United States opposed Hezbollah's progressively increased participation in peaceful Lebanese politics. In March 2005, President George W. Bush indicated that the United States might accept Hezbollah as a legitimate political force in Lebanon if it disarms. In the

[37] Hezbollah is believed responsible for the October 1983 bombing of the U.S. Marine barracks in Beirut, as well as attacks on U.S. Embassy Beirut facilities in April 1983 and September 1984, and for the hijacking of TWA Flight 847 in June 1985 in which Navy diver Robert Stetham was killed. Hezbollah is also believed to have committed the March 17, 1992, bombing of Israel's embassy in that city, which killed 29 people. Its last known terrorist attack outside Lebanon was the July 18, 1994, bombing of a Jewish community center in Buenos Aires, which killed 85. On October 31, 2006, Argentine prosecutors asked a federal judge to seek the arrest of Rafsanjani, former Intelligence Minister Ali Fallahian, former Foreign Minister Ali Akbar Velayati, and four other Iranian officials for this attack.

[38]"Israel's Peres Says Iran Arming Hizbollah." Reuters, February 4, 2002. [39] Rotella, Sebastian. "In Lebanon, Hezbollah Arms Stockpile Bigger, Deadlier." *Los Angeles Times*, May 4, 2008. [40] Shadid, Anthony. "Armed With Iran's Millions, Fighters Turn to Rebuilding." *Washington Post*, August 16, 2006.

Lebanese parliamentary elections of May—June 2005, Hezbollah expanded its presence in the parliament to 14 out of the 128-seat body, and it gained two cabinet seats. In mid May 2008, Hezbollah, for the first time ever, used its militia wing for domestic purposes. Its fighters took over large parts of Beirut in response to an attempt by the U.S. and Saudi-backed Lebanese government to curb Hezbollah's media and commercial

For additional analytical, business and investment opportunities information, please contact Global Investment & Business Center, USA at (703) 370-8082. Fax: (703) 370-8083. E-mail: ibpusa3@gmail.com
Global Business and Investment Info Databank - www.ibpus.com

operations. The success of its fighters contributed to a Qatar-brokered settlement on May 21, 2008, in which the majority coalition agreed to give Hezbollah and its allies enough seats in a new cabinet (one Hezbollah cabinet seat and seven allies holding cabinet seats as well) to be able to veto government decisions. Hezbollah agreed to the compromise candidate of Lebanese Army commander Michel Suleiman to become president.

Based on the strength, Hezbollah was viewed as a likely winner in June 7, 2009, parliamentary elections in Lebanon. However, its coalition won 57 seats in the elections, failing to overturn the majority of the pro-U.S. factions led by Sa'd al-Hariri, son of assassinated leader Rafiq Hariri, which won 71 seats (one more than they had previously). A new cabinet was formed in November 2009, but Hezbollah's political strength in that government was reduced only slightly compared to the pre-election government. Nonetheless, the election defeat for Hezbollah allies set back Tehran's regional influence. As a matter of policy, the United States does not meet with any Hezbollah members, even those in the parliament or cabinet. Hezbollah is a designated FTO, but that designation bars financial transactions with the group and does not specifically ban meeting members of the group.

SYRIA

Iran's support for Hezbollah is linked in many ways to its alliance with Syria. Syria is the transit point for the Iranian weapons shipments to Hezbollah and both countries see Hezbollah as leverage against Israel to achieve their regional and territorial aims. In order to preserve its links to Syria, which is one of Iran's few real allies, Iran purportedly has acted as an intermediary with North Korea to supply Syria with various forms of WMD and missile technology. Some see Israel-Syria negotiations—and recent Obama Administration engagement with Syria—as means to wean Syria away from its alliance with Iran. However, Iran is a major investor in the Syrian economy, which attracts very little western investment, and some believe the Iran-Syria alliance is not easily severed. On December 13, 2009, the Syrian and Iranian defense ministers signed a defense agreement to "face common enemies and challenges."

CENTRAL ASIA AND THE CASPIAN

Iran's policy in Central Asia has thus far emphasized Iran's rights to Caspian Sea resources, particularly against Azerbaijan. That country's population, like Iran's, is mostly Shiite Muslim, but its leadership is secular. In addition, Azerbaijan is ethnically Turkic, and Iran fears that Azerbaijan nationalists might stoke separatism among Iran's large Azeri Turkic population, which demonstrated some unrest in 2006. These factors could explain why Iran has generally tilted toward Armenia, which is Christian, even though it has been at odds with Azerbaijan over territory and control of ethnic Armenians. In July 2001, Iranian warships and combat aircraft threatened a British Petroleum (BP) ship on contract to Azerbaijan out of an area of the Caspian that Iran considers its own. The United States called that action provocative, and it is engaged in border security and defense cooperation with Azerbaijan directed against Iran (and Russia). The United States successfully backed construction of the Baku-Tblisi-Ceyhan oil pipeline, intended in part to provide alternatives to Iranian oil. Along with India and Pakistan, Iran has been given observer status at the Central Asian security grouping called the Shanghai Cooperation Organization (SCO—Russia, China, Kazakhstan, Kyrgyzstan, Uzbekistan, and Tajikistan). In April 2008, Iran applied for full membership in the organization, which opposes a long-term U.S. presence in Central Asia.

AFGHANISTAN AND PAKISTAN[41]

Iran is viewed by U.S. officials as pursuing a multi-track strategy—attempting to help develop Afghanistan and enhance its influence there, while also building leverage against the United States by arming anti-U.S. militant groups. Iran is particularly interested in restoring some of its traditional sway in eastern, central, and northern Afghanistan where Persian-speaking Afghans predominate. Iran may want to be in position to threaten the air base at Shindand, in Herat Province, which is now used by U.S. and allied forces and which Iran believes could be used for surveillance of or strikes on Iran.

The State Department terrorism report for 2008 again accused the Qods Force of supplying various munitions, including 107mm rockets, to Taliban and other militants in Afghanistan; some Taliban commanders openly say they are obtaining Iranian weapons. The 2008 reports also, and for the first time, accuses Iran of training Taliban fighters in small unit tactics, small arms use, explosives, and indirect weapons fire. Among specific shipments noted by the United States: on April 17, 2007, U.S. military personnel in Afghanistan captured a shipment of Iranian weapons that purportedly was bound for Taliban fighters. On several occasions in 2007, NATO officers said they directly intercepted Iranian shipments of heavy arms, C4 explosives, and advanced roadside bombs (explosively forced projectiles, or EFPs, such as those found in Iraq) to Taliban fighters in Afghanistan. U.S. commanders in Afghanistan maintain that the intercepted shipments are large enough that the Iranian government would have to have known about them. U.S. and Afghan officials say the shipments continue, but are not consistent or necessarily decisive in the Afghanistan war.

These shipments and contacts have caused debate over Iran's goals because Iran long opposed the regime of the Taliban in Afghanistan on the grounds that it oppressed Shiite Muslim and other Persian-speaking minorities. Iran nearly launched a military attack against the Taliban in September 1998 after Taliban fighters captured and killed nine Iranian diplomats based in northern Afghanistan, and Iran provided military aid to the Northern Alliance factions. During the major combat phase of the post-September 11 U.S.-led war in Afghanistan, Iran offered search and rescue of any downed service persons and the transshipment to Afghanistan of humanitarian assistance. Iran and U.S. diplomats were in continuous contact in forging a post-Taliban government in Afghanistan at the December 2001 "Bonn Conference." In March 2002, Iran expelled Gulbuddin Hikmatyar, an Afghan militant leader; it froze his assets in January 2005.

After 2004, Iran's influence waned somewhat as Northern Alliance figures were marginalized in Afghan politics. To build financial and alternative political influence in Afghanistan, Iran has funded projects that total about $1.2 billion million since 2001 (close to a pledged amount in international donors conferences), mostly in neighboring Herat but also in Kabul (Shiite theological seminaries there). Afghan officials and observers in Herat Province say Iran's influence is substantial there but not necessarily against the Afghan government.[42] Iran's

[41] See CRS Report RL30588, *Afghanistan: Post-Taliban Governance, Security, and U.S. Policy*, by Kenneth Katzman. [42] Conversations with observers and officials in Herat during CRS visit there. October 2009.

construction of Shiite mosques and seminaries could indicate Iran is trying to support Afghanistan's Shiite (Hazara tribe) minority, and Iran has funded several media outlets in Afghanistan catering to Shiites.

At the same time, some commanders, including CENTCOM Commander Gen. David Petraeus, have said that U.S. engagement with Iran on Afghanistan might help U.S. stabilization efforts there. Others say that working with Iran on Afghanistan might help build a broader understanding with Iran on other issues, including the nuclear issue.

Perhaps in recognition of Iran's role in Afghanistan, or as part of a broader effort to build dialogue with Iran, the United States invited Iran to an international conference on Afghanistan held in the Netherlands on March 31, 2009. Iran's representatives there had a brief side exchange there with U.S. special representative for Afghanistan and Pakistan Ambassador Richard Holbrooke. At the meeting, Iran pledged cooperation on preventing drug smuggling out of Afghanistan and in helping economically develop that country.

PAKISTAN

Iran's relations with Pakistan have been partly a function of events in Afghanistan, although relations have worsened somewhat in late 2009 as Iran has accused Pakistan of supporting Sunni Muslim rebels in Iran's Baluchistan region. These Sunni guerrillas have conducted a number of attacks on Iranian regime targets in 2009, as discussed above ("Jundullah").

Iran had a burgeoning military cooperation with Pakistan in the early 1990s, and as noted Iran's nuclear program benefitted from the A.Q. Khan network. However, Iran-Pakistan relations became strained in the 1990s when Pakistan was supporting the Taliban in Afghanistan, which committed alleged atrocities against Shiite Afghans (Hazara tribe), and which seized control of Persian-speaking areas of Afghanistan. Currently, Iran remains suspicious that Pakistan might want to again implant the Taliban in power in Afghanistan—and Iran itself is aiding the Taliban to some extent—but Iran and Pakistan now have a broad agenda that includes a potential major gas pipeline project, discussed further below.

AL QAEDA

Iran is not a natural ally of Al Qaeda, largely because Al Qaeda is an orthodox Sunni Muslim organization. However, some experts believe that hardliners in Iran might want to use Al Qaeda activists as leverage against the United States and its allies. Some say Iran might want to exchange them for a U.S. hand-over of PMOI activists under U.S.

For additional analytical, business and investment opportunities information, please contact Global Investment & Business Center, USA at (703) 370-8082. Fax: (703) 370-8083. E-mail: ibpusa3@gmail.com Global Business and Investment Info Databank - www.ibpus.com

control in Iraq. The 9/11 Commission report said several of the September 11 hijackers and other plotters, possibly with official help, might have transited Iran, but the report does not assert that the Iranian government cooperated with or knew about the plot. Another bin Laden ally, Abu Musab al-Zarqawi, killed by

U.S. forces in Iraq on June 7, 2006, reportedly transited Iran after the September 11 attacks and took root in Iraq, becoming an insurgent leader there.

However, Iran might see possibilities for tactical alliance with Al Qaeda. Iran asserted on July 23, 2003, that it had "in custody" senior Al Qaeda figures. On July 16, 2005, Iran's Intelligence Minister said that 200 Al Qaeda members are in Iranian jails.[43] U.S. officials have said since January 2002 that Iran has not prosecuted or extradited any senior Al Qaeda operatives. The three major Al Qaeda figures believed to have been in Iran include spokesman Sulayman Abu Ghaith, top operative Sayf Al Adl, and Osama bin Laden's son, Saad.[44] although some U.S. officials said in January 2009 that Saad bin Laden might have left Iran and could be in Pakistan. That information was publicized a few days after the Treasury Department (on January 16, 2009) designated four Al Qaeda operatives in Iran, including Saad bin Laden (and three lesser known figures) as terrorist entities under Executive Order 13224. (U.S. officials blamed Saad bin Laden, Adl, and Abu Ghaith for the May 12, 2003, bombings in Riyadh, Saudi Arabia, against four expatriate housing complexes on these operatives, saying they have been able to contact associates outside Iran.[45]) Saad bin Laden was subsequently said to have possibly been killed in a

U.S. air strike against Al Qaeda locations in Pakistan, although there has been no confirmation of that.

In December 2009, Iran's Foreign Minister confirmed that a teenage daughter of Osama bin Laden had sought refuge in the Saudi embassy in Tehran—the first official confirmation that members of bin Laden's family have been in Iran. Other family members are said to have been living in a compound in Iran since the September 11, 2001, attacks. Some family members have said the young bin Ladens have never been affiliated with Al Qaeda.

LATIN AMERICA

A growing concern has been Iran's developing relations with countries and leaders in Latin America considered adversaries of the United States, particularly Cuba and Venezuela's Hugo Chavez. Ahmadinejad made a high profile visit to five Latin American countries in November 2009, including Brazil but also including, as expected, Venezuela. On January 27, 2009, Secretary of Defense Gates said Iran was trying to build influence in Latin America by expanding front companies and opening offices in countries there. Recent State Department terrorism reports have said that Cuba maintains "close relationships with other state sponsors of terrorism such as Iran." Iran has offered Bolivia $1 billion in aid and investment, according to an *Associated Press* report of November 23, 2008.

For additional analytical, business and investment opportunities information, please contact Global Investment & Business Center, USA at (703) 370-8082. Fax: (703) 370-8083. E-mail: ibpusa3@gmail.com Global Business and Investment Info Databank - www.ibpus.com

Chavez has visited Iran on several occasions, offering Iran additional gasoline during Iran's fuel shortages in 2007 as well as joint oil and gas projects. A firm deal for Petroleos de Venezuela to supply Iran with gasoline was signed in September 2009, apparently in a joint effort to circumvent any potential worldwide ban on sales of gasoline to Iran. The two countries have established direct air links, and 400 Iranian engineers have reportedly been sent to Venezuela to work on infrastructure projects there. However, many accounts say that most of the agreements between Iran and Venezuela are agreements in principle that have not been implemented in reality. On October 30, 2007, then Secretary of Homeland Security Michael Chertoff said that Iran's relationship with Venezuela is an emerging threat because it represents a "marriage" of Iran's extremist ideology with "those who have anti-American views."

[43] "Tehran Pledges to Crack Down on Militants." Associated Press, July 18, 2005. [44] Gertz, Bill. "Al Qaeda Terrorists Being Held by Iran." *Washington Times*, July 24, 2003. [45] Gertz, Bill. "CIA Points to Continuing Iran Tie to Al Qaeda." *Washington Times*, July 23, 2004.

INDIA

Iran and India have cultivated good relations with each other in order to enable each to pursue its own interests and avoid mutual conflict. The two backed similar anti-Taliban factions in Afghanistan during 1996-2001 and have a number of mutual economic and even military-tomilitary relationships and projects, discussed further in CRS Report RS22486, *India-Iran Relations and U.S. Interests*, by K. Alan Kronstadt and Kenneth Katzman.

One aspect of the relationship involves not only the potential building of a natural gas pipeline from Iran, through Pakistan, to India, but also the supplies of gasoline to Iran. A key supplier is Reliance Industries Ltd., which by some accounts supplies up to 40% of Iran's imports of gasoline. In December 2008, some Members of Congress expressed opposition to a decision by the Export-Import Bank to provide up to $900 million in loan guarantees to Reliance, because of its gasoline sales to Iran. A provision of H.R. 3081, a FY2010 foreign aid appropriation, would end provision of such export credits to companies that sell gasoline to Iran. Another source of U.S. concern has been visits to India by some Iranian naval personnel.

AFRICA

Some Members of Congress are concerned that Iran is support radical Islamist movements in Africa. In the 111th Congress, H.Con.Res. 16 cites Hezbollah for engaging in raising funds in Africa by trafficking in "conflict diamonds." Iran also might have supplied Islamists in Somalia with anti-aircraft and anti-tank weaponry. The possible transfer of weaponry to Hamas via Sudan was discussed above.

NATIONAL SECURITY

DURING THE 1970s, imperial Iran developed one of the most impressive military forces in the Middle East, and it used those forces to assume a security role in the Persian Gulf after the British military withdrawal in 1971. The defense of the strategic Strait of Hormuz preoccupied the shah, as it did the other conservative monarchs in the area. Freedom of navigation in the Gulf was important for international shipping, and the shah was perceived, at least in certain quarters, as the undeclared "policeman of the West in the Gulf."

When independent observers concluded that Iran's military buildup exceeded its defensive needs, the shah declared that his responsibilities extended beyond Iran and included the protection of the Gulf. Increasingly, the military played a pivotal role in promoting this policy and, in doing so, gained a privileged position in society. Under the Nixon Doctrine of 1969, according to which aiding local armed forces was considered preferable to direct United States military intervention, Washington played an important part in upgrading the Iranian military forces. The United States supplied Iran with sophisticated hardware and sent thousands of military advisers and technicians to help Iran absorb the technology.

By 1979 the United States military presence in Iran had drawn the wrath of Iranians. Ayatollah Sayyid Ruhollah Musavi Khomeini specifically identified the shah's pro-American policies as detrimental to Iranian interests and called on his supporters to oppose the United States presence. He cited special legal privileges granted United States personnel in Iran as an example of the shah's excessive identification of Iran's interests with those of Washington.

Following the Islamic Revolution of 1979, the armed forces underwent fundamental changes. The revolutionary government purged high-ranking officials as well as many mid-ranking officers identified with the Pahlavi regime and created a loyal military force, the Pasdaran (Pasdaran-e Enghelab-e Islami, or Islamic Revolutionary Guard Corps, or Revolutionary Guards), whose purpose was to defend the Revolution. When the Iran-Iraq War began, however, the revolutionary government had to acknowledge its need for the professional services of many of the purged officers to lead the armed forces in defending the country against Iraq. The army was unexpectedly successful in the war, even though, as of 1987, the regular armed forces continued to be regarded with considerable suspicion. Within the Iranian military there was competition between the regular and irregular armed forces. The Islamic clergy (see Glossary) continued to rely more heavily on the loyal Pasdaran to defend the regime. Moreover, most of the casualties were members of the Pasdaran and Basij volunteers who composed the irregular armed forces. In the late 1980s, in addition to defending the Revolution, Iran continued to follow certain national security policies that had remained constant during the previous four decades.

INTERNAL SECURITY

The Islamic Revolution destroyed the structures on which the shah's internal security policies depended. Mohammad Reza Shah had not tolerated dissent, had reacted strongly when challenged, and had relied on an elaborate internal security police force to enforce his absolute authority. Over the years, Khomeini had vigorously condemned the shah's secret police operations and continually called on Iranians to rise against a perceived tyrannical ruler. By the late 1970s, the shah's internal security organizations were in disgrace because of their abuses. In early 1979, the revolutionary regime dismantled existing security organizations and called on loyal citizens to protect the Revolution. Yet, like the shah, the revolutionary regime faced clear opposition to its authority.

INTERNAL SECURITY IN THE 1970S

The Pahlavi regime identified the Fadayan, the Tudeh, and several ethnic groups as opponents to the shah's rule. To meet their rising challenge, the shah relied on security forces whose agents infiltrated many underground organizations. By early 1970, a sophisticated intelligence-gathering system was in place, reporting all currents of political dissent directly to the monarch.

In 1970 opposition forces took the initiative by launching a terrorist campaign against the regime. At the time, this was perceived as a nuisance and an embarrassment to the shah, because the monarchy was not "threatened." Nevertheless, opposition to the shah grew stronger when the monarch authorized unrelenting punishment of those accused of security violations. Hundreds of young Iranians were arrested, tried, and sentenced. Many were tortured and some executed for their unwavering opposition. In 1976 opposition forces clashed with the police in a series of gun battles that mobilized thousands in the streets of Tehran. With heightened visibility, terrorist groups mounted successful attacks on police posts, further threatening the regime's hold on internal security. By 1978 organized opposition to the monarchy reached a high point with ideologically incompatible groups joining in efforts to overthrow the shah. Leftist guerrillas joined student and religious organizations in calling for political change.

The two most important leftist guerrilla groups operating in Iran in 1978 were the Mojahedin and the Fadayan The Mojahedin had changed its name at least three times since its formation in 1960 under the name of Nehzat-e Azadi-yi Iran, or the Iran Freedom Movement (IFM). Although it was not formally a religious party, its rank-and-file membership was religiously oriented, a fact that helped mobilize clerical support in 1978. Unlike the clerical forces, however, the Mojahedin and the Fadayan conducted a systematic assassination campaign in 1977 and 1978 against Iranian security officials and United States military and defense-related personnel stationed in Tehran. The shah was also a target, as evidenced by periodic uncoverings of assassination plots.

This wave of violence was met by an equally strong and determined campaign of arrests and executions. Iranian students abroad also became part of a cycle of action and counteraction: in the United States and Western Europe, students who protested against the shah were kept under surveillance so that punitive action could later be taken against them. In addition, the Mojahedin and the Fadayan conducted a propaganda campaign in support of "the Iranian armed struggle" and against the shah, SAVAK, and what was termed "institutionalized repression in Iran."

Within Iran's borders, stiff government security measures notwithstanding, organized opposition was never eliminated. Although the shah had declared illegal all opposition political parties, labor unions, peasant organizations, and university student groups, antigovernment sentiments remained high, especially among the clerical community. By late 1977, student demonstrations increased in frequency, with a vocal minority calling on Iranians to "raise their voices against absolute rule." These protests, timed to call President Jimmy Carter's attention to the human rights situation in Iran, resulted in the arrest of hundreds of demonstrators, many of whom were allegedly tortured by SAVAK forces.

In January 1978, conservative religious students demonstrated in the holy city of Qom to express the long-standing clerical opposition to the shah's land reform policies, which had resulted in the expropriation of *vaqf* (religious endowment) and other lands. Religious leaders were also outraged at what they perceived to be the shah's violations of sacred Islamic laws in such areas as the role of women in society and the imposition of a secular legal system that usurped clerical authority. Attempts by the police to disperse demonstrators resulted in several deaths.

The religious leadership called for a general strike across the country for February 18, to highlight the forty-day mourning period for those killed in Qom. Far more serious disturbances erupted on that day in Tabriz and Tehran, precipitating the worst riots since 1963. After several days of widespread arson directed at banks, movie theaters, and hotels in Tabriz, the army moved in to restore order. Similar measures were taken in Tehran and other major cities. According to the government 12 persons were killed in Tabriz and 250 persons arrested. In reality, the casualty figure was much higher and the arrests more numerous. Ironically, the deaths presented the next opportunity for confrontation. When demonstrators, commemorating the forty-day mourning period, defiantly marched through the streets of Tabriz, the armed forces reacted as expected. To protect themselves and restore order, they opened fire, killing and injuring more civilians. The result was a sequence of events in which the opposition, led by influential clerics, conducted "religious commemorations," and the government interpreted them as challenges to law and order. With neither side relenting, the cycle of violence spread.

Observers of these tragic events pointed out that the reemergence of large-scale protest demonstrations was only made possible because of the shah's more liberal policies toward the nonviolent expression of dissent. Indeed, the shah confirmed on several occasions his commitment to more "liberal" political reforms, but at the same time he warned that the dissident movement was "completely illegal" and that he would "not let it get out of hand." Illegal or not, mass protest demonstrations did get out of control when the shah openly chastised the clerics for "destroying the country." The shah could not end these demonstrations, which gathered more support throughout 1978. Workers from the oil industry, heeding the call of the religious authorities, slowly paralyzed Iran's economic sector. It became only a matter of time before the shah lost control over Iran's internal security.

LAW ENFORCEMENT AGENCIES

Intensely concerned with matters of internal security in the post-1953 environment, the shah authorized the development of one of the most extensive systems of law enforcement agencies in the developing world. The Gendarmerie--the rural police--and the National Police gained in numbers and responsibilities. The secret police organization, SAVAK, gained special notoriety for its excessive zeal in "maintaining" internal security. But as in the regular armed forces, the shah's management style virtually eliminated all coordination among these agencies. A favorite approach was to shuffle army personnel back and forth between their ordinary duties and temporary positions in internal security agencies, in order to minimize the possibility of any organized coups against the throne. Added to this list of institutional shortcomings was agencies' all- important public image, cloaked in mystery and fear. Iranians in and out of the country came to perceive these agencies as "arms" of the shah's absolute power and resented them deeply.

SAVAK

Formed under the guidance of United States and Israeli intelligence officers in 1957, SAVAK developed into an effective secret agency. General Teymur Bakhtiar was appointed its first director, only to be dismissed in 1961, allegedly for organizing a coup; he was assassinated in 1970 under mysterious circumstances, probably on the shah's direct order. His successor, General Hosain Pakravan, was dismissed in 1966, allegedly for having failed to crush the clerical opposition in the early 1960s. The shah turned to his childhood friend and classmate, General Nematollah Nassiri, to rebuild SAVAK and properly "serve" the monarch. Mansur Rafizadeh, the SAVAK director in the United States throughout the 1970s, claimed that General Nassiri's telephone was tapped by SAVAK agents reporting directly to the shah, an example of the level of mistrust pervading the government on the eve of the Revolution.

In 1987 accurate information concerning SAVAK remained publicly unavailable. A flurry of pamphlets issued by the revolutionary regime after 1979 indicated that SAVAK had been a full-scale intelligence agency with more than 15,000 full-time personnel and thousands of part-time informants. SAVAK was attached to the Office of the Prime Minister, and its director assumed the title of deputy to the prime minister for national security affairs. Although officially a civilian agency, SAVAK had close ties to the military; many of its officers served simultaneously in branches of the armed forces. Another childhood friend and close confidant of the shah, Major General Hosain Fardust, was deputy director of SAVAK until the early 1970s, when the shah promoted him to the directorship of the Special Intelligence Bureau, which operated inside Niavaran Palace, independently of SAVAK.

Founded to round up members of the outlawed Tudeh, SAVAK expanded its activities to include gathering intelligence and neutralizing the regime's opponents. An elaborate system was created to monitor all facets of political life. For example, a censorship office was established to monitor journalists, literary figures, and academics throughout the country; it took appropriate measures against those who fell out of line. Universities, labor unions, and peasant organizations, among others, were all subjected to intense surveillance by SAVAK agents and paid informants. The agency was also active abroad, especially in monitoring Iranian students who publicly opposed Pahlavi rule.

Over the years, SAVAK became a law unto itself, having legal authority to arrest and detain suspected persons indefinitely. SAVAK operated its own prisons in Tehran (the

For additional analytical, business and investment opportunities information, please contact Global Investment & Business Center, USA at (703) 370-8082. Fax: (703) 370-8083. E-mail: ibpusa3@gmail.com Global Business and Investment Info Databank - www.ibpus.com

Komiteh and Evin facilities) and, many suspected, throughout the country as well. Many of these activities were carried out without any institutional checks. Thus, it came as no surprise when, in 1979, SAVAK was singled out as a primary target for reprisals, its headquarters overrun, and prominent leaders tried and executed by *komiteh* representatives. High-ranking SAVAK agents were purged between 1979 and 1981; there were 61 SAVAK officials among 248 military personnel executed between February and September 1979. The organization was officially dissolved by Khomeini shortly after he came to power in 1979.

SAVAMA

Little information existed in 1987 on SAVAK's successor agency, SAVAMA. According to General Robert E. Huyser, President Jimmy Carter's last special envoy to imperial Iran, SAVAMA's first director was Major General Fardust, who was arrested in December 1985 for being a "Soviet informer." But after this major arrest the revolutionary government's keen desire to gain an upper hand over leftist guerrilla organizations may have influenced certain IRP leaders to relax their previously unrelenting pursuit of military intelligence personnel. Key religious leaders, including Majlis speaker Hashemi-Rafsanjani, insisted on recalling former agents to help the regime eliminate domestic opposition. Consequently, some intelligence officers and low-ranking SAVAK and army intelligence officials were asked to return to government service because of their specialized knowledge of the Iranian left. Others had acquired in-depth knowledge of Iraq's Baath Party and proved to be invaluable in helping decision makers.

Although it is impossible to verify, in 1987 observers speculated that some of SAVAK's intelligence-gathering operations were turned over to SAVAMA. It remained to be determined whether these newly authorized operations proved effective and whether there was coordination with other branches of government, including the powerful Pasdaran

GENDARMERIE AND NATIONAL POLICE

The Gendarmerie, numbering nearly 74,000 in 1979, was subordinate to the Ministry of Interior. Its law enforcement responsibilities extended to all rural areas and to small towns and villages of fewer than 5,000 inhabitants. The International Institute for Strategic Studies estimated its manpower at 70,000 in 1986.

The National Police operated with approximately 200,000 men in 1979, a figure that has not fluctuated much since. Like the Gendarmerie, the National Police was under the Ministry of Interior, and its responsibilities included all cities with more than 5,000 in population--a total of 20 percent of the population. In addition, the National Police was responsible for passport and immigration procedures, issuance and control of citizens' identification cards, driver and vehicle licensing and registration, and railroad and airport policing. Some of these duties were absorbed into the Ministry of the Pasdaran during the early years of the Revolution, and cooperation between these two branches seemed extensive.

Since 1979 both these paramilitary organizations have undergone complete reorganizations. IRP leaders quickly appointed Gendarmerie and police officers loyal to

For additional analytical, business and investment opportunities information, please contact Global Investment & Business Center, USA at (703) 370-8082. Fax: (703) 370-8083. E-mail: ibpusa3@gmail.com Global Business and Investment Info Databank - www.ibpus.com

the Revolution to revive and reorganize the two bodies under the Republic. Between 1979 and 1983, no fewer than seven officers were given top National Police portfolios. Colonel Khalil Samimi, appointed in 1983 by the influential Hojjatoleslam Nategh-e Nuri, then minister of interior, was credited with reorganizing the National Police according to the IRP's Islamic guidelines. The Gendarmerie followed a similar path. Seven appointments were made between 1979 and 1986, leading to a full reorganization. In addition to Brigadier General Ahmad Mohagheghi, the commander in the early republican period who was executed in late summer of 1980, five colonels were purged. Colonel Ali Kuchekzadeh played a major role in reorganizing and strengthening the Gendarmerie after its near collapse in the early revolutionary period. The commander in 1987, Colonel Mohammad Sohrabi, had served in that position since February 1985 and was the first top officer to have risen from the ranks.

As of 1987, the National Police and the Gendarmerie reflected the ideology of the state. Despite their valuable internal security operations, the roles of both bodies were restricted by the rising influence of the Pasdaran and the Basij.

ANTIREGIME OPPOSITION GROUPS

The Khomeini regime has faced severe challenges from several opposition groups, including royalists, National Front bureaucrats, intellectuals and professionals, communists, guerrilla organizations, Kurdish rebels, and distinguished *mujtahids* (Shia clerics whose demonstrated erudition in religious law has earned them the privilege to interpret law). Of these, the royalists and the National Front leaders have operated mainly from foreign bases or underground cells. The communists were purged in 1983 when the Tudeh's leadership was almost entirely eliminated. The main guerrilla group, the Mojahedin, claimed to have made strides in organizing a war of attrition against the regime. But because it has operated since July 1986 primarily from Baghdad, thus giving the impression of collaboration with Iraq, the Mojahedin's effectiveness and credibility may have been lessened by the war. The Kurds have been fighting the regime since their 1979 rebellion, even though Tehran has kept them off balance by using Pasdaran forces. Finally, National Front politicians have openly displayed their differing views, mostly in West European capitals, although the group led by former Prime Minister Bazargan was the only domestic "opposition" party tolerated by the regime.

MOJAHEDIN

In the early 1970s, supporters of Khomeini decided to create the Mojahedin movement to organize operations against the shah's government. Initial demands made by Mojahedin leaders, who included clerical officials like Hashemi-Rafsanjani, covered such points as the cancellation of all security agreements with the United States; expropriation of multinational corporations; nationalization of agricultural and urban land, banks, and large industries; administration of the army and other institutions by people's councils; creation of a "people's army"; regional autonomy for Iran's ethnic minorities; and various measures to benefit workers and peasants. Unlike other anti-shah organizations, the Mojahedin channeled its efforts into gaining supporters and developing an effective party network. The members were not ideologically inspired by outside sources but focused on strong nationalistic arguments and attacked the shah and his perceived abuses. By 1979 the membership of the Mojahedin had reached a record high of 25,000, and it had

For additional analytical, business and investment opportunities information, please contact Global Investment & Business Center, USA at (703) 370-8082. Fax: (703) 370-8083. E-mail: ibpusa3@gmail.com Global Business and Investment Info Databank - www.ibpus.com

hundreds of thousands of supporters. The movement frequently mobilized these masses against the shah.

The organization fell out of favor immediately after the Revolution, however, when its new leader, Masud Rajavi, boycotted the referendum on the new Constitution and advocated the total separation of the religious establishment and the state. Khomeini considered this a calculated and direct challenge to the IRP and the revolutionary regime. Rumors spread that the Mojahedin organization was a pawn of foreign powers, especially the United States. In response, the Mojahedin launched its own anti-Khomeini campaign by calling on the government to purify the Revolution.

President Bani Sadr supported the Mojahedin. When he lost the support of Khomeini, Bani Sadr sought refuge with Mojahedin leaders and was smuggled out of Iran, along with Rajavi and other senior representatives. In July 1981, the two leaders announced the formation of the National Council of Resistance (NCR) and launched a campaign to overthrow the Khomeini regime. From its headquarters in France, the NCR recruited additional support both within and outside Iran and welcomed ethnic minority leaders to its ranks. Its published charter was almost identical to the program of the Mojahedin. Partly to satisfy its diverse constituency and partly to distinguish itself from the Khomeini regime, the NCR offered a new agenda that reflected special concern for the interests of the lower middle class. In its attempt to gain the support of minor civil servants, shopkeepers, artisans, and small merchants, it adopted a slightly more moderate position than the one the Khomeini government had espoused concerning private property. The charter also promised to respect individual liberties, "except for persons identified with the shah's or Khomeini's regime," and guaranteed special rights for ethnic minorities, particularly the Kurds.

A score of other promises were made, including the return of land to farmers who would, however, be encouraged to consolidate their holdings in collective farms; the increase of available housing, education, and health services; the guarantee of equality for women; and the establishment of a "democratic army" in which the rank and file would be consulted on decisions and selections of officers. Yet, these promises could not be implemented because the NCR was not in power. The organization had to operate inside Iran, and the process strained the leadership's unity; disagreements over goals eventually led to the dissolution of the NCR. By March 1984, Bani Sadr and Kurdish leaders withdrew from the coalition. The French government asked Rajavi to leave France in July 1986. The Mojahedin set up their headquarters in Baghdad, whence they continued to launch military and propaganda offensives against the Khomeini regime.

In June 1987, Rajavi announced the formation of the Iranian National Army of Liberation, open to non-Mojahedin members, that would escalate attacks. Subsequently, Mojahedin sources claimed to have set up military training camps near the war front and to have launched numerous attacks against Pasdaran outposts. The Mojahedin has also been active in Western Europe and the United States; it has organized numerous rallies, distributed anti-Khomeini literature, and recruited Iranians living abroad

FADAYAN

For additional analytical, business and investment opportunities information,
please contact Global Investment & Business Center, USA
at (703) 370-8082. Fax: (703) 370-8083. E-mail: ibpusa3@gmail.com
Global Business and Investment Info Databank - www.ibpus.com

Among the armed leftist guerrilla groups operating in Iran in 1987, the Fadayan was the most active. The Fadayan was established when smaller groups operating in Tabriz, Mashhad, and Tehran merged in 1970. Its founders were university students and graduates who saw violence as the only means to oppose the shah. As Iran's economic situation deteriorated in the mid-1970s, the Fadayan recruited workers from large manufacturing industries and the oil sector. Recruitment expanded to include such national and ethnic movements as those of Kurdish, Turkoman, Baluch, and Arab minorities. The Fadayan opposed both imperial and republican regimes but did participate fully in the Revolution, taking over various military barracks and police stations in Tehran, Tabriz, Hamadan, Abadan, and Shiraz in 1979. In early June 1980, the Fadayan split into two factions: the Fadayan "Minority" and the Fadayan " Majority." The "Minority" faction, which was actually the larger of the two, has consistently opposed the Republic and considered Khomeini "reactionary." It vehemently condemned the Tudeh's cooperation with Khomeini prior to 1983. It also rejected the armed activities of the Mojahedin and advocated instead the expansion of underground cells. The "Minority" faction refused to join the NCR because of Bani Sadr's past association with the Khomeini regime. Subsequently, the "Minority" faction, along with a number of smaller leftist groups, established a new organization known as the Organization of Revolutionary Workers of Iran.

The Fadayan "Majority" faction moved closer to the views held by the Tudeh and supported Khomeini because of his anti-imperialist stance. This support of Khomeini changed in early 1983 when Khomeini turned against the Tudeh. In late 1987, the "Majority" faction was a satellite of the Tudeh .

The falling out of the Fadayan with the Islamic government within the first year of the Revolution was attributed to the ideological rift that emerged between the Fadayan's leftist-secular agenda and the religious and ideological views of the clerical leadership. Khomeini's *velayat-e faqih* (see Glossary) was a powerful concept that swept aside all leftist arguments; the Khomeini view of the Revolution was appealing precisely because of its nationalist aspects, which were easily assimilated by the Iranian population.

PAYKAR

The Paykar (Struggle) Organization was formed in 1979 from a Mojahedin splinter group that advocated the total separation of the religious establishment and the state. It considered Khomeini's policies backward and damaging to Iran's long-term socioeconomic development. The Paykar, perceived by other leftist groups as a dogmatic movement, called for an end to the Iran-Iraq War, viewing it as a diversionary tactic "waged by two reactionary and unpopular regimes." In 1982, when several Paykar leaders were arrested, the organization ceased to function overtly, but in 1987 it was still suspected of operating underground cells in major Iranian cities.

For additional analytical, business and investment opportunities information, please contact Global Investment & Business Center, USA at (703) 370-8082. Fax: (703) 370-8083. E-mail: ibpusa3@gmail.com Global Business and Investment Info Databank - www.ibpus.com

ARMY GROUND FORCES WEAPON SYSTEMS

INFANTRY WEAPONS - SMALL ARMS

Model	Type	Quantity	Acquired	Origin	Notes
PC-9 ZOAF	Semi-automatic pistol			Iran	9 mm pistol, unlicensed local production variant of the Swiss SIG Sauer P226.
M1911A1	Semi-automatic pistol			United States	.45 ACP pistol.
MPT-9	Submachine gun			Germany/ Iran	Heckler & Koch MP5 manufactured under licence
Uzi	Submachine gun			Israel	
Nakhjir	Sniper rifle			Soviet Union/ Iran	SVD manufactured under license; A new upgraded version was unveiled during the Muhammad Rasulullah 4 exercises held on 12 December 2016.
Siyavash sniper rifle	Sniper rifle			Iran	Domestically produced lightweight sniper weighing 6.5 kg (14 lb) loaded
Taher	Sniper rifle			Iran	Domestically developed sniper rifle with maximum range of 1200 m
Steyr HS .50/Sayyad	Anti-material rifle			Austria/ Iran	
Shaher	Anti-material rifle			Iran	Iranian 14.5 mm anti material rifle.

For additional analytical, business and investment opportunities information, please contact Global Investment & Business Center, USA at (703) 370-8082. Fax: (703) 370-8083. E-mail: ibpusa3@gmail.com Global Business and Investment Info Databank - www.ibpus.com

Taktab	Anti-material rifle			Iran	Iranian 20 mm anti material sniper rifle
S.5'56	Assault rifle			Iran	Copy of the Norinco CQ. In service with Saberin unit.
Arash	Anti-material rifle			Iran	Iranian 20 mm bullpup Anti-Material rifle.
KH-2002	Assault rifle			Iran	Iranian designed bullpup configuration of the Chinese Norinco CQ 5.56×45mm rifle. Limited service.
Fateh	Assault rifle			Iran	Iranian 5.56x45mm clone of American XCR-L and FN SCAR .
AKM	Assault rifle			Soviet Union	
Type 56	Assault rifle			People's Republic of China	Chinese AKM clone
KL-7.62	Assault rifle			Iran	Iranian copy of the Chinese Type 56 and AKM. Possibly produced under license. IRGC main service rifle.
H&K G3A6	Battle rifle			Germany/ Iran	Licensed production of G3A3 Battle Rifle, Army main service rifle
MGA3	General purpose machine gun			Germany/ Iran	Licensed production
PKM-T80	General Purpose Machine Gun			Soviet Union/ Iran	Local production
MGD	Heavy machine gun			Soviet Union/ Iran	Local production

For additional analytical, business and investment opportunities information, please contact Global Investment & Business Center, USA
at (703) 370-8082. Fax: (703) 370-8083. E-mail: ibpusa3@gmail.com
Global Business and Investment Info Databank - www.ibpus.com

RPK	Light machine gun			Soviet Union	Local production
Akhgar	Heavy machine gun			Iran	Locally produced 7.62 mm 6-barrelled rotary machine gun.
Moharram	Heavy machine gun			Iran	Locally produced 12.7 mm 6-barrelled rotary machine gun.
Nasir	automatic grenade launcher			Iran	40mm automatic grenade launcher.
Star Model Z84	Submachine gun			Spain	Amphibious Submachine-Gun is using by IRGCN frogmen.
FAJR 224	Assault rifle			Iran/ United States	Iranian copy of American M4 carbine
Sayad 5.56	Assault rifle			Iran	Carbine version of the Norinco CQ produced by Iran

PC-9 ZOAF

Production history	
Designed	1980-1983
Manufacturer	SIG Sauer
Produced	1983-present
Variants	See Variants
Specifications	
Weight	964 g (34.0 oz) (w/ magazine)

For additional analytical, business and investment opportunities information, please contact Global Investment & Business Center, USA at (703) 370-8082. Fax: (703) 370-8083. E-mail: ibpusa3@gmail.com
Global Business and Investment Info Databank - www.ibpus.com

Length	196 mm (7.7 in)
Barrel length	112 mm (4.4 in)
Width	38.1 mm (1.50 in)
Height	140 mm (5.5 in)
Cartridge	• .40 S&W • 9×19mm Parabellum • .357 SIG • .22 Long Rifle (Classic 22 model only)
Action	Mechanically locked, recoil operated (DA/SA, SAO, or DAO)
Feed system	10-, 12-, 13-, or 15-round magazine (.40 S&W, .357 SIG); 10-, 15-, 17-, 18-, or 20-round magazine (9×19mm Parabellum); 10-round polymer magazine (Classic 22 only)
Sights	Iron sights

The **SIG Sauer P226** is a full-sized, service-type pistol made by SIG Sauer. It is chambered for the 9×19mm Parabellum, .40 S&W, .357 SIG, and .22 Long Rifle. It is essentially the same basic design of the SIG Sauer P220, but developed to use higher capacity, double stack magazines in place of the single stack magazines of the P220. The P226 itself has spawned further sub-variants; the P228 and P229 are both compact versions of the double stack P226 design. The SIG Sauer P226 and its variants are in service with numerous law enforcement and military organizations worldwide

M1911A1

The **M1911**, also known as the "Government" or "Colt Government", is a single-action, semi-automatic, magazine-fed, recoil-operated pistol chambered for the .45 ACP cartridge. It served as the standard-issue sidearm for the United States Armed Forces from 1911 to 1986. It was widely used in World War I, World War II, the Korean War, and the Vietnam War. The pistol's formal designation as of 1940 was **Automatic Pistol, Caliber .45, M1911** for the original model of 1911 or **Automatic Pistol, Caliber .45, M1911A1** for the M1911A1, adopted in 1924. The designation changed to **Pistol, Caliber .45, Automatic, M1911A1** in the Vietnam War era.

The U.S. procured around 2.7 million M1911 and M1911A1 pistols in military contracts during its service life. The M1911 was replaced by the 9mm Beretta M9 pistol as the standard U.S. sidearm in October 1986, but due to its popularity among users, it has not been completely phased out. Modernized derivative variants of the M1911 are still in use by some units of the U.S. Army Special Forces and the U.S. Navy.

Designed by John Browning, the M1911 is the best-known of his designs to use the short recoil principle in its basic design. The pistol was widely copied, and this operating system rose to become the preeminent type of the 20th century and of nearly all modern centerfire pistols. It is popular with civilian shooters in competitive events such as USPSA, IDPA, International Practical Shooting Confederation, and Bullseye shooting. Compact variants are popular civilian concealed carry weapons in the U.S. because of the design's relatively slim width and the stopping power of the .45 ACP cartridge

Type	Semi-automatic pistol
Place of origin	United States
	Service history
In service	1911–present
Used by	Over 20 nations, see Users below for details
Wars	As standard U.S. service pistol: • World War I • Banana Wars • World War II • Korean War • Vietnam War In non-standard use: • Chaco war • Indonesian National Revolution • Algerian War • Laotian Civil War • Rhodesian Bush War • Cambodian Civil War • Cambodian–Vietnamese War • Sino-Vietnamese War • Falklands War • Gulf War • War in Afghanistan • Iraq War • Syrian Civil War
	Production history
Designer	John Browning
Designed	1911 and 1924 (A1)

Manufacturer	Colt Manufacturing Company
Produced	1911–present
No. built	Over 2.7 million
Variants	• M1911A1 • M1911A2 • RIA Officers • Kongsberg Colt
	Specifications
Weight	39 oz (1,100 g) empty, with magazine
Length	8.25 in (210 mm)
Barrel length	• Government model: 5.03 in (127 mm) • Commander model: 4.25 in (108 mm) • Officer's ACP model: 3.5 in (89 mm)
Cartridge	.45 ACP
Action	Short recoil operation
Muzzle velocity	830 ft/s (253 m/s)
Feed system	7 round standard detachable box magazine

MPT-9

The **MP5** (German: ***M**aschinen**p**istole **5***) is a 9mm submachine gun, developed in the 1960s by a team of engineers from the German small arms manufacturer Heckler & Koch GmbH (H&K) of Oberndorf am Neckar. There are over 100 variants of the MP5, including some semi-automatic versions. The MP5 is one of the most widely used submachine guns in the world, having been adopted by 40 nations and numerous military, law enforcement, intelligence, and security organizations. It was widely used by SWAT teams in North America, but has largely been replaced by AR-15 variants in the 21st century. In 1999, Heckler & Koch developed the Heckler & Koch UMP, the MP5's successor; both are available as of 2018.

Type	Submachine gun
Place of origin	West Germany
	Service history
In service	1966–present
Used by	See Users
Wars	The Troubles Iranian Embassy siege Operation Eagle Claw Lebanese Civil War Internal conflict in Peru Colombian conflict Sri Lankan Civil War Gulf War War in Afghanistan Iraq War Boko Haram insurgency Libyan Civil War
	Production history
Designer	Tilo Möller, Manfred Guhring, Georg Seidl, Helmut Baureuter
Designed	1964–1966
Manufacturer	Heckler & Koch
Produced	1966–present
Variants	See Variants
	Specifications
Weight	• 2.5 kg (5.5 lb) (MP5A2) • 3.1 kg (6.8 lb) (MP5A3) • 2.9 kg (6.4 lb) (MP5A4) • 3.1 kg (6.8 lb) (MP5A5) • 2.7 kg (6.0 lb) fixed stock / 2.85 kg (6.3 lb) retractable stock (MP5/10) • 2.7 kg (6.0 lb) fixed stock / 2.85 kg (6.3 lb) retractable stock (MP5/40) • 2.8 kg (6.2 lb) (MP5SD1) • 3.1 kg (6.8 lb) (MP5SD2) • 2.8 kg (6.2 lb) (MP5SD3) • 2.8 kg (6.2 lb) (MP5SD4) • 3.1 kg (6.8 lb) (MP5SD5) 3.4 kg (7.5 lb) (MP5SD6) • 2.0 kg (4.4 lb) (MP5K, MP5KA1, MP5KA4, MP5KA5) • 2.5 kg (5.5 lb) (MP5K-PDW)
Length	Fixed stock: • 680 mm (27 in) (MP5A2, MP5A4, MP5/10, MP5/40) • 790 mm (31.1 in) (MP5SD2, MP5SD5)

For additional analytical, business and investment opportunities information, please contact Global Investment & Business Center, USA at (703) 370-8082. Fax: (703) 370-8083. E-mail: ibpusa3@gmail.com Global Business and Investment Info Databank - www.ibpus.com

	• 634 mm (25.0 in) (T-94 ZSG) Telescoping stock: • 700 mm (27.6 in) stock extended / 550 mm (21.7 in) stock collapsed (MP5A3, MP5A5) • 660 mm (26.0 in) stock extended / 490 mm (19.3 in) stock collapsed (MP5/10, MP5/40) • 805 mm (31.7 in) stock extended / 670 mm (26.4 in) stock collapsed (MP5SD3, MP5SD6) • 603 mm (23.7 in) stock extended / 368 mm (14.5 in) stock folded (MP5K-PDW) Receiver end cap: • 550 mm (21.7 in) (MP5SD1, MP5SD4) • 325 mm (12.8 in) (MP5K, MP5KA1, MP5KA4, MP5KA5) • 349 mm (13.7 in) (MP5K-PDW)
Barrel length	• 225 mm (8.9 in) (MP5A2, MP5A3, MP5A4, MP5A5, MP5/10, MP5/40) • 146 mm (5.7 in) (MP5SD1, MP5SD2, MP5SD3, MP5SD4, MP5SD5, MP5SD6) • 140 mm (5.5 in) (T-94 ZSG) • 115 mm (4.5 in) (MP5K, MP5KA1, MP5KA4, MP5KA5) • 148 mm (5.8 in) (MP5K-PDW)
Width	• 50 mm (2.0 in) (MP5A2, MP5A3, MP5A4, MP5A5, MP5K, MP5KA1, MP5KA4, MP5KA5, MP5K-PDW, MP5/10, MP5/40) • 60 mm (2.4 in) (MP5SD1, MP5SD2, MP5SD3, MP5SD4, MP5SD5, MP5SD6)
Height	• 260 mm (10.2 in) (MP5A2, MP5A3, MP5A4, MP5A5, MP5SD1, MP5SD2, MP5SD3, MP5SD4, MP5SD5, MP5SD6, MP5/10, MP5/40) • 210 mm (8.3 in) (MP5K, MP5KA1, MP5KA4, MP5KA5, MP5K-PDW)
Cartridge	• 9×19mm Parabellum • 10mm Auto (MP5/10) • .40 S&W (MP5/40)
Action	Roller-delayed blowback, closed bolt
Rate of fire	• 800 rounds/min (MP5A series, MP5/10 and MP5/40) • 700 rounds/min (MP5SD series) • 900 rounds/min (MP5K series)

Muzzle velocity	• 400 m/s (1,312 ft/s) (MP5A2, MP5A3, MP5A4, MP5A5) • 425 m/s (1,394 ft/s) (MP5/10) • 315 m/s (1,033 ft/s) (MP5/40) • 285 m/s (935 ft/s) (MP5SD1, MP5SD2, MP5SD3, MP5SD4, MP5SD5, MP5SD6) • 375 m/s (1,230 ft/s) (MP5K, MP5KA1, MP5KA4, MP5KA5, MP5K-PDW)
Effective firing range	• 200 m (656 ft) (MP5A2, MP5A3, MP5A4, MP5A5) • 125 m (410 ft) (MP5/10) • 100 m (328 ft) (MP5/40) • 100 m (328 ft) (MP5K, MP5KA1, MP5KA4, MP5KA5, MP5K-PDW)
Feed system	15, 30 or 40 round detachable box magazine and 100-round Beta C-Mag drum magazine
Sights	Iron sights. Rear: rotary drum; front: hooded post

UZI

Type	Submachine gun Machine pistol (Mini Uzi, Micro Uzi)
Place of origin	Israel
	Service history
In service	1954–present
Used by	See Users
Wars	Suez Crisis Six-Day War The Troubles Vietnam War War of Attrition Yom Kippur War Colombian internal conflict Internal conflict in Peru Portuguese Colonial War Angolan Civil War

For additional analytical, business and investment opportunities information,
please contact Global Investment & Business Center, USA
at (703) 370-8082. Fax: (703) 370-8083. E-mail: ibpusa3@gmail.com
Global Business and Investment Info Databank - www.ibpus.com

	Shaba II Falklands War Sri Lankan Civil War Invasion of Grenada Lebanese Civil War 1982 Lebanon war South African Border War Rhodesian Bush War Yugoslav Wars Somali Civil War Burundian Civil War First Congo War War in Darfur Mexican Drug War Kivu Conflict First Ivorian Civil War Syrian Civil War Miami Drug Wars
	Production history
Designer	Uziel Gal
Designed	1950
Manufacturer	Israel Military Industries Israel Weapon Industries FN Herstal Norinco Lyttleton Engineering Works (under Vektor Arms) RH-ALAN Group Industries
Produced	1950–present
No. built	10,000,000+
Variants	See Variants
	Specifications
Weight	3.5 kg (7.72 lb)
Length	• 445 mm (17.5 in) stockless • 470 mm (18.5 in) folding stock collapsed • 640 mm (25 in) folding stock extended
Barrel length	260 mm (10.2 in)
Cartridge	9mm Parabellum .22 LR .45 ACP .41 AE 9×21mm IMI
Action	Blowback, open bolt
Rate of fire	600 rounds/min
Muzzle velocity	400 m/s (1,300 ft/s) (9mm)

For additional analytical, business and investment opportunities information, please contact Global Investment & Business Center, USA at (703) 370-8082. Fax: (703) 370-8083. E-mail: ibpusa3@gmail.com Global Business and Investment Info Databank - www.ibpus.com

Effective firing range	200 m
Feed system	•10-round box magazine (.22 and .41 AE) •16-round box (.45 ACP) •20-, 25-, 32-, 40-, or 50-round box
Sights	Iron sights

The **Uzi** officially cased as **UZI**) /ˈuːzi/ (listen) is a family of Israeli open-bolt, blowback-operated submachine guns. Smaller variants are often considered to be machine pistols. The Uzi was one of the first weapons to use a telescoping bolt design which allows the magazine to be housed in the pistol grip for a shorter weapon.

The first Uzi submachine gun was designed by Major Uziel Gal in the late 1940s. The prototype was finished in 1950. First introduced to IDF special forces in 1954, the weapon was placed into general issue two years later. The Uzi has found use as a personal defense weapon by rear-echelon troops, officers, artillery troops and tankers, as well as a frontline weapon by elite light infantry assault forces.

The Uzi has been exported to over 90 countries. Over its service lifetime, it has been manufactured by Israel Military Industries, FN Herstal, and other manufacturers. From the 1960s through the 1980s, more Uzi submachine guns were sold to more military, law enforcement and security markets than any other submachine gun ever made

NAKHJIR

Type	Semi-automatic sniper rifle, designated marksman rifle
Place of origin	Soviet Union
	Service history
In service	1963–present
Used by	See Users
Wars	• Vietnam War • Cambodian–Vietnamese War • Sino-Vietnamese War • Soviet–Afghan War • Nagorno-Karabakh War • Salvadorian Civil War

For additional analytical, business and investment opportunities information, please contact Global Investment & Business Center, USA at (703) 370-8082. Fax: (703) 370-8083. E-mail: ibpusa3@gmail.com
Global Business and Investment Info Databank - www.ibpus.com

	• Iran–Iraq War • Gulf War • Somali Civil War • Operation Restore Hope • Burundian Civil War • War in Afghanistan (2001–14) • Iraq War • Yugoslav Wars • First Chechen War • Second Chechen Wars • Cambodian–Thai border dispute • 2008 South Ossetia War • Kargil War • 2011 Libyan Civil War • Northern Mali conflict • Syrian Civil War • Boko Haram insurgency • Iraqi Civil War (2014–present) • War in Donbass • Yemeni Civil War (2015) • Saudi-led intervention in Yemen (2015–present) • Conflict in Najran, Jizan and Asir
Production history	
Designer	Yevgeny Dragunov
Designed	1958–1963
Manufacturer	• Kalashnikov Concern • Norinco
Produced	1963–present
Variants	See Variants
Specifications	
Weight	• 4.30 kg (9.48 lb) (with scope and unloaded magazine) • 4.68 kg (10.3 lb) (SVDS) • 4.40 kg (9.7 lb) (SVU) • 5.30 kg (11.7 lb) (SVDM) • 5.02 kg (11.1 lb) (SWD-M)
Length	• 1,225 mm (48.2 in) (SVD) • 1,135 mm (44.7 in) stock extended / 815 mm (32.1 in) stock folded (SVDS) • 900 mm (35.4 in) (SVU) • 1,135 mm (44.7 in) stock extended / 975 mm (38.4 in) stock folded (SVDM) • 1,125 mm (44.3 in) (SWD-M)
Barrel length	• 620 mm (24.4 in) (SVD, SWD-M) • 565 mm (22.2 in) (SVDS) • 600 mm (23.6 in) (SVU) • 550 mm (21.7 in) (SVDM)

For additional analytical, business and investment opportunities information, please contact Global Investment & Business Center, USA at (703) 370-8082. Fax: (703) 370-8083. E-mail: ibpusa3@gmail.com Global Business and Investment Info Databank - www.ibpus.com

Cartridge	7.62×54mmR
Action	Gas-operated, rotating bolt
Rate of fire	30 rounds/min
Muzzle velocity	• 830 m/s (2,723 ft/s) (SVD) • 810 m/s (2,657.5 ft/s) (SVDS) • 800 m/s (2,624.7 ft/s) (SVU)
Effective firing range	800 m (875 yd)
Feed system	10-round detachable box magazine
Sights	PSO-1 telescopic sight, 1PN51/1PN58 night vision sights and iron sights with an adjustable rear notch sight

SIYAVASH SNIPER RIFLE

The Siyavash sniper rifle is a light rifle designed for and deployed by the Iranian Army. It carries a 5-round magazine and weighs 14 pounds (6.5 kg)

Siyavash Sniper Rifle	
Type	Sniper rifle
Place of origin	Islamic Republic of Iran
Service history	
In service	2013 - present
Used by	Islamic Republic of Iran Army
Specifications	
Weight	6.5 kg (14 lbs)
Action	bolt-action
Feed system	5-round

TAHER

For additional analytical, business and investment opportunities information,
please contact Global Investment & Business Center, USA
at (703) 370-8082. Fax: (703) 370-8083. E-mail: ibpusa3@gmail.com
Global Business and Investment Info Databank - www.ibpus.com

The **Taher** is a sniper rifle developed by Iran. It was revealed during the country's *Muhammad Rasulullah*-4 military exercises held 11-13 December, 2016. Iran announced that the weapon has a maximum range of 1,200 meters

The Taher is a bolt action gun which operated manually by the opening and closing of the breech with a small handle, placed on the right-hand side of the weapon. It is chambered for the 7.62x51mm ammunition.

The top of the receiver is fitted with a Picatinny rail which is fitted with an optical sight. There is a bipod in the forearm with independent adjustment for each leg. The Taher is also fitted with an adjustable length stock.

The new Iranian-made Taher sniper has a total weight of 4,4kg and can fire at a maximum range of 1,200 m with an effective range of 800m.

STEYR HS .50/SAYYAD

The **Steyr HS .50** is a .50 BMG single-shot anti-materiel sniper rifle manufactured by Steyr Mannlicher.

Type	Anti Materiel Rifle/Sniper Rifle
Place of origin	Austria
	Service history
Used by	See Users
Wars	Iraq War Syrian Civil War Iraqi Civil War (2014-2017) Yemeni Civil War (2015-present) Saudi-led intervention in Yemen (2015-present) Conflict in Najran, Jizan and Asir
	Production history
Manufacturer	Steyr Mannlicher
Unit cost	$5,299
Produced	2004
Variants	HS .460 HS .50 M1
	Specifications (HS .50)
Weight	12.4 kg (28.5 lbs)
Length	1,370 mm (54 inches)
Barrel length	833 mm (33 inches)
Cartridge	.50 BMG .460 Steyr
Caliber	.50 BMG
Action	Bolt action
Effective firing range	2500 m – 1500 m
Feed system	Single shot

SHAHER

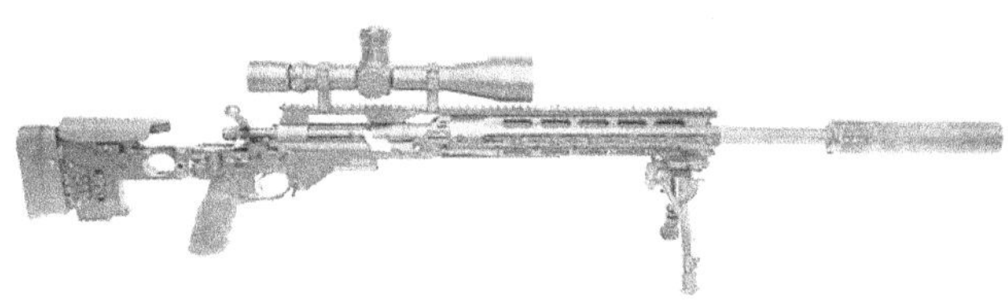

Shaher is an Iranian-made 14.5mm anti-materiel sniper rifle capable of penetrating concrete strongholds, armored vehicles and helicopters. It has a maximum effective range of 4 kilometres (2.5 mi). The weapon weighs 22 kilograms (49 lb) and is 1.85 metres (6.1 ft) long. It can engage helicopters and other low flying aircraft. The anti-armor rounds used by the Shaher are capable of penetrating 50 mm (2.0 in) thick armor and come in different armor-piercing varieties.

S.5'56

For additional analytical, business and investment opportunities information,
please contact Global Investment & Business Center, USA
at (703) 370-8082. Fax: (703) 370-8083. E-mail: ibpusa3@gmail.com
Global Business and Investment Info Databank - www.ibpus.com

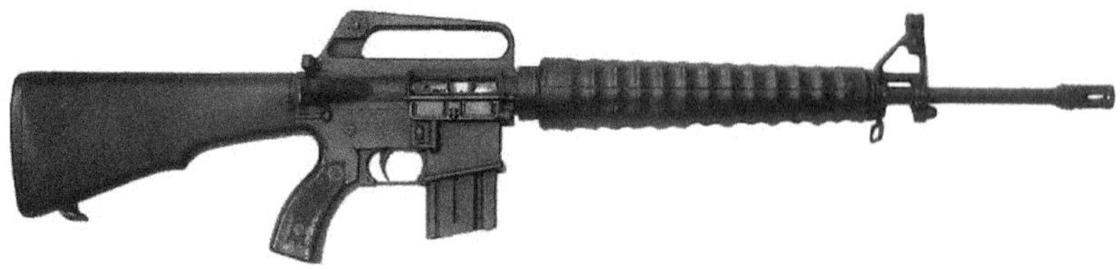

Type	Assault rifle
Place of origin	China
	Service history
Used by	See Users
Wars	Soviet–Afghan War War in Darfur Syrian Civil War
	Production history
Designer	Norinco
Manufacturer	Norinco
Produced	1980s–present
Variants	See Variants
	Specifications
Weight	2.9 kg (Empty)
Length	987 mm
Barrel length	504 mm
Cartridge	5.56×45mm NATO (only non-NATO standard 55-grain M193 "Ball" cartridge), .223 Remington (Semi-automatic sporter model)
Caliber	5.56mm
Action	Gas operated, rotating bolt
Rate of fire	900 RPM (Select-fire version only)
Muzzle velocity	990 m/s
Maximum firing range	460 m
Feed system	20/30-round detachable box magazine (STANAG 4179)
Sights	Iron sights

The **Type CQ** is an unlicensed Chinese variant of the M16 rifle manufactured by Norinco. According to the Norinco website, the rifle is officially known as **CQ 5.56**.

It can be distinguished from other AR-15 and M-16 pattern rifles by its long, revolver-like pistol grip, somewhat rounded handguards, and the unique shape of its stock.

Though it has the same look as the M16 rifle, there are some modifications to various parts. The most immediately recognizable distinguishing features that tell the Type CQ apart from an M16 rifle are its distinctive handguard and stock, curved pistol grip, and hooded front sight.

For additional analytical, business and investment opportunities information, please contact Global Investment & Business Center, USA at (703) 370-8082. Fax: (703) 370-8083. E-mail: ibpusa3@gmail.com Global Business and Investment Info Databank - www.ibpus.com

The Type CQ rifle, in both its Military/LE and Civilian variants, has a 1:12 rifling pitch which allows it to properly stabilize the M193 "Ball" variant of the 5.56mm ammunition or the **Type CJ** Chinese clone, as well as any .223 Remington commercial cartridge variant that can be stabilized by the 1:12 pitch rifling barrel (normally Varmint or other simple sporter cartridges, up to a maximum bullet weight of 55 Grains). The M193 "Ball" 5.56mm cartridge was never a NATO standard until the adoption of this weapon system by other nations. Type CQ is chambered in "5.56×45mm NATO", but it will not properly stabilize the NATO standard 5.56mm ammunition (the SS109, M855 in US service), which requires a 1:9 or 1:7 pitch rifling barrel due to a bullet weight of 62 Grains. However, in an emergency situation these barrels **will** safely fire the heavier rounds, just the aggregate group size will be much larger and a greater amount of tumbling and "key holing" (the bullet arriving at target sideways due to instability from improper spin rate).

ARASH

Arash is an Iranian semi-automatic anti-material sniper rifle. This weapon is used by the armed forces of Iran, Hezbollah and Iraq. The Arash sniper rifle is a semi-automatic weapon with rotating bolt and gunpowder gas system has an eight Khan straight back from left to right. It is 180 cm-long weapon, and it is equipped with optical cameras. It is a typically used as a shoulder-fired weapon. The rifle weighs between 18 and 20 kilograms, and fires 20mm bullets.

KH-2002

Type	Bullpup assault rifle
Place of origin	Iran
	Service history
Used by	Islamic Republic of Iran Army in limited numbers (Primary User) See Users for more details
	Production history
Designed	2001
Manufacturer	Defense Industries Organization
Produced	2003–2012
Variants	See Variants
	Specifications
Weight	3.7kg (with long barrel and empty 30-round magazine)
Length	780 mm, 730 mm, 680 mm (Assault Rifle, Carbine, DMR)
Cartridge	5.56×45mm NATO

For additional analytical, business and investment opportunities information, please contact Global Investment & Business Center, USA at (703) 370-8082. Fax: (703) 370-8083. E-mail: ibpusa3@gmail.com Global Business and Investment Info Databank - www.ibpus.com

Caliber	5.56mm
Action	Gas-operated, rotating bolt
Rate of fire	800 to 850 round/min, cyclic
Muzzle velocity	900 to 950 m/s
Effective firing range	450 m
Feed system	Various STANAG Magazines
Sights	Iron sights Various scopes/sights can be attached on the picatinny rail via carry handle. Two picatinny rails on both sides of upper receiver (Sama model only)

The **KH-2002 *Khaybar*** is an Iranian-designed assault rifle, derived from the DIO S 5.56 assault rifle (an unlicensed clone of the Chinese Norinco CQ, which in turn is an unlicensed copy of the American M16) and further developed by Iran's Defense Industries Organization (DIO). It was designed in 2001 with samples produced in 2003 with the eventual production of the KH2002 commencing in 2004. It is similar in appearance to the FAMAS and Steyr AUG assault rifles.

Its improved version, released in 2009, was known as "Sama"

AKM

Type	Assault rifle
Place of origin	Soviet Union
	Service history
In service	1959–present
Used by	See Users below
Wars	Vietnam War Laotian Civil War Portuguese Colonial War Rhodesian Bush War Cambodian Civil War Nigerian Civil War

For additional analytical, business and investment opportunities information, please contact Global Investment & Business Center, USA at (703) 370-8082. Fax: (703) 370-8083. E-mail: ibpusa3@gmail.com Global Business and Investment Info Databank - www.ibpus.com

	The Troubles Angolan Civil War Yom Kippur War Lebanese Civil War Cambodian–Vietnamese War Chadian–Libyan conflict Sino-Vietnamese War Soviet–Afghan War Nicaraguan Revolution Iran–Iraq War LRA insurgency First Liberian Civil War Persian Gulf War Somali Civil War Georgian Civil War Yugoslav Wars First Chechen War Second Chechen War Second Liberian Civil War 2001 Afghanistan War Ivorian Civil Wars Iraq War War in Darfur Mexican Drug War Russo-Georgian War Boko Haram insurgency Libyan Civil War Syrian Civil War War in Donbass Iraqi Civil War (2014–2017) 2015 Yemeni Civil War
Production history	
Designer	Mikhail Kalashnikov
Designed	1950s
Manufacturer	Kalashnikov Concern Tula Arms Plant others
Produced	1959–1978 (USSR)
No. built	More than 10,278,300
Variants	AKM AKMS AKMSU
Specifications (Updated information)	
Weight	AKM: 3.1 kg (6.83 lb) w/unloaded magazine AKML: 3.80 kg (8.4 lb) AKMS: 3.3 kg (7.3 lb) AKMSN: 3.77 kg (8.3 lb)

For additional analytical, business and investment opportunities information,
please contact Global Investment & Business Center, USA
at (703) 370-8082. Fax: (703) 370-8083. E-mail: ibpusa3@gmail.com
Global Business and Investment Info Databank - www.ibpus.com

	AKMS: 3.8 kg (8.4 lb) with full magazine 30-rnd magazine: 0.33 kg (0.73 lb) 6H4 bayonet: 0.32 kg (0.71 lb)
Length	AKM, AKML: 880 mm (34.6 in) AKMS, AKMSN: 920 mm (36.2 in) stock extended / 655 mm (25.8 in) stock folded
Barrel length	415 mm (16.3 in)
Cartridge	7.62×39mm M43
Action	Gas operated, rotating bolt
Rate of fire	Cyclic rate of fire: 600 rds/min Practical rate of fire: Semi-auto 40 rds/min Full-auto 100 rds/min
Muzzle velocity	715 m/s (2,346 ft/s)
Effective firing range	350 m (383 yd)
Feed system	10, 20, or 30 round detachable box magazines. Also compatible with 40 round box magazines and 75-round drum magazines from the RPK.
Sights	Rear sight notch on sliding tangent, front post 100–1,000 m sight adjustments Sight radius: 378 mm (14.9 in)

The **AKM** (*Modernized Kalashnikov Automatic Rifle*) is a 7.62mm assault rifle designed by Mikhail Kalashnikov. It is a common modernized variant of the AK-47 rifle developed in the 1940s.

For additional analytical, business and investment opportunities information, please contact Global Investment & Business Center, USA at (703) 370-8082. Fax: (703) 370-8083. E-mail: ibpusa3@gmail.com Global Business and Investment Info Databank - www.ibpus.com

Introduced into service with the Soviet Army in 1959, the AKM is the most ubiquitous variant of the entire AK series of firearms and it has found widespread use with most member states of the former Warsaw Pact and its African and Asian allies as well as being widely exported and produced in many other countries. The production of these rifles was carried out at both the Tula Arms Plant and Izhmash. It was officially replaced in Soviet frontline service by the AK-74 in the late 1970s, but remains in use worldwide.

TYPE 56

Type	Assault rifle
Place of origin	People's Republic of China
	Service history
In service	1956–present
Used by	See Users
Wars	Vietnam War Laotian Civil War Sino-Indian War Rhodesian Bush War Cambodian Civil War Cambodian–Vietnamese War Sino-Vietnamese War Soviet–Afghan War Nicaraguan Revolution Iran–Iraq War Sri Lankan Civil War Lord's Resistance Army insurgency Somali Civil War Tuareg rebellion (1990–1995) Persian Gulf War Baren Township riot Croatian War of Independence Bosnian War Burundian Civil War Kosovo War Liberian Civil Wars 2001 Afghanistan War Iraq War Mexican Drug War Cambodian–Thai border dispute Kivu Conflict War in Darfur

	2011 Libyan Civil War Syrian Civil War 2011 Iraqi Insurgency Northern Mali conflict Boko Haram insurgency South Sudanese Civil War Iraqi Civil War (2014–2017)
	Production history
Designed	1956
Produced	1956–present
Variants	Type 56 Type 56-1 Type 56-2
	Specifications
Weight	Type 56: 3.8 kg (8.38 lb) Type 56-1: 3.7 kg (8.16 lb) Type 56-2/56-4: 3.9 kg (8.60 lb) QBZ-56C: 2.85 kg (6.28 lb)
Length	Type 56: 874 mm (34.4 in) Type 56-1/56-2: 874 mm (34.4 in) w/ stock extended,654 mm (25.7 in) w/ stock folded. QBZ-56C: 764 mm (30.1 in) w/ stock extended,557 mm (21.9 in) w/ stock folded.
Barrel length	Type 56, Type 56-I, Type 56-II: 414 mm (16.3 in) QBZ-56C: 280 mm (11.0 in)
Cartridge	7.62×39mm
Caliber	7.62mm
Rate of fire	650 rounds/min
Muzzle velocity	Type 56, Type 56-I, Type 56-II: 735 m/s (2,411 ft/s) QBZ-56C: 665 m/s (2182 ft/s)
Effective firing range	100–800 m sight adjustments. Effective range 300-400 meters
Feed system	20, 30, or 40-round detachable box magazine
Sights	Adjustable Iron sights

The **Type 56** is a Chinese 7.62×39mm assault rifle. It is a variant of the Soviet-designed AK-47 and AKM assault rifles. Production started in 1956 at State Factory 66 but was eventually handed over to Norinco, who continues to manufacture the rifle primarily for export.

H&K G3A6

Type	Battle rifle
Place of origin	West Germany
	Service history
In service	1959–present
Used by	See Users
	Production history
Designer	CETME Mauser Heckler & Koch
Designed	1950s
Manufacturer	Heckler & Koch (original) Rheinmetall MIC SEDENA Kongsberg Gruppen and others
Produced	1958–present
No. built	7,000,000
Variants	See Variants
	Specifications
Cartridge	7.62×51mm NATO
Action	Roller-delayed blowback
Rate of fire	500–600 rounds/min
Muzzle velocity	800 m/s (2,625 ft/s)
Effective firing range	100–400 metres (109–437 yd)
Maximum firing range	3,700 metres (4,046 yd)

For additional analytical, business and investment opportunities information,
please contact Global Investment & Business Center, USA
at (703) 370-8082. Fax: (703) 370-8083. E-mail: ibpusa3@gmail.com
Global Business and Investment Info Databank - www.ibpus.com

Feed system	20-round or 30-round detachable box, and 50-round and 100-round drum magazine

The **G3** (**G**ewehr **3**) is a 7.62×51mm NATO, select-fire battle rifle developed in the 1950s by the German armament manufacturer Heckler & Koch (H&K) in collaboration with the Spanish state-owned design and development agency CETME (*Centro de Estudios Técnicos de Materiales Especiales*

The G3A3 (A4) is a selective-fire automatic weapon that employs a roller-delayed blowback operating system. The two-piece bolt assembly consists of a breech (bolt head) and bolt carrier. The bolt is held in battery by two sliding cylindrical rollers that engage locking recesses in the barrel extension. The breech is opened when both rollers are compressed inward against camming surfaces driven by the rearward pressure of the expanding gases upon the bolt head. As the rollers move inward, recoil energy is transferred to the locking piece and bolt carrier which begin to withdraw while the bolt head slowly moves rearward in relation to the bolt carrier. As the bolt carrier clears the rollers, pressure in the bore drops to a safe level, the bolt head is caught by the bolt carrier and moves to the rear as one unit, continuing the operating cycle. The bolt features an anti-bounce mechanism that prevents the bolt from bouncing off the barrel's breech surface. The "bolt head locking lever" is a spring-loaded claw mounted on the bolt carrier that grabs the bolt head as the bolt carrier group goes into battery. The lever essentially ratchets into place with friction, providing enough resistance to being re-opened that the bolt carrier does not rebound. The spring-powered claw extractor is also contained inside the bolt while the lever ejector is located inside the trigger housing (actuated by the recoiling bolt)

MGA3

Type	General-purpose machine gun
Place of origin	West Germany
	Service history
In service	1960–present
Used by	See Users
Wars	Nigerian Civil War Iran–Iraq War

	Lebanese Civil War Turkey-PKK conflict Somali Civil War War in Afghanistan War in North-West Pakistan Syrian Civil War Boko Haram insurgency Libyan Civil War Iraqi Civil War (2014–present) Yemeni Civil War (2015–present) Saudi Arabian-led intervention in Yemen Conflict in Najran, Jizan and Asir
	Production history
Designed	1959
Manufacturer	Rheinmetall License-built by: Beretta, MKEK, Ellinika Amyntika Systimata, Defense Industries Organization, Military Industry Corporation, Pakistan Ordnance Factories, General Dynamics Santa Bárbara Sistemas
Produced	1960–present
No. built	1million+
Variants	See Variants
	Specifications
Weight	11.5 kg (25.35 lb) 27.5 kg (61 lb) (mounted on tripod)
Length	1,225 mm (48.2 in) 1,097 mm (43.2 in) (without stock)
Barrel length	565 mm (22.2 in)
Cartridge	7.62×51mm NATO
Action	Recoil-operated, roller locked
Rate of fire	1,000–1,300 rpm
Muzzle velocity	820 m/s (2,690 ft/s)
Effective firing range	200–1,200 m sight adjustments
Maximum firing range	600 m (1,969 ft) (bipod) 1,200 m (3,937 ft) (tripod mounted) 3,000 m (9,843 ft) (gun carriage) 3,750 m (12,303 ft) (terminal)
Feed system	50-Round non-disintegrating DM1 belt (can be combined in a drum); 100-Round disintegrating DM6/M13 belt
Sights	Open tangent iron sights

he **MG 3** is a German general-purpose machine gun chambered for the 7.62×51mm NATO cartridge. The weapon's design is derived from the World War II era MG 42 universal machine gun that fired the 7.92×57mm Mauser round.

The MG 3 was standardized in the late 1950s and adopted into service with the newly formed *Bundeswehr*, where it continues to serve to this day as a squad support weapon and a vehicle-mounted machine gun. The weapon and its derivatives have also been acquired by the armed forces of over 30 countries. Production rights to the machine gun were purchased by Italy (MG 42/59), Spain, Pakistan (MG 1A3), Greece, Iran, Sudan and Turkey.

PKM-T80

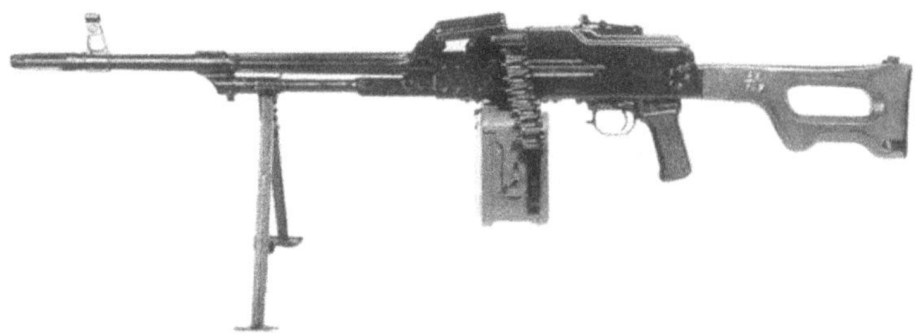

Type	General-purpose machine gun
Place of origin	Soviet Union
	Service history
In service	1961–present
Used by	See Users
Wars	South African Border War Cambodian Civil War Libyan–Egyptian War Cambodian–Vietnamese War Sino-Vietnamese War Soviet–Afghan War Iran–Iraq War Lord's Resistance Army insurgency Tuareg rebellion (1990–1995) Nagorno-Karabakh War Gulf War Somali Civil War Yugoslav Wars Burundian Civil War First Chechen War Second Chechen War War in Afghanistan Iraq conflict Northern Mali Conflict Cambodian–Thai border dispute Russo-Georgian War Lebanese Civil War

	First Libyan Civil War Second Libyan Civil War Boko Haram insurgency Syrian Civil War War in Donbass Yemeni Civil War Saudi-led intervention in Yemen (2015-present) Conflict in Najran, Jizan and Asir
	Production history
Designer	Mikhail Kalashnikov
Designed	PK: 1961 PKM: 1969
Manufacturer	Degtyarev plant
Produced	PK: 1961–present PKM: 1969–present
No. built	1 million+
Variants	PK PKS PKT PKM PKMS
	Specifications
Weight	PK: 9 kg (19.84 lb) (gun + integral bipod) + 7.7 kg (16.98 lb) (tripod). PKM: 7.5 kg (16.53 lb) (gun + integral bipod) + 4.5 kg (9.92 lb) (tripod). PKTM (tank): 10.5 kg (23.15 lb)
Length	PK: 1,203 mm (47.4 in) PKM: 1,192 mm (46.9 in) PKT: 1,098 mm (43.2 in)
Barrel length	PK(M): 605 mm (23.8 in) (without muzzle device) PKT: 772 mm (30.4 in)
Cartridge	7.62×54mmR
Action	Gas-operated, open bolt
Rate of fire	PK, PKM: 650 rounds/min PKT: 700–800 rounds/min Practical: 250 rounds/min
Muzzle velocity	PK, PKM: 825 m/s (2,707 ft/s) PKT: 855 m/s (2,805 ft/s)
Effective firing range	PK(M): 1,000 m (1,094 yd) (100–1,500 m sight adjustments) PKT: 1,500 m (1,640 yd) (100–1,500 m sight adjustments)
Maximum firing range	PK(M): 3,800 m (4,156 yd) PKT: 4,000 m (4,374 yd)

For additional analytical, business and investment opportunities information, please contact Global Investment & Business Center, USA at (703) 370-8082. Fax: (703) 370-8083. E-mail: ibpusa3@gmail.com Global Business and Investment Info Databank - www.ibpus.com

Feed system	Non-disintegrating metal 50 round belts in 100 and 200/250 round ammunition boxes
Sights	Tangent iron sights (default); Optical, Night-vision, Thermal and Radar sights

The **PK** is a 7.62×54mmR general-purpose machine gun designed in the Soviet Union and currently in production in Russia. The original PK machine gun was introduced in 1961 and then the improved PKM in 1969 to replace the SGM and RP-46 machine guns in Soviet service. It remains in use as a front-line infantry and vehicle-mounted weapon with Russia's armed forces. The PK has been exported extensively and produced in several other countries under license.

MGD

Type	Heavy machine gun
Place of origin	Soviet Union
	Service history
In service	1938–present
Used by	See Users
Wars	Winter War World War II Korean War Chinese Civil War First Indochina War Operation Trikora Indonesia–Malaysia confrontation Vietnam War Laotian Civil War Dhofar Rebellion Cambodian Civil War Cambodian-Vietnamese War Sino-Vietnamese War Six-Day War

	Yom Kippur War Western Sahara War Angolan Civil War Iran–Iraq War The Troubles Lebanese Civil War Chadian–Libyan conflict Somali Civil War Tuareg rebellion (1990–1995) Gulf War Yugoslav Wars Kargil War Iraq War Wars in Afghanistan Cambodian–Thai border dispute Operation Enduring Freedom Liberian Civil Wars Operation Linda Nchi Chechen Wars First Libyan Civil War Second Libyan Civil War 2014 pro-Russian conflict in Ukraine South African Border War Syrian Civil War Iraqi Civil War (2014–2017) Yemeni Civil War (2015–present) Conflict in Najran, Jizan and Asir
	Production history
Designer	Vasily Degtyaryov, Georgi Shpagin
Designed	1938
Manufacturer	Tula
Unit cost	US$2,250 (2012)
No. built	1 million
Variants	DK, DShKM, DSHKS, Type 54 HMG
	Specifications
Weight	34 kg (74.96 lb) (gun only) 157 kg (346.13 lb) on wheeled mounting
Length	1,625 mm (64.0 in)
Barrel length	1,070 mm (42.1 in)
Cartridge	12.7×108mm
Action	Gas-operated, flapper-locked
Rate of fire	600 rounds/min
Muzzle velocity	850 m/s (2,788 ft/s)
Effective firing range	2,000 m

Maximum firing range	2,500 m
Feed system	50 round belt
Sights	Iron/optical

The **DShK 1938** is a Soviet heavy machine gun with V-shaped "butterfly" trigger, firing the 12.7×108mm cartridge. The weapon was also used as a heavy infantry machine gun, in which case it was frequently deployed with a two-wheeled mounting and a single-sheet armour-plate shield. It took its name from the weapons designers Vasily Degtyaryov, who designed the original weapon, and Georgi Shpagin, who improved the cartridge feed mechanism. It is sometimes nicknamed *Dushka* (a dear or beloved person) in Russian-speaking countries, from the abbreviation

RPK

Type	Light machine gun Squad automatic weapon
Place of origin	Soviet Union
	Service history
In service	1960- present
Used by	See Users
Wars	Vietnam War South African Border War Yom Kippur War Lebanese Civil War Angolan Civil War Afghan Wars Salvadoran Civil War Iran–Iraq War Lord's Resistance Army insurgency Tuareg rebellion (1990–1995) Gulf War The Troubles Yugoslav Wars Burundian Civil War

	Iraqi conflict Syrian Civil War
	Production history
Designer	Mikhail Kalashnikov
Designed	1961
Manufacturer	Vyatskiye Polyany Machine-Building Plant
Produced	1961–1978
Variants	See Variants
	Specifications
Weight	4.8 kg (10.6 lb) (RPK) 5.1 kg (11 lb) (RPKS)
Length	1,040 mm (40.9 in) (stock extended) (RPK, RPKS) 820 mm (32.3 in) (stock folded) (RPKS)
Barrel length	590 mm (23.2 in)
Cartridge	7.62×39mm M43
Action	Gas operated, rotating bolt; closed bolt
Rate of fire	600 RPM
Muzzle velocity	745 m/s (2,444 ft/s)
Effective firing range	100–1,000 m sight adjustments
Feed system	20-, 30-, 40-round curved magazine, 75-round drum magazine
Sights	Iron sights: semi-shrouded front post and rear sliding tangent with an adjustable notch Sight radius: 555 mm (21.9 in)

The **RPK** "Kalashnikov hand-held machine gun") is a 7.62×39mm light machine gun of Soviet design, developed by Mikhail Kalashnikov in the late 1950s, parallel with the AKM assault rifle. It was created as part of a program designed to standardize the small arms inventory of the Red Army, where it replaced the 7.62×39mm RPD light machine gun. The RPK continues to be used by the armed forces of countries of the former Soviet Union and certain African and Asian nations. The RPK is also manufactured in Bulgaria, Romania and Yugoslavia.

AKHGAR

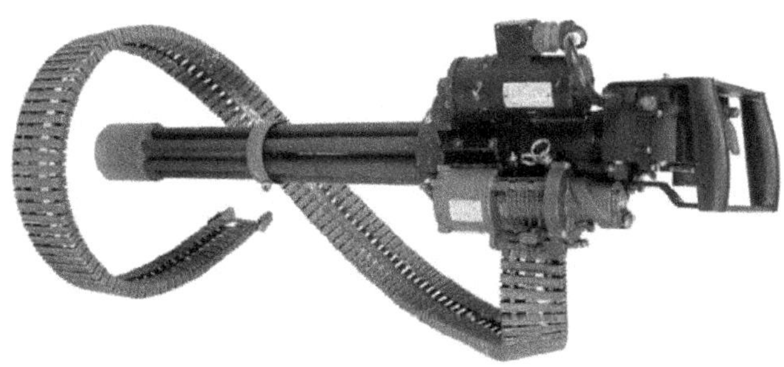

The **Akhgar machine gun** is a Minigun of Iranian origin. The weapon is a copy of the M134 Minigun. This weapon gets its design from the larger M61 Vulcan. It is scaled down to fire 7.62 x 51 mm NATO rounds. It is known for its high rate of fire and is most commonly used mounted in aerial vehicles such as helicopters and aircraft.

MOHARRAM

The Muharram is an externally powered 12.7x108mm gatling derived machine gun of Iranian origin. Moharram is a 6-barrel 12.7 mm Gatling-type machine gun. During the military parade in Tehran on April 18, 2014, the Moharram was mounted at the rear of a local-made neinava 4x4 light tactical vehicle.

NASIR

It is a 40mm automatic grenade launcher with an integrated fire control system, capable of launching smart programmable 40mm shells in addition to various unguided rounds.

STAR MODEL Z84

Type	Submachine gun
Place of origin	Spain
Service history	
In service	1980s–present

Used by	See Users
Wars	Iran–Iraq War
	Production history
Designed	1984
Manufacturer	Star Bonifacio Echeverria, S.A.
Produced	1984–present
Variants	See Variants
	Specifications
Weight	Short barrel: 3.10 kg (6.8 lb) Standard barrel: 3.15 kg (6.9 lb) 25-round magazine: • Empty: 0.22 kg (0.49 lb) • Full: 0.532 kg (1.17 lb) 30-round magazine: • Empty: 0.24 kg (0.53 lb) • Full: 0.607 kg (1.34 lb)
Length	Standard barrel: • 465 mm (18.3 in) with stock retracted • 670 mm (26 in) with stock extended Short barrel: • 410 mm (16 in) with stock retracted • 615 mm (24.2 in) with stock extended
Barrel length	Standard barrel: 270 mm (11 in) Short barrel: 215 mm (8.5 in)
Cartridge	9×19mm Parabellum
Caliber	9mm
Action	Blowback-operated, open bolt, telescoping bolt
Rate of fire	600 rounds/min
Muzzle velocity	400 metres per second (1,300 ft/s)
Effective firing range	150–200m
Feed system	25/30-round detachable box magazine
Sights	Diopter-type iron sights

For additional analytical, business and investment opportunities information, please contact Global Investment & Business Center, USA at (703) 370-8082. Fax: (703) 370-8083. E-mail: ibpusa3@gmail.com Global Business and Investment Info Databank - www.ibpus.com

The **Star Z-84** is a Spanish selective-fire submachine gun originally manufactured by the now defunct Star Bonifacio Echeverria, S.A.. The Z-84 is a sturdy well designed weapon that never saw high production due to politics. Originally manufactured for use by SCUBA divers, the Z-84 could be used right out of the water without any need to drain the working parts or magazine. (OTB capability)

Star S.A. developed the weapon after a successful run of submachine guns based on the German MP-40 design. Realizing they couldn't rebuild the same weapon over and over, they built the Z-84 completely from scratch using modern designs and engineering. At the time of the Z-84's design, Star was building and importing large numbers of cheap handguns into the US. The 1994 Assault Weapons Ban (now repealed), banned the importation of many of their designs. This proved disastrous for Star and by 1996 had driven them into bankruptcy. Less than 1000 Z-84 were manufactured before the company went bankrupt, but many were sold on a testing basis to various countries in South and Central America.

Iranian Takavar commandos still use Z-84 as it is found to be reliable in amphibious warfare.

FAJR 224

Type	Assault rifle Carbine

Place of origin	United States
	Service history
In service	1994–present
Used by	See Users below
Wars	Colombian conflict Moro conflict Burundian Civil War Kosovo War War in Afghanistan (2001–present) Iraq War Syrian Civil War 2013 Lahad Datu standoff Iraqi Civil War (2014–present) Yemeni Civil War (2015-present) Battle of Marawi
	Production history
Designed	1984–1993
Manufacturer	See Manufacturers below
Unit cost	$700 (avg. cost)
Produced	1993–present
Variants	M4A1 Mark 18 Mod 0 CQBR
	Specifications
Weight	6.5 lb (2.9 kg) empty 7.49 lb (3.40 kg) with 30 rounds
Length	33 in (840 mm) (stock extended) 29.75 in (756 mm) (stock retracted)
Barrel length	14.5 in (370 mm)
Cartridge	5.56×45mm NATO
Caliber	5.56 mm (.223 in)
Barrels	1
Action	Gas-operated, rotating bolt (Direct impingement)
Rate of fire	700–950 round/min cyclic
Muzzle velocity	2,970 ft/s (910 m/s) (M855A1 round)
Effective firing range	500 m (550 yd)
Feed system	30-round box magazine or other STANAG magazines. Magazines with different capacities also available.
Sights	Iron sights or various optics

The **M4 carbine** is a shorter and lighter variant of the M16A2 assault rifle. The M4 is a 5.56×45mm NATO, air-cooled, direct impingement gas-operated, magazine-fed carbine. It has a 14.5 in (370 mm) barrel and a telescoping stock.

For additional analytical, business and investment opportunities information, please contact Global Investment & Business Center, USA at (703) 370-8082. Fax: (703) 370-8083. E-mail: ibpusa3@gmail.com Global Business and Investment Info Databank - www.ibpus.com

The M4 carbine is extensively used by the United States Armed Forces and is largely replacing the M16 rifle in United States Army and United States Marine Corps combat units as the primary infantry weapon and service rifle.

The M4 is also capable of mounting the M203 and M320 grenade launchers. The distinctive step in its barrel is for mounting the M203 with the standard hardware. The **M4** is capable of firing in semi-automatic and three-round burst modes (like the M16A2 and M16A4), while the **M4A1** is capable of firing in semi-automatic and fully automatic modes (like the M16A1 and M16A3).

SAYAD 5.56

The **Type CQ** is an unlicensed Chinese variant of the M16 rifle manufactured by Norinco. According to the Norinco website, the rifle is officially known as **CQ 5.56**. It can be distinguished from other AR-15 and M-16 pattern rifles by its long, revolver-like pistol grip, somewhat rounded handguards, and the unique shape of its stock.

ANTI-TANK WEAPONS - UNGUIDED

Model	Type	Quantity	Acquired	Origin
SPG-9	Recoilless rifle			Soviet Union/ Iran
M40	Recoilless rifle			United States/ Iran
RPG-7				Soviet Union/ Iran
Type 69 RPG				People's Republic of China
Saegheh				Iran

RPG-29				Soviet Union

ANTI-TANK GUIDED MISSILE

Model	Type	Quantity	Acquired	Origin	Notes
Saeghe 1/2	Anti-tank guided missile	Unknown		Iran	Reverse engineered M47 Dragon.
Toophan Toophan 2 Toophan 2B Toophan 2M Toophan 3 Toophan 4 Toophan 5 Toophan 6 Toophan 7	Anti-tank guided missile	Unknown	Entered production 1987/1988. Revealed 2000. N/A N/A Introduced 2016 First shown to the public in 2017 but in use since at least 2015. Began development in 2002 and entered production in 2010. Shown to the Public in 2017 Planned Variant, currently in development.	Iran	

Toophan 1 Anti-Tank Guided Missile
Toophan 5 Anti-Tank Guided Missile
||Considered to be the BGM-71A TOW clone the Toophan-1's payload is a 3.6 kg HEAT warhead. the top speed 310 m/s. Toophan-1 marketing material claims a hit probability of 96%

The Toophan 2 is a derivative of BGM-71C TOW missile with a tandem HEAT warhead; possibly incorporates elements of BGM-71E TOW 2A missile.

The Toophan 2B is an upgraded model of the Toophan 2 with heavier warhead.

The Toophan 2M is an upgraded model of the Toophan 2B equipped with a tandem-warhead.

The Toophan 3 is a reverse-engineered American BGM-71F TOW 2B top-attack missile.

The Toophan 4 is a variant of the Toophan family which is equipped with a thermobaric fuel-air warhead.

Considered the premier Toophan variant the Toophan-5 has laser guidance, tandem-warheadand canards. As a laser-riding missile, it uses a different launcher. Not a copy of any TOW variant.

The Toophan 6 is a variant of the Toophan family which is equipped with an anti-bunker thermobaric warhead and is said to be laser-riding.

The Toophan 7 is a planned variant of the Toophan family, it's equipped warhead is unclear some sources claim it is perhaps fragmentation thermobaric.

Qaem Qaem-M	Anti-aircraft missile	Unknown	Entered mass production in 2009	Iran
9K11 Malyutka/Raad	Anti-tank guided missile	Unknown	Soviet Union/ Iran	Manufactured in Iran under the name Raad.
9K111 Fagot	Anti-tank guided missile	Unknown	Soviet Union	
9M113 Konkurs	Anti-tank guided missile	Unkown	Soviet Union/ Iran	Built as Towsan-1 or M-113 in Iran.
9K115-2 Metis-M	Anti-tank guided missile	Unknown	Russia/ Iran	Produced under license from Russia.
MILAN	Anti-tank guided missile	Unknown	France	Captured during the Iran-Iraq War. Probably no longer in service.
Dehlavie	Anti-tank guided missile	Unknown	Iran	Iranian copy of Kornet. Available as Pirooz vehicle-mounted weapon station.

SAEGHE 1/2

The **Saegheh** ("Lightning" or "Thunder" in Persian) (also spelled Saegre, Saeghe, Saeqeh, etc) refers to at least six completely separate Iranian weapons systems: a RPG

For additional analytical, business and investment opportunities information,
please contact Global Investment & Business Center, USA
at (703) 370-8082. Fax: (703) 370-8083. E-mail: ibpusa3@gmail.com
Global Business and Investment Info Databank - www.ibpus.com

warhead, an anti-tank guided missile family, a surface-to-surface rocket, a target drone family, an air-to-air missile and a claimed stealth Unmanned aerial vehicle.

The first system, the *Saeghe 1*, is an Iranian reverse-engineered clone of the American M47 Dragon anti-tank rocket, introduced in 2001. It seems to have entered production in 2002. Iran later introduced the *Saeghe 2*, a clone of a more advanced M47 Dragon variant, and the *Saeghe-4*, with a thermobaric warhead. The *Saeghe-1* weights 6.1 kilograms (13 lb) and can penetrate armor up to 500 millimetres (20 in). The 7.4-kilogram (16 lb) *Saeghe 2* missile has a tandem warhead and can penetrate up to 760 millimetres (30 in) of armor. Like the M47 Dragon, the *Saeghe 1* and *Saeghe 2* ATGMs have a range of 75 to 1,000 metres (250 to 3,280 ft).

Despite being essentially obsolete, the Saegheh anti-tank missiles have been exported to Syria, Hezbollah, and Shia militias in Iraq. The saeghe ATGM is extremely hard to aim and in Iranian service it appears to be limited to IRGC and rapid response forces.

In 2006, Iran tested a completely unrelated short-range surface-to-surface missile that is also named "Saegheh." It has a range of 80 to 250 kilometres (50 to 155 mi).

Under the Saegheh name, Iran has also built a variant warhead for RPG-7 style rocket launchers. Iran also uses the Saeghe name for a target drone (which comes in two variants: Saeghe 1 and Saeghe 2) and an air-to-air missile.

The semi-official Tasnim news agency of Iran reported in September 2016 that an unmanned aerial vehicle (UAV, drone) named Saegheh similar to the US RQ-170 Sentinel spy drone had been built. It was said to be able to carry four precision-guided bombs; range was not stated. An RQ-170 had been captured by Iran in 2011

TOOPHAN

ype	Anti-tank missile
Place of origin	Iran
	Service history
In service	1987-Present
Wars	Iran-Iraq War 2006 Lebanon War Syrian Civil War Iraqi Civil War Yemeni Civil War Saudi-led intervention in Yemen
	Production history
Designer	Hughes Missile Systems
Designed	Early to mid 1980s
Manufacturer	Aerospace Industries Organization (missiles, launchers) Iran Electronics Industries (guidance units)
Produced	1985-Present
Variants	Toophan 1/2/2B/2M/3/4/5/6/7/Qaem/Qaem-M
	Specifications

For additional analytical, business and investment opportunities information, please contact Global Investment & Business Center, USA at (703) 370-8082. Fax: (703) 370-8083. E-mail: ibpusa3@gmail.com Global Business and Investment Info Databank - www.ibpus.com

Length	varies based on variant
Diameter	0.152 m
Maximum firing range	3500m – 3750m
Warhead	HE, HEAT, or thermobaric
Warhead weight	3.6 kg
Speed	310 m/s (peak) 180 m/s (average)
Guidance system	Wire-guidance. Laser guidance for some variants

The **Toophan** (Persian: طوفان "Storm", rarely **Toofan**) is an Iranian SACLOS anti-tank guided missile reverse-engineered from the American BGM-71 TOW missile. The Toophan 1, an unlicensed copy of the BGM-71A TOW missile, began mass production in 1988 and the Toophan 2, a BGM-71C ITOW variant, was publicly shown in 2000. The Toophan comes in at least 11 variants, many of which are poorly documented, including variants with laser guidance, thermobaric warheads, and tandem-warheads with increased penetration. The Toophan is manufactured jointly by the Aerospace Industries Organization of Iran and Iran Electronics Industries.

The Toophan is normally deployed from ground-based tripods, and can also be mounted on fighting vehicles and helicopters. Like the BGM-71 TOW missile, the Toophan is a large, rugged, powerful, and reliable anti-tank guided missile deployed by small teams against tanks, armored vehicles, buildings, and other targets. The Toophan forms the backbone of the Iranian Armed Forces's ATGM inventory and is procured in large quantities in a variety of variants. The Toophan has been exported to the governments of Iraq and Syria and to a large number of non-state actors in the Middle East, and has been used in the Iran-Iraq War, the 2006 Lebanon War and the Iraqi, Syrian, and Yemeni Civil Wars.

VARIANTS

Variant	Range	Penetration (RHA)	Length	Weight	Notes
Toophan 1	3.5 km	550 mm	116 cm	18.5 kg	BGM-71A TOW clone. The Toophan-1's payload is a 3.6 kg HEAT warhead. the top speed 310 m/s. Exported to Hezbollah of Lebanon in the 2000s and Iraqi forces in the Iraqi Civil War. Toophan-1 marketing material claims a hit probability of 96%.Entered production 1987/1988.
Toophan 2	3.5 km	760 mm	145 cm	19.1 kg	derivative of BGM-71C TOW missile with a tandem HEAT

					warhead; possibly incorporates elements of BGM-71E TOW 2A missile. Revealed 2000
Toophan 2B	3.5 km	900 mm	145 cm	19.1 kg	Upgraded Toophan 2 with heavier warhead. Exported to Iraq and used in the Battle of Mosul.
Toophan 2M	3.75 km	650 mm	147 cm	21 kg	tandem-warhead. Exported to Iraq.
Toophan 3	3.5 km	80 mm	116 cm	19.1 kg	derivative of American BGM-71F TOW 2B top-attack missile albeit with worse performance, introduced c. 2016. Possibly exported to Hezbollah (Lebanon) and Kata'ib Hezbollah.
Toophan 4	3.75 km	N/A	117.2 cm	20 kg	Variant with thermobaric fuel-air warhead. Exported to PMU forces in Iraq and used in the battle of Mosul. Also exported to Houthis in Yemen. First shown to the public in 2017 but in use since at least 2015. Like all Iranian thermobaric weapons, has a distinctive red band.
Toophan 5	3.5 km	900 mm	145 cm	19.1 kg	Considered the premier Toophan variant, the Toophan-5 has laser guidance, tandem-warhead and canards. Was apparently in development in 2002 and entered production in 2010. Exported to Iraq and used by Iraqi Federal Police in Ninawa province and elsewhere. As a laser-riding missile, it requires a different launcher. Not a copy of any TOW variant.
Qaem					anti-helicopter variant with laser guidance and secondary flight motor. Mass production began in 2010.
Qaem-M (or Ghaem-M)	6 km	N/A	116 cm	19.5 kg	Qaem variant with proximity fuze.
Toophan 6	3.5 km	N/A	117.2 cm	21 kg	Anti-bunker thermobaric warhead. First shown to the public in 2017. perhaps laser-riding. Unclear differences compared to Toophan-4.

Toophan 7	3.75 km		117.2 cm	21 kg	Unclear warhead, perhaps fragmentation thermobaric

QAEM

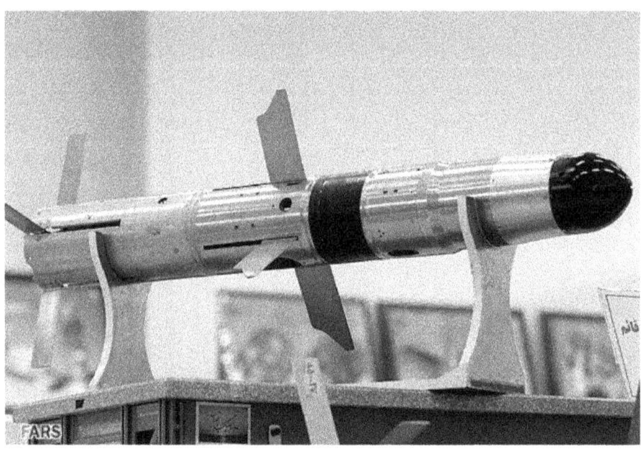

The **Qaem** or **Ghaem**, is an Iranian SACLOS beam-riding SHORAD surface-to-air missile. With a range of six kilometers and a maximum altitude of two kilometers, the Qaem is intended for use against UAVs and low flying or stationary helicopters. The Qaem is a development of the Toophan missile, itself an unlicensed copy of the American BGM-71 TOW missile, and entered mass production in 2009.

The missiles can be used by Ghods Mohajer UAVs.
The Qaem anti-aircraft missile uses a laser guidance system. Iran also produces a variant, the **Qaem-M**, which adds a proximity fuse

**For additional analytical, business and investment opportunities information, please contact Global Investment & Business Center, USA at (703) 370-8082. Fax: (703) 370-8083. E-mail: ibpusa3@gmail.com
Global Business and Investment Info Databank - www.ibpus.com**

9M14 Malyutka

Type	Anti-tank missile
Place of origin	Soviet Union
	Service history
In service	1963–present
Used by	Soviet Union and others
Wars	Vietnam War Yom Kippur War Western Sahara War Ethiopian Civil War Lebanese Civil War Iran–Iraq War Gulf War Croatian War of Independence 2006 Lebanon War First Chechen War Second Chechen War (by Chechen militants) Libyan Civil War Syrian Civil War Iraqi Civil War (2014–present) Yemeni Civil War (2015-present) Saudi Arabian-led intervention in Yemen (2015-present) Conflict in Najran, Jizan and Asir
	Production history
Designer	Design Bureau of Machine-Building (KBM, Kolomna)
Designed	1961–1962
Manufacturer	Soviet Union, Russia as successor state and other countries under license and domestic versions
Produced	1963
Variants	9M14M, 9M14P1, Malyutka-2, Malyutka-2F
	Specifications

Weight	10.9 kg (9M14M) 11.4 kg (9M14P1) 12.5 kg (Malyutka-2) ~12 kg (Malyutka-2F)
Length	860 mm 1,005 mm combat ready (Malyutka-2)
Width	393 mm (wingspan)
Diameter	125 mm
Effective firing range	500–3,000 m
Warhead weight	2.6 kg (9M14M, 9M14P1) 3.5 kg (Malyutka-2, Malyutka-2F)
Speed	115 m/s (410 km/h) (9M14M, 9M14P1) 130 m/s (470 km/h) (Malyutka-2, Malyutka-2F)
Guidance system	MCLOS, SACLOS (Later variants)

The **9M14 Malyutka** (Russian: Малютка; "Little one", NATO reporting name: **AT-3 Sagger**) is a *manual command to line of sight* (MCLOS) wire-guided anti-tank guided missile (ATGM) system developed in the Soviet Union. It was the first man-portable anti-tank guided missile of the Soviet Union and is probably the most widely produced ATGM of all time—with Soviet production peaking at 25,000 missiles a year during the 1960s and 1970s. In addition, copies of the missile have been manufactured under various names by at least five countries.

Since supplemented by more advanced anti-tank guided missiles, the Sagger and its variants have seen widespread use in nearly every regional conflict since the 1960s.

The **9M113 *Konkurs*** NATO reporting name **AT-5 *Spandrel***) is a Soviet SACLOS wire-guided anti-tank missile. A development of the 9K111 Fagot with greater firepower, the 9M113 Konkurs can use the same launchers and is very similar visually, distinguishable only by a slight bulge towards the end of the Konkurs' missile tube.

The missile is designed to be fired from vehicles, although it can also be fired from the later models of 9M111 launchers. It is an integral part of the BMP-2, BMD-2 and BRDM-2 vehicles. The missile is stored and carried in a fiberglass container/launch tube.

The system uses a gas generator to push the missile out of the launch tube. The gas also exits from the rear of the launch tube in a similar manner to a recoilless rifle. The missile leaves the launch tube at 80 meters per second, and is quickly accelerated to 200 meters per second by its solid fuel motor. This initial high speed reduces the missile's deadzone, since it can be launched directly at the target, rather than in an upward arc. In flight, the missile spins at between five and seven revolutions per second.

For additional analytical, business and investment opportunities information, please contact Global Investment & Business Center, USA at (703) 370-8082. Fax: (703) 370-8083. E-mail: ibpusa3@gmail.com Global Business and Investment Info Databank - www.ibpus.com

The launcher tracks the position of an incandescent infrared bulb on the back of the missile relative to the target and transmits appropriate commands to the missile via a thin wire that trails behind the missile. The system has an alarm that activates when it detects jamming from a system like Shtora. The operator can then take manual control, reducing the missile to MCLOS. The SACLOS guidance system has many benefits over MCLOS. The system's accuracy is quoted in some sources as 90%, though its performance is probably comparable to the BGM-71 TOW or later SACLOS versions of the 9K11 Malyutka.

ARMORED FIGHTING VEHICLES

Model	Type	In Service		Origin	
Boragh/BMP-1	Armored personnel carrier	250	1997	Iran	
Sayyad	Armored fast attack vehicle	Unknown		Iran	
M113	Armored personnel carrier	300		United States	
EE-9 Cascavel	Armored car	35		Brazil	35 are in service.
BTR-50 BTR-60 BTR-80	Amphibious Armored personnel carrier Armored Personnel Carrier	480	1966–2017(BTR-80)	Soviet Union	KPVT 14.5 mm machine gun replaced with DShKM 12.7 mm machine gun or ZSU-23 gun on some vehicles. ATGM launchers added to some vehicles.BTR-82 Variant
BMP-2	Infantry fighting vehicle	650	1991–2001	Soviet Union	1,500 ordered in 1991 from Russia and 413 were delivered between 1993 and 2001 of which 82 were delivered directly by Russia and 331 were assembled in Iran. 100 were in service in 1995, 140 in 2000 and 400 in 2002, 2005 and 2008. 400 are currently in service. Some sources claim that production is ongoing.
FV101 Scorpion	Combat Vehicle Reconnaissance	80	1997	United Kingdom	Tosan is a domestically produced light Tank, based on the FV101 Scorpion

For additional analytical, business and investment opportunities information, please contact Global Investment & Business Center, USA at (703) 370-8082. Fax: (703) 370-8083. E-mail: ibpusa3@gmail.com
Global Business and Investment Info Databank - www.ibpus.com

BORAGH/BMP-1

Type	Armoured personnel carrier
Place of origin	Iran
	Service history
Used by	See Operators
	Production history
Manufacturer	Defense Industries Organization (Iran) MIC (Sudan)
Produced	1997 - Present
	Specifications
Weight	13 tons
Length	6.72 m
Width	3.10 m
Height	1.66 m
Crew	3 (+8 passengers)
Armor	Welded rolled steel
Main armament	12.7 mm DShK 1938/46 heavy machine gun (1,000 rounds), 30mm cannon, 120mm mortar or a Toophan ATGM launcher
Secondary armament	unknown
Engine	V-8 diesel 330 hp (246 kW)
Power/weight	25.4 hp/tonne (18.9 kW/tonne)
Suspension	torsion bar
Operational	550km

range	
Speed	65km/h (road) 45km/h (off-road)

Boragh or **Boraq** (Persian: نفربر براق) is an Iranian-made armoured personnel carrier. Boragh is believed to be a reverse engineered and upgraded model of the Chinese Type 86 (BMP-1). The upgrades include a reduction in weight, a higher road speed, and stronger armor. The vehicle is fully amphibious and is fitted with an NBC protection system and infra-red night vision equipment.

It was reported in May 2002 that three additional variants are produced by the Vehicle and Equipment Group (VEIG) of the Iranian Defence Industries Organisation (DIO). These are a 120 mm mortar carrier, an ammunition resupply vehicle, and an armoured personnel carrier (APC) fitted with improved armaments

SAYYAD

Sayyad	
Type	Quick reaction armored vehicle
Place of origin	Iran
	Service history
Used by	Iran
	Production history
Manufacturer	Defense Industries Organization
Produced	2010
	Specifications
Armor	Steel
Main armament	Single or double Toophan anti-tank missile launchers or two 23x 77 millimetres (3.0 in) rocket launchers
Engine	Diesel
Suspension	Torsion bar

The **Sayyad AFV** is an Iranian light, multi-purpose, tracked armored vehicle, sometimes described as a "quick reaction tank".

The overall design is similar to that of the British FV102 Striker, and it is often mistaken for the Tosan tank. However, there are some major differences between the Sayyad and the Striker. The Sayyad is shorter in length than the Striker, and it has one less road wheel. The hull is slightly redesigned and storage baskets have also been added.

There are two variants of the Sayyad. One with either a single or a double Toophan anti-tank missile launcher, with six reload missiles in storage baskets. The other is a multiple rocket launcher variant with two 23 tube launchers for 77mm rockets.

The vehicle is intended to be used to provide a fast platform for anti-tank missiles and small artillery rockets. It entered service in 2010

M113

Type	Armored personnel carrier
Place of origin	United States
	Service history
In service	1960–present
Used by	See Operators
Wars	• Vietnam War • Cambodian Civil War • Cambodian–Vietnamese War • Sino-Vietnamese War • Six-Day War • Indo-Pakistani War of 1965 • Civil conflict in the Philippines • Indo-Pakistani War of 1971 • Yom Kippur War • Lebanese Civil War • 1982 Lebanon War • South Lebanon conflict (1985–2000) • Invasion of Panama

- Iran–Iraq War
- Persian Gulf War
- Kosovo War
- First Chechen War
- War in Afghanistan
- Iraq War
- Second Chechen War
- Waziristan War
- Second Intifada
- 2006 Lebanon War
- Gaza War
- Libyan Civil War
- Operation Protective Edge
- Iraqi insurgency
- Central African Republic Civil War (2012–2014)
- Iraqi Civil War (2014–present)
- Syrian Civil War
- Yemeni Civil War (2015–present)
- Saudi-led intervention in Yemen
- Conflict in Najran, Jizan and Asir
- Battle of Marawi

Production history	
No. built	≈80,000 (all variants)
Variants	Numerous, see text
Specifications	
Weight	12.3 tonnes (13.6 short tons; 12.1 long tons)
Length	4.863 metres (15 ft 11.5 in)
Width	2.686 metres (8 ft 9.7 in)
Height	2.5 metres (8 ft 2 in)
Crew	2
Passengers	11 passengers
Armor	aluminum 12–38 millimetres (0.47–1.50 in)
Main armament	M2 Browning machine gun
Secondary armament	varies (see text)
Engine	Detroit Diesel 6V53T, 6-cylinder diesel engine 275 hp (205 kW)
Power/weight	22.36 hp/tonne
Suspension	torsion bar, 5 road wheels
Operational range	480 km (300 mi)
Speed	67.6 km/h (42.0 mph), 5.8 km/h (3.6 mph) swimming

For additional analytical, business and investment opportunities information, please contact Global Investment & Business Center, USA at (703) 370-8082. Fax: (703) 370-8083. E-mail: ibpusa3@gmail.com Global Business and Investment Info Databank - www.ibpus.com

The **M113** is a fully tracked armored personnel carrier (APC) that was developed by Food Machinery Corp (FMC). The vehicle was first fielded by the United States Army's mechanized infantry units in Vietnam in April 1962. The M113 was the most widely used armored vehicle of the U.S. Army in the Vietnam War, earning the nickname 'Green Dragon' by the Viet Cong as it was used to break through heavy thickets in the midst of the jungle to attack and overrun enemy positions. It was largely known as an "APC" or an "ACAV" (armored cavalry assault vehicle) by the allied forces.

The M113 introduced new aluminum armor that made the vehicle much lighter than earlier vehicles; it was thick enough to protect the crew and passengers against small arms fire but light enough that the vehicle was air transportable and moderately amphibious. In the U.S. Army, the M113 series have long been replaced as front-line combat vehicles by the M2 and M3 Bradleys, but large numbers are still used in support roles such as armored ambulance, mortar carrier, engineer vehicle, and command vehicle. The U.S. Army's heavy brigade combat teams are equipped with approximately 6,000 M113s and 4,000 Bradleys.

The M113's versatility spawned a wide variety of adaptations that live on worldwide, and in U.S. service. These variants together currently represent about half of U.S. Army armored vehicles. To date, it is estimated that over 80,000 M113s of all types have been produced and used by over 50 countries worldwide, making it one of the most widely used armored fighting vehicles of all time. The Military Channel's *Top Ten* series named the M113 the most significant infantry vehicle in history.

The U.S. Army planned to retire the M113 family of vehicles by 2018, seeking replacement with the GCV Infantry Fighting Vehicle program, but now replacement of the M113 has fallen to the Armored Multi-Purpose Vehicle (AMPV) program. Thousands of M113s continue to see combat service in the IDF, although as of 2014 the IDF was seeking to gradually replace many of its vehicles with Namer APCs

EE-9 CASCAVEL

Type	Armoured Car
Place of origin	Brazil
	Service history
In service	1974–present
Used by	See Operators
Wars	Colombian Civil War Western Sahara War Libyan–Egyptian War Chadian–Libyan conflict Iran–Iraq War Gulf War Second Congo War Iraq War Internal conflict in Burma 2011 Libyan Civil War Libyan Civil War (2014–present) Iraqi Civil War (2014–present)
	Production history
Designer	Engesa
Designed	1970
Manufacturer	Engesa
Unit cost	USD $500,000 (new)
Produced	1974–1993
No. built	1,715
Variants	See Variants
	Specifications
Weight	12 tonnes (13 short tons; 12 long tons)
Length	6.29 m (20 ft 8 in)
length	5.25 m (17 ft 3 in) (hull)
Width	2.59 m (8 ft 6 in)
Height	2.60 m (8 ft 6 in)
Crew	3 (commander, driver, gunner)
Main armament	90mm Engesa EC-90 (44 rounds)
Secondary armament	2× 7.62mm machine guns (2200–2400 rounds)
Engine	Detroit Diesel 6V-53N 5.2 l (320 in^3) 6-cylinder water-cooled diesel 158 kW (212 hp) at 2,800 rpm
Power/weight	15.82hp/tonne
Suspension	6X6 double axle boomerang drive
Ground clearance	0.375 m (1 ft 2.8 in)

For additional analytical, business and investment opportunities information,
please contact Global Investment & Business Center, USA
at (703) 370-8082. Fax: (703) 370-8083. E-mail: ibpusa3@gmail.com
Global Business and Investment Info Databank - www.ibpus.com

Fuel capacity	360 L (95 US gal)
Operational range	750 km (470 mi)
Speed	100 km/h (62 mph)

The **EE-9 *Cascavel*)** is a six-wheeled Brazilian armoured car developed primarily for reconnaissance. It was engineered by Engesa in 1970 as a replacement for Brazil's ageing fleet of M8 Greyhounds. The vehicle was first fitted with the Greyhound's 37mm main gun, and subsequently, a French turret adopted from the Panhard AML-90. Later models carry unique Engesa turrets with a Belgian 90mm Cockerill Mk.3 cannon produced under licence as the *EC-90*.

The Cascavel shares many components with the EE-11 Urutu, its armoured personnel carrier counterpart; both entered production in 1974 and are now operated by over 20 nations in South America, Africa, and the Middle East. Rights to the design were also sold to the United States via the FMC Corporation. About 2,767 Cascavels and Urutus were manufactured before Engesa ceased operations in 1993

BTR-60

Type	Amphibious Tracked Armored Personnel Carrier
Place of origin	Soviet Union
	Service history
In service	1954 – late 1970s (USSR)
Used by	See Operators.
Wars	Six-Day War, Vietnam War, War of Attrition, Lebanese Civil War, Iran–Iraq War, Syrian Civil War
	Production history

For additional analytical, business and investment opportunities information, please contact Global Investment & Business Center, USA at (703) 370-8082. Fax: (703) 370-8083. E-mail: ibpusa3@gmail.com
Global Business and Investment Info Databank - www.ibpus.com

Designed	1952
Produced	1954 – 1970
Variants	See Variants
	Specifications
Weight	14.5 tonnes
Length	7.08 m
Width	3.14 m
Height	2.03 m
Crew	2 (driver and commander) (+20 passengers)
Armor	Homogeneous, cold rolled, welded steel 13 mm front 10 mm sides 10 mm top 7 mm rear
Main armament	None or 7.62 mm SGMB medium machine gun (BTR-50P) (1,250 rounds) 14.5 mm KPV heavy machine gun (BTR-50PA) 7.62 mm SGMB medium machine gun (BTR-50PK) (1,250 rounds)
Secondary armament	none
Engine	V-6 6-cylinder 4-stroke in line water-cooled diesel 240 hp (179 kW) at 1,800 rpm
Power/weight	16.6 hp/t
Suspension	torsion bar
Ground clearance	370 mm
Fuel capacity	400 l
Operational range	400 km
Speed	44 km/h (road) 11 km/h (water)

The **BTR-50** (BTR stands for *Bronetransporter* (БТР, Бронетранспортер), literally "armored transporter") is a Soviet amphibious armored personnel carrier (APC) based on the PT-76 light tank. The BTR-50 is tracked, unlike most in the BTR series, which are wheeled. The BTR-50 shares many similarities with two other APCs, the OT-62 TOPAS and the Type 77. While the OT-62 is an improved copy of the BTR-50 developed jointly by Czechoslovakia and Poland, the Type 77, based on the Type 63 amphibious light tank developed by the People's Republic of China (PRC), is not a copy of the BTR-50.

BTR-80

Type	Armored personnel carrier
Place of origin	Soviet Union Russia
	Service history
In service	1986–present
Used by	See Operators
Wars	Soviet–Afghan War Nagorno-Karabakh War Georgian Civil War Kurdish–Turkish conflict (1978–present) Transnistria War Tajikistan Civil War War in Afghanistan Iraq War First Chechen War War of Dagestan Second Chechen War 2008 South Ossetian War Iraqi insurgency (2011–13) War in Donbass
	Production history
Manufacturer	Arzamas Machinery Plant, Nizhniy Novgorod
Produced	1984–present
No. built	5,000+
	Specifications
Weight	13.6 tonnes (15.0 tons)
Length	7.7 m (25.3 ft)
Width	2.9 m (9.5 ft)

For additional analytical, business and investment opportunities information, please contact Global Investment & Business Center, USA at (703) 370-8082. Fax: (703) 370-8083. E-mail: ibpusa3@gmail.com Global Business and Investment Info Databank - www.ibpus.com

Height	2.41 m (7.9 ft)
Crew	3 (+7 passengers)
Main armament	14.5 mm KPVT machine gun or 30mm 2A72 automatic cannon
Secondary armament	7.62 mm PKT machine gun
Engine	diesel KamAZ-7403 260 hp (190 kW)
Power/weight	19 hp/tonne
Suspension	wheeled 8×8
Operational range	600 km (372.8 mi)
Speed	80–90 km/h (49.7–55.9 m/h) swim 10 km/h (6.2 m/h)

The **BTR-80** (Russian: бронетранспортер/Bronetransporter, literally "Armoured Transporter") is an 8×8 wheeled amphibious armoured personnel carrier (APC) designed in the USSR. It was adopted in 1986 and replaced the previous vehicles, the BTR-60 and BTR-70, in the Soviet Army. It was first deployed during the Soviet–Afghan War

BMP-2

Type	Infantry fighting vehicle
Place of origin	Soviet Union
Service history	

In service	1980–present
Wars	Gulf War Syrian Civil War
	Production history
Manufacturer	Kurganmashzavod
Produced	1980–present
	Specifications
Weight	14.3 tonnes (15.8 short tons; 14.1 long tons)
Length	6.735 metres (22 ft 1.2 in)
Width	3.15 metres (10 ft 4 in)
Height	2.45 metres (8 ft 0 in)
Crew	3 (+7 passengers)
Armor	33 millimetres (1.3 in) (max)
Main armament	30 mm automatic cannon 2A42 9M113 Konkurs ATGM
Secondary armament	7.62 mm machine gun (PKTM)
Engine	diesel UTD-20/3 300 hp (225 kW)
Power/weight	21 hp/tonne
Suspension	torsion bar
Operational range	600 km (370 mi)
Speed	65 km/h (40 mph) (road) 45 km/h (28 mph) (off-road) 7 km/h (4.3 mph) (water)

The **BMP-2** (*Boyevaya Mashina Pekhoty*, Russian: Боевая Машина Пехоты, literally "infantry combat vehicle") is a second-generation, amphibious infantry fighting vehicle introduced in the 1980s in the Soviet Union, following on from the BMP-1 of the 1960s

FV101 SCORPION

Type	Reconnaissance vehicle
Place of origin	United Kingdom
	Service history
In service	1973–present
Used by	Operators
Wars	Iran–Iraq War Falklands war Gulf war
	Production history
Manufacturer	Alvis Vehicles Ltd, Coventry, England

For additional analytical, business and investment opportunities information,
please contact Global Investment & Business Center, USA
at (703) 370-8082. Fax: (703) 370-8083. E-mail: ibpusa3@gmail.com
Global Business and Investment Info Databank - www.ibpus.com

Variants	Scorpion 90
	Specifications
Weight	17,800 lb (8.074 tonnes)
Length	5.288 m (17 ft 4.2 in)
Width	2.134 m (7 ft 0 in)
Height	2.102 m (6 ft 10.8 in)
Crew	3
Armour	Aluminium armour, Cast and 1318b plate
Main armament	ROF 76mm L23A1 gun 90 mm in Scorpion 90
Secondary armament	Coaxial 7.62 mm L43A1 machine gun
Engine	Cummins BTA 5.9-litre (diesel) 190 hp (140 kW)
Power/weight	22.92 hp (17.3 kW) / tonne
Transmission	Self Change Gears TN15X
Suspension	Torsion-bar
Operational range	756 km (470 mi)
Speed	72.5 km/h (45.0 mph

The **FV101 Scorpion** is a British armoured reconnaissance vehicle. It was the lead vehicle and the fire support type in the Combat Vehicle Reconnaissance (Tracked), CVR(T), family of seven armoured vehicles. Manufactured by Alvis, it was introduced into service with the British Army in 1973 and served until 1994. The base model was

For additional analytical, business and investment opportunities information,
please contact Global Investment & Business Center, USA
at (703) 370-8082. Fax: (703) 370-8083. E-mail: ibpusa3@gmail.com
Global Business and Investment Info Databank - www.ibpus.com

retired from active service, but the army retains a number of base Scorpions in reserve as training vehicles. More than 3,000 were produced and used as a reconnaissance vehicle or a light tank. It holds the Guinness world record for the fastest production tank; recorded doing 82.23 km/h (51.10 mph) at the QinetiQ vehicle test track, Chertsey, Surrey, on 26 January 2002

TANKS

Tosan Tank	Light Tank	20	1997	Iran	

Zulfiqar MBT 3	Main Battle Tank	200 (More Scheduled for Production)	1996–present	Iran
Zulfiqar MBT 2		1(prototype)		
Zulfiqar MBT 1		100		

Zulfiqar 1
Zulfiqar 3 Based on M60 and T-72. Featuring EFCS-3 fire control system and autoloader. The Zulfiqar 3 is the latest model in the family which has been heavily modernized with advanced technologies and armaments. It features considerable upgrades to the fire control system, chassis, engine and main gun. The new variant is equipped with the 2A46 125 mm smoothbore cannon, a laser rangefinder, RAM camouflage and a new fire control system. It is also fitted with a reinforced turret and the wheels are covered by an armoured skirt. 300+ in service according to Global Security.

Chieftain Mobarez	Main battle tank	100(Chieftain) - Mobarez ~50		United Kingdom/Iran	707 Mk-3P and Mk-5P, 125–189 FV-4030-1, 41 ARV and 14 AVLB obtained before the 1979 revolution. Further planned deliveries of the more capable 4030 series were cancelled at that point. 100 in service as of 2005.Many others upgraded to Mobarez
M60 Patton	Main Battle Tank	200		United States/Iran	

T-72S	Main Battle	563(25 T-72M1s)	1994–1999	Iran/ Soviet Union	Iran produced 2538 T-72S tanks under

For additional analytical, business and investment opportunities information,
please contact Global Investment & Business Center, USA
at (703) 370-8082. Fax: (703) 370-8083. E-mail: ibpusa3@gmail.com
Global Business and Investment Info Databank - www.ibpus.com

T-72 Khorrhamshahr	Tank Main Battle Tank	-10?	1990s	Iran	licence from Russia from 1993-2012, received 104 T-72M1 tanks from Poland from 1994-1995 and 37 T-72M1 tanks from Belarus starting in 2000,T-72M1 used in limited services. Possible unlicensed production,around 2000 in inventory including 1500 T-72S and 500 less capable T-72M/M1.T-72 fitted with T-80 turret and using Kontakt-5 ERA
T-72Z Safir-74	Main Battle Tank	Approximatly 400 with around 10 said to still be in service	1990s	Iran/ Soviet Union	Modernized T-62 which have been replaced with the Zulfiqar 3 tanks and soon the Karrar tank.

Karrar	Main Battle Tank	800 (scheduled)	2016	Iran	Both IRGC and Iran armed forces order about 800 Karrar tanks from local industry

TOSAN TANK

Type	Light tank
Place of origin	Iran

Service history

In service	1997–
Used by	Iranian Army IRGCGF
Production history	
Produced	1997
No. built	~ 20
Specifications	
Weight	~ 8 tonnes
Length	4.9 m
Width	2.2 m
Height	2.1 m
Crew	3
Armour	12.7 mm
Main armament	90 mm gun
Secondary armament	Toophan
Engine	Diesel
Suspension	Torsion bar

The **Tosan** (Also written Towsan, meaning Wild Horse or Fury) is an Iranian light tank, for unconventional warfare. Iran calls it a 'Quick Reaction' tank because the tank is said to be capable of rapid response and is built for strategic missions. It appears to be based on the British FV101 Scorpion (where Iran has 80 in service), the tank is fitted with a 90 mm gun, Toophan missile launchers and an improved firing and targeting systems. The tank can drive long distances on its tracks and does not need to be carried on trucks

ZULFIQAR MBT 3

Type	Main battle tank (MBT)
Place of origin	Iran
	Service history
Used by	Islamic Republic of Iran
	Production history
Designed	1993
Manufacturer	Shahid Kolah Dooz Industrial Complex
Produced	1996–present
No. built	~150 Zulfiqar 1 in 2012 100 Zulfiqar 3
Variants	Zulfiqar 1, Zulfiqar 2, Zulfiqar 3
	Specifications (Zulfiqar 3)
Weight	52 tonnes
Length	9.20 m (30 ft 2 in)
Width	3.6 m (11 ft 10 in)
Height	2.5 m (8 ft 2 in)
Crew	3
Armour	composite armour
Main armament	125 mm smoothbore tank gun
Secondary armament	12.7 mm and 7.62 mm machine guns
Engine	12-cyl. diesel Zulfiqar 1: 780 hp (630 kW) Zulfiqar 3: AVDS-1790 1000 hp
Power/weight	21.7 hp/ton (Zulfiqar 1),17.85 hp/ton (zulfiqar 3)
Transmission	6-gear SPAT 1200 automatic transmission
Suspension	torsion-bar
Operational range	450 km (280 mi)
Speed	70 km/h (43 mph)

Zulfiqar is an Iranian main battle tank (MBT), conceived by Brigadier General Mir-Younes Masoumzadeh, deputy ground force commander for research and self-sufficiency of the armed forces. It is named after Zulfiqar, the legendary sword of Ali, the fourth Caliph and the first Shiite Imam. The test prototypes of the tank were evaluated in 1993. Six semi-industrial prototypes of the tank were produced and tested in 1997

The tank has a distinctive box-shaped, steel-welded turret of local design. The Zulfiqar is believed to be developed from major components of the Soviet T-72 and American M48 and M60 tanks. The suspension is modelled on the M48 /M60 Patton tanks supplied to Iran by the U.S. The SPAT 1200 transmission also seems to be a local development of that of the M-60. Zulfiqar-1's combat weight has been reported to be 36 tonnes with a 780 hp diesel engine; giving the tank a 21.7 hp per ton ratio. Some sources see

For additional analytical, business and investment opportunities information, please contact Global Investment & Business Center, USA at (703) 370-8082. Fax: (703) 370-8083. E-mail: ibpusa3@gmail.com Global Business and Investment Info Databank - www.ibpus.com

resemblances between the Zulfiqar design and the Brazilian prototype Osório. The Zulfiqar is operated by a crew of three personnel. The automatic loader is believed to be the same one from the T-72 tank.

In October 2016, Iran claimed they had successfully tested an active protection system on the Zulfiqar, based on pulse-doppler and phased-array radar systems equipped with four arms systems that can cover a full 360-degrees of sight.

The tank is armed with a 125 mm smoothbore gun 2A46 derived from that of the T-72, which is fitted with a fume extractor. Its secondary armament consists of a 7.62 mm coaxial and a 12.7 mm machine gun. For the Zulfiqar/T-72 fleet, the Ammunition Group of the Iranian Defense Industries Organization mass-produces a standard high explosive 23 kilograms (51 lb) propellant charge which fires the 3 kg warhead at a muzzle velocity of 850 metres per second (2,800 ft/s).
The Zulfiqar-1 uses the Slovenian EFCS-3 fire control system, the same model used on the Type 72Z ("Safir-74"), providing 'fire-on-the-move' technology. The Zulfiqar allegedly mounts a laser-warning pod on the turret. Its design enables the tank to use an Iranian-made package of reactive armor

CHIEFTAIN

Type	Main battle tank
Place of origin	United Kingdom
	Service history
In service	1966–present
Used by	UK, Iran, Iraq, Jordan, Kuwait, Oman
Wars	Iran–Iraq War Persian Gulf War
	Production history
Manufacturer	Leyland Motors
Unit cost	£90,000-£100,000 (March 1967)
	Specifications

Weight	55 long tons (62 short tons; 56 t)
Length	35 ft 4 in (10.77 m) – gun forward 7.5 m (24 ft 7 in) – hull
Width	12 ft 0 in (3.66 m)
Height	2.9 m (9 ft 6 in)
Crew	4
Armour	Glacis: 120 mm (4.7 in) (72°) Hull sides: 38 mm (1.5 in) (10°) Turret: 195 mm (7.7 in) (60°)
Main armament	L11A5 120 mm rifled gun
Secondary armament	2 × L7 Machine Gun
Engine	Leyland L60 (multifuel 2-stroke opposed-piston compression-ignition) 750 hp (560 kW) 6 Cyl, 19 litres.
Power/weight	11.1 hp (8.3 kW)/ton (at sprocket)
Transmission	TN 12
Suspension	Horstmann: Horizontal Coil Spring Suspension Bogies
Ground clearance	1 ft 10 in (0.56 m))
Fuel capacity	195 imp gal (890 l; 234 US gal)
Operational range	500 km (310 miles) on roads
Speed	Road: 48 km/h (30 mph) Off road: 30 km/h (19 mph)

The FV4201 **Chieftain** was the main battle tank of the United Kingdom during the 1960s, 1970s and 1980s. The main battle tank was further improved by being the first tank in service to incorporate the Chobham armour upgrades as part of the "Stillbrew" package.

A development of the Centurion, the Chieftain introduced the supine (reclining) driver position to British design enabling a heavily sloped hull with reduced height. A new powerpack and improved transmission gave it higher speed than the Centurion despite being heavier due to major upgrades to armour protection and the armament. It remained in service until replaced by the Challenger 1 which shared a large number of the Chieftain's features.

MOBAREZ

Type	Main battle tank
Place of origin	Iran
	Service history
Used by	Iran
	Production history
Produced	2006–present
	Specifications (Mobarez)
Weight	55 long tons (62 short tons; 56 t)
Length	7.5 m (24 ft 7 in) (hull)
Width	3.5 m (11 ft 6 in)
Height	2.9 m (9 ft 6 in)

Mobarez (meaning "Warrior") is a domestically upgraded version of the British Chieftain tank by Iran. The hull of the tank has been modified at the back and sides. The fuel tank has been replaced by a new, repairable one. Also, additional vibration dampening systems have been added to protect sensitive electronic components. Other modifications include a laser range finder, a more powerful engine and the addition of light amplifying and infra-red systems.

M60 PATTON

Type	Main battle tank
Place of origin	United States
	Service history
In service	1960–present
Used by	See Operators
Wars	Yom Kippur War • Cold War • Iran–Iraq War

	• 1982 Lebanon War • Invasion of Grenada • Persian Gulf War • Restore Hope, Somalia • Western Sahara War • Houthi insurgency in Yemen • Turkey–PKK conflict • Sinai insurgency • Yemeni Civil War (2015) • Saudi Arabian-led intervention in Yemen • Syrian Civil War
Production history	
Manufacturer	Detroit Arsenal Tank Plant, Chrysler
Produced	M60: 1960–1962 M60A1: 1962-1980 M60A2: 1969-1975 M60A3: 1978-1983
No. built	Over 15,000 (all variants)
Variants	See Variants
Specifications	
Weight	M60: 50.7 short tons (46.0 t; 45.3 long tons) M60A1: 52 to 54 short tons (47 to 49 t; 46 to 48 long tons) depending on turret design.
Length	M60: 6.946 meters (22 ft 9.5 in) (hull), 9.309 meters (30 ft 6.5 in) (gun forward)
Width	M60: 3.631 meters (11 ft 11.0 in)
Height	M60: 3.213 meters (10 ft 6.5 in)
Crew	4
Armor	Upper Glacis • M60: 3.67 in (93 mm) at 65° 8.68 in (220 mm) LoS • M60A1: 4.29 in (109 mm) at 65° 10.15 in (258 mm) LoS • M60A2: same as M60A1 • M60A3: same as M60A1 Turret Front • M60: equals 7 in (180 mm) • M60A1: equals 10 in (250 mm) • M60A2: equals 11.5 in (290 mm) • M60A3: same as M60A1

For additional analytical, business and investment opportunities information, please contact Global Investment & Business Center, USA at (703) 370-8082. Fax: (703) 370-8083. E-mail: ibpusa3@gmail.com Global Business and Investment Info Databank - www.ibpus.com

Main armament	• M60 / M60A1 / M60A3: 105 mm (4.1 in) M68 gun (M60/A1/A3) • M60A2: 152 mm (6.0 in) M162 Gun/Launcher
Secondary armament	• .50 BMG (12.7×99mm) M85 mounted on M19 Commanders Cupola • 7.62×51mm NATO M73 machine gun
Engine	Continental AVDS-1790-2 V12, air-cooled Twin-turbo diesel engine 750 bhp (560 kW)
Power/weight	15.08 bhp/st (12.4 kW/tonne)
Transmission	General Motors, cross-drive, single-stage with 2 forward and 1 reverse ranges
Suspension	Torsion bar suspension
Ground clearance	1 foot 6.2 inches (0.463 m)
Fuel capacity	385 U.S. gallons (1,457 L)
Operational range	300 miles (500 km)
Speed	30 mph (48 km/h) (road)

The **M60 Patton** is a main battle tank (MBT) introduced in December 1960. With the United States Army's deactivation of their last (M103) heavy tank battalion in 1963, the M60 became the Army's primary tank during the Cold War. Although developed from the M48 Patton, the M60 series was never *officially* classified as a Patton tank, but as a "product-improved descendant" of the Patton series. In March 1959, the tank was officially standardized as the **105 mm Gun Full Tracked Combat Tank M60**. Over

15,000 M60s were built by Chrysler. Hull production ended in 1983, but 5,400 older models were converted to the M60A3 variant ending in 1990.

The M60 underwent many updates over its service life. The interior layout, based on the design of the M48, provided ample room for updates and improvements, extending the vehicle's service life for over four decades. It was widely used by the U.S. and its Cold War allies, especially those in NATO, and remains in service throughout the world today, despite having been superseded by the M1 Abrams in the U.S. military. Egypt is currently the largest operator with 1,716 upgraded M60A3s, Turkey is second with 866 upgraded units in service, and Israel is third with over 700 units of Israeli variants.

T-72S

Type	Main battle tank
Place of origin	Soviet Union
Service history	
In service	1973–present
Production history	
Designer	Kartsev-Venediktov
Designed	1967–73
Manufacturer	Uralvagonzavod
Produced	1971–present
No. built	25,000+

The **T-72** is a Soviet-designed main battle tank that entered production in 1971. It replaced the T-54/55 series as the workhorse of Soviet tank forces (while the T-64 and T-80 served as the Soviet high-technology tanks). In front-line Russian service, T-72s are being upgraded or augmented by the T-90 (itself, a modernized version of the T-72B). The T-72 has been exported and produced in many countries.

T-72Z SAFIR-74

Type	Main battle tank
Place of origin	Iran
	Service history
Used by	See Operators
	Production history
Manufacturer	Defense Industries Organization, Military Industry Corporation
Produced	1996–present
Variants	See Variants
	Specifications
Weight	36 tonnes
Length	6.45m
Width	3.37m
Height	2.40m
Crew	3-4
Armor	203 mm front of the turret 150 mm sides of the turret 64 mm rear of the turret 39 mm top of the turret 97 mm upper front of the hull 99 mm lower front of the hull 79 mm upper sides of the hull 20 mm lower sides of the hull 46 mm rear of the hull 20 mm floor of the hull fitted with ERA

For additional analytical, business and investment opportunities information, please contact Global Investment & Business Center, USA at (703) 370-8082. Fax: (703) 370-8083. E-mail: ibpusa3@gmail.com Global Business and Investment Info Databank - www.ibpus.com

Main armament	105mm M68 rifled tank gun
Secondary armament	7.62mm coaxial PKT and roof-mounted 12.7mm DShKM machine guns
Engine	V-46-6 V-12 diesel 780 hp (630 kW)
Power/weight	21.66hp/tonne
Suspension	Torsion bar
Operational range	440 km
Speed	65 km/h

The **Type 72Z** (also known as the **T-72Z** and the **Safir-74**, and the **Al-Zubair I** in Sudan) is a highly modernized version of the Type 59 and T-54/T-55 tanks, with upgrades carried out by the Iranian Defense Industries Organization

ARTILLERY

MORTARS

Model	Type	Quantity	Acquired	Origin	Notes
37mm Marsh Mortar	37mm Mortar	+		Iran	
HM 12	60mm Mortar	+		Iran	
HM 13	60mm Mortar	+		Iran	
HM 14	60mm Mortar	+		Iran	
HM 15	81mm Mortar	+		Iran	
HM 16	120mm Mortar	+		Iran	
Razm Mortar	120mm Mortar	+		Iran	
Vafa Mortar	160mm Mortar	+		Iran	

Mortars Reference 1: Mortars Reference 2:

37MM MARSH MORTAR

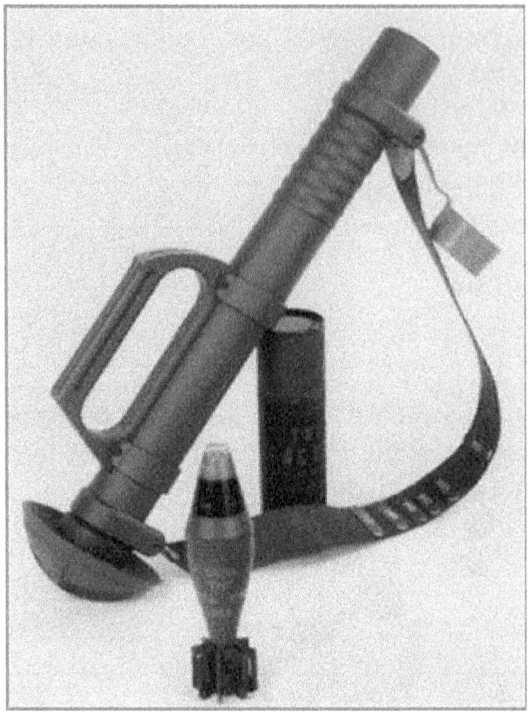

The **37mm marsh mortar** was a compact commando mortar developed by the Iranian Army during the Iran–Iraq War. It is very similar in concept to the World War II Soviet 37mm spade mortar. Though not officially designated as *marsh mortar*, the term is used by academics in describing this mortar. Though small for a mortar, 37mm was the maximum shell size for which recoil did not drive the mortar into the soft ground

HM 12

Type	Mortar
Place of origin	Iran
Service history	
Used by	Iran
Wars	Syrian Civil War
Production history	
Manufacturer	Defense Industries Organization
Specifications	
Weight	6,5 kg
Barrel length	677mm
Crew	2
Caliber	60 mm
Elevation	45° to 85°

For additional analytical, business and investment opportunities information, please contact Global Investment & Business Center, USA at (703) 370-8082. Fax: (703) 370-8083. E-mail: ibpusa3@gmail.com Global Business and Investment Info Databank - www.ibpus.com

Traverse	360°
Rate of fire	20 round per minute
Maximum firing range	1050m

The **HM 12 Fateh** (or **Hadid**) is an Iranian 60mm mortar manufactured by the Ammunition & Metallurgy Industries Group, part of Iran's Defense Industries Organization. It is an unlicensed copy of Israel's Soltam 60 mm mortar. It is generally operated by two people but in urgent cases it can be operated by one as well. It has been exported to Syria and used by the National Defence Forces in the Syrian Civil War.

RAZM MORTAR

Type	Heavy mortar
Place of origin	Iran
	Service history
In service	Iranian Army
	Production history
Manufacturer	DIO
Produced	2010–Present
	Specifications
Calibre	120 mm (4.7 in)
Carriage	Vehicle
Effective firing range	16,000 m (17,000 yd) with rocket assisted projectile

Razm is an Iranian 120 mm heavy mortar unveiled in 2010 and produced by Iran's Defense Industries Organization. It is a long range mortar with range of 16 km with rocket-assisted munitions and can be used alongside tube artillery. To achieve this range, Razm uses an unusually long barrel, and is very heavy. The overall design of the mortar is similar to that of 120 mm HM 16. Due to its long barrel, it is too heavy to be carried by infantry, and therefore it is vehicle-mounted

VAFA MORTAR

TOWED ARTILLERY

Model	Type	Quantity	Acquired	Origin	Notes
M101A1	105mm howitzer	130		United States	
2A18M	122mm howitzer	550		Soviet Union	
Type-54	122mm howitzer	100		China	
M1954/Type 59-1	130mm howitzer	985		Soviet Union/ China	In 2002, Iran had 1,100 M-46 in conditional use. By 2012 this number has dropped to 985.
M1955	152mm howitzer	30		Soviet Union/ China	
WAC-21	155mm howitzer	15		China	
GHN-45	155mm howitzer	120		Canada	
M-114	155mm howitzer	70		United States	
122mm HM 40	122mm howitzer	+		Iran	
155mm HM 41	155mm howitzer	+		Iran	
FH-77B	155mm howitzer	18		Sweden	
G-5	155mm howitzer	50		South Africa	In 1990, Iran had 50 G-5. Howerver, there is no current information on the condition of these howitzer.
M-115	203mm howitzer	20		United States	
Type 63 MRL/Fajr 1	107mm MRL	1300	1986	Iran/ China	

M101A1

Type	Howitzer
Place of origin	United States
	Service history
Used by	United States
Wars	World War II Korean War First Indochina War Vietnam War Insurgency in the Philippines
	Production history
Manufacturer	Rock Island Arsenal
Produced	1941–1953
No. built	10,200
	Specifications
Weight	4,980 lb (2,260 kg)
Length	19 ft 6 in (5.94 m)
Barrel length	7 ft 7 in (2.31 m) L/22
Width	7 ft 3 in (2.21 m)
Height	5 ft 8 in (1.73 m)
Shell	105x372R
Caliber	105 mm (4.1 in)
Breech	Horizontal-block
Recoil	Hydro-pneumatic, constant, 42 in (110 cm)
Carriage	split trail
Elevation	-5° to +66°
Traverse	46°
Muzzle velocity	1,550 ft/s (472 m/s)

For additional analytical, business and investment opportunities information, please contact Global Investment & Business Center, USA at (703) 370-8082. Fax: (703) 370-8083. E-mail: ibpusa3@gmail.com Global Business and Investment Info Databank - www.ibpus.com

Maximum firing range	7.00 mi (11,270 m)

The **105 mm M101A1 howitzer** (previously designated **M2A1**) was an artillery piece developed and used by the United States. It was the standard U.S. light field howitzer in World War II and saw action in both the European and Pacific theaters. Entering production in 1941, it quickly gained a reputation for accuracy and a powerful punch. The M101A1 fired 105 mm (4.1 in) high explosive (HE) semi-fixed ammunition and had a range of 12,330 yards (11,270 m), making it suitable for supporting infantry.

All of these qualities of the weapon, along with its widespread production, led to its adoption by many countries after the war. Its ammunition type also became the standard for many foreign countries' later models.

2A18M

Type	Howitzer
Place of origin	Soviet Union
	Service history
In service	1960–present
Used by	Soviet Union and allies as well as nonaligned and post-Soviet states.
Wars	Soviet–Afghan War Iran–Iraq War Lebanese Civil War Western Sahara War Uganda–Tanzania War Gulf War Somali Civil War Yugoslav War Syrian Civil War

	Iraqi Civil War (2014–present) Yemeni Civil War (2015–present) Saudi-led intervention in Yemen Conflict in Najran, Jizan and Asir, many regional conflicts.
	Production history
Designer	F.F. Petrov
Designed	1950s
Manufacturer	PJSC «Plant № 9»
Produced	1960–present
Variants	See variants
	Specifications
Weight	Combat: 3,210 kg (7,080 lb)
Length	Transport: 5.4 m (17 ft 9 in)
Barrel length	Bore: 4.8 m (15 ft 9 in) 38 calibres
Width	Transport: 1.9 m (6 ft 3 in)
Height	Transport: 1.6 m (5 ft 3 in)
Crew	1+7
Shell	Separate loading charge and projectile
Caliber	122 mm (4.8 in)
Breech	Semi-automatic vertical sliding-wedge
Recoil	Hydro-pneumatic
Carriage	tripod
Elevation	−7° to 70°
Traverse	360°
Rate of fire	Maximum: 10–12 rpm Sustained: 5–6 rpm
Effective firing range	15.4 km (9.6 mi) 21.9 km (13.6 mi) (with rocket-assisted projectile)

The **122-mm howitzer D-30** (GRAU index 2A18) is a Soviet howitzer that first entered service in the 1960. It is a robust piece that focuses on the essential features of a towed field gun suitable for all conditions. The D-30 has a maximum range of 15.4 kilometers, or over 21 km using RAP ammunition.

With its striking three-leg mounting, the D-30 can be rapidly traversed through 360 degrees. Although no longer manufactured in the nations of the former Soviet Union, the D-30 is still manufactured internationally and is in service in more than 60 countries' armed forces.

The barrel assembly of the 2A18 gun is used by the 2S1 self-propelled howitzer. There are also Egyptian, Chinese, Serbian and Syrian self-propelled variants and conversions. The Syrian conversion utilizes the hull of a T-34 tank.

For additional analytical, business and investment opportunities information, please contact Global Investment & Business Center, USA at (703) 370-8082. Fax: (703) 370-8083. E-mail: ibpusa3@gmail.com
Global Business and Investment Info Databank - www.ibpus.com

TYPE-54

Type	Field howitzer
Place of origin	Soviet Union
	Service history
Wars	Syrian Civil War
	Production history
Designer	Design bureau of Motovilikha Plants, headed by F. F. Petrov
Designed	1938
Manufacturer	Plants No. 92 & No. 9
Produced	1939–1960
No. built	19,266
Variants	M-30S, Chinese Type 54
	Specifications
Weight	combat: 2,450 kg (5,401 lbs) travel: 3,100 kg (6,834 lbs)
Length	5.9 m (19 ft 4 in) (with limber)
Barrel length	bore: 2.67 m (8 ft 9 in) L/21.9 overall: 2.8 m (9 ft 2 in) L/23 (without breech block)
Width	1.98 m (6 ft 6 in)
Height	1.82 m (6 ft)
Crew	8
Shell	Separate loading charge and projectile
Caliber	121.92 mm (4.8 in)
Breech	Interrupted screw
Recoil	Hydro-pneumatic

Carriage	Split trail
Elevation	-3° to 63.5°
Traverse	49°
Rate of fire	5-6 rounds per minute
Maximum firing range	11.8 km (7.33 mi)

The **122 mm howitzer M1938 (M-30)** was a Soviet 121.92 mm (4.8 inch) howitzer. The weapon was developed by the design bureau of Motovilikha Plants, headed by F. F. Petrov, in the late 1930s, and was in production from 1939 to 1955. The M-30 saw action in World War II, mainly as a divisional artillery piece of the Red Army (RKKA). Captured guns were also employed later in the conflict by the German Wehrmacht and the Finnish Army. Post World War II the M-30 saw combat in numerous conflicts of the mid- to late twentieth century in service of other countries' armies, notably in the Middle East.

M1954/TYPE 59-1

Type	Field gun
Place of origin	Soviet Union
	Service history
Wars	Vietnam War Angolan Civil War South African Border War Yom Kippur War Yugoslav Wars Syrian Civil War Yemeni Civil War (2015–present)
	Production history
Designed	1946–1950
Manufacturer	MOTZ
Produced	1951–1971

For additional analytical, business and investment opportunities information, please contact Global Investment & Business Center, USA at (703) 370-8082. Fax: (703) 370-8083. E-mail: ibpusa3@gmail.com
Global Business and Investment Info Databank - www.ibpus.com

	Specifications
Weight	7.7 t (16,975 lbs)
Length	11.73 m (38 ft 6 in)
Barrel length	6.76 m (22 ft 2 in) L/52
Width	2.45 m (8 ft)
Height	2.55 m (8 ft 4 in)
Crew	8
Shell	separate-loading charge and projectile
Caliber	130 mm (5.1 in)
Breech	Horizontal sliding-wedge
Recoil	hydro-pneumatic
Carriage	Split-trail
Elevation	-2.5° to 45°
Traverse	50°
Rate of fire	6 (normal) 8 (burst) 5 (sustained)
Muzzle velocity	930 m/s (3,051 ft/s)
Maximum firing range	27.5 km (17 mi) (unassisted) 38 km (23.61 mi) (assisted)

The **130 mm towed field gun M-46** (Russian: 130-мм пушка М-46) is a manually loaded, towed 130 mm artillery piece, manufactured in the Soviet Union in the 1950s. It was first observed by the west in 1954. There is also a Chinese copy, called the **Type 59**. For many years, the M-46 was one of the longest range artillery systems around, with a range of more than 27 km.

M1955

Type	Towed howitzer

For additional analytical, business and investment opportunities information, please contact Global Investment & Business Center, USA at (703) 370-8082. Fax: (703) 370-8083. E-mail: ibpusa3@gmail.com Global Business and Investment Info Databank - www.ibpus.com

Place of origin	Soviet Union
	Service history
Used by	Soviet Union and numerous others
Wars	Vietnam War, Six-Day War, Yom Kippur War, Soviet–Afghan War, Syrian Civil War and numerous others
	Production history
Designer	Petrov Artillery Design Bureau
Designed	Circa 1947
Manufacturer	Artillery Plant Number 9, Yekaterinburg
	Specifications
Weight	5,700 kg (12,566 lbs)
Length	8.69 m (28 ft 6 in)
Barrel length	5.195 m (20 ft)
Width	2.35 m (7 ft 9 in)
Height	1.93 m (6 ft 4 in)
Crew	8
Shell	Separate loading charge and projectile
Caliber	152.4 mm (6 in)
Breech	Vertical semi-automatic sliding-wedge
Recoil	hydraulic buffer and hydro-pneumatic recuperator
Carriage	Split trail
Elevation	-5° to 45°
Traverse	58°
Rate of fire	Burst: 5–6 rpm Sustained: 1 rpm
Muzzle velocity	650 m/s (2,132 ft/s) (typical)
Effective firing range	17.4 km (11 mi)
Maximum firing range	24 km (15 mi) (rocket assisted projectile)
Sights	PG1M indirect sight and OP4M direct fire sight

The **152 mm gun-howitzer M1955**, also known as the **D-20**, (Russian: 152-мм пушка-гаубица Д-20 обр. 1955 г.) is a manually loaded, towed 152 mm artillery piece, manufactured in the Soviet Union during the 1950s. It was first observed by the west in 1955, at which time it was designated the M1955. Its GRAU index is **52-P-546**

For additional analytical, business and investment opportunities information, please contact Global Investment & Business Center, USA at (703) 370-8082. Fax: (703) 370-8083. E-mail: ibpusa3@gmail.com Global Business and Investment Info Databank - www.ibpus.com

WAC-21

Also known as the WAC-021, this 155 mm howitzer is used by the Iranian army as towed artillery. Built to fire NATO-compatible ammunition, it was originally designed and built in China by the NORINCO corporation. It is one of the newest artillery pieces fielded by Iran and comes with a pivot so the weapon can be rapidly relaid.

The WAC-21 is very similar in many respects to the Austrian NORICUM GH N-45 gun-howitzer, to the extent that the carriage of the Type WA-021 can accommodate the ordnance of the NORICUM weapon. The NORINCO Type WA-021 has an auto-frettaged barrel 45 calibres long, fitted with a multibaffle muzzle brake, which has an efficiency of 30 percent. A screw-type breech mechanism opening to the right is employed and the chamber volume is 22.95 litres. The rifling employs 48 grooves with a twist of 1 in 20 calibres, and the grooves are understood to be three times deeper than the rifling depths found on comparable Western 155 mm designs.

GHN-45

The **GC-45** (*Gun, Canada, 45-calibre*) is a 155 mm howitzer designed by Gerald Bull's Space Research Corporation (SRC) in the 1970s. Versions were produced by a number of companies during the 1980s, notably in Austria and South Africa.

The most publicized use of the design was in Iraq, where the GHN-45 variant used by some Iraqi artillery units had a longer range than any coalition cannon systems. This initially caused considerable worry on the part of the allied forces in the Persian Gulf War.

Type	Howitzer
Place of origin	Canada
	Service history
In service	1970s-present
Used by	See users
Wars	Iran–Iraq War, Gulf War, Cambodian–Thai border stand-off
	Production history
Designer	Gerald Bull
Designed	1970s
Manufacturer	Space Research Corporation, Noricum, NORINCO
Produced	1980s-Present
Variants	GHN-45, PLL01
	Specifications
Weight	8,220 kg (18,120 lb)
Caliber	155 mm (6.1 in.)
Carriage	Split trail
Elevation	-89 to 1,280 mils
Traverse	Left 534 mils, Right 711 mils
Rate of fire	maximum: 5 rpm sustained: 2 rpm
Muzzle velocity	897 m/s (2,943 ft/sec)
Maximum firing range	39.6 km (24.6 mi) with Base bleed

The gun designed to fire it had a 23,000 cm^3 (1,400 cu in) chamber, a 45-calibre rifled barrel with 1/20 right hand twist fitted with a conventional muzzle brake. Its breech was a conventional screw with interrupted thread.

Key performance data, from the Firing Table are:

- ERFB-BB shell, weight 48.0 kg (105.9 lb), M11 Zone 10 muzzle velocity 897 m/s (2,940 ft/s), QE 898 mils, time of flight 112 s, range 39.6 km (24.6 mi; 130,000 ft). Probable error in range 212 m (696 ft), in line 36 m (118 ft).
- ERFB shell, weight 45.5 kg (100.4 lb), M11 Zone 10 muzzle velocity 897 m/s (2,940 ft/s), QE 881 mils, time of flight 99 s, range 29.9 km (18.6 mi; 98,000 ft). Probable error in range 189 metres (620 ft), in line 42 metres (138 ft).
- HE M107 shell, weight 43 kg (95 lb), M119 Zone 8 muzzle velocity 675 m/s (2,210 ft/s), QE 764 mils, time of flight 65 s, range 17.8 km (11.1 mi; 58,000 ft). Probable error in range 59 m (194 ft), in line 12 m (39 ft).

The dispersion of the EFRB shell is more than three times that of the FH-70 field howitzer at its maximum range of only 5 km less, and is twice as great as FH-70s at

20 km (66,000 ft; 12 mi). Its maximum range with the M107 projectile is the same as any 39 calibre 155-mm gun and its dispersion about the same. (The "dispersion" figure means that 50% of shells will fall up to the stated distance either side of the mean point of impact, but 100% will fall within 4 times the probable error either side.) Dispersion of this magnitude significantly reduces the tactical value of the equipment.

M-114

The **M114 155 mm howitzer** was a towed howitzer developed and used by the United States Army. It was first produced in 1942 as a medium artillery piece under the designation of **155 mm Howitzer M1**. It saw service with the US Army during World War II, the Korean War, and the Vietnam War, before being replaced by the M198 howitzer. The gun was also used by the armed forces of many nations. In some countries, the M114A1 still remains in service

Type	Howitzer
Place of origin	United States
	Service history
In service	1942–present
Used by	See operators
Wars	World War II, Korean War, Vietnam War, Cambodian Civil War, Laotian Civil War, Lebanese Civil War
	Production history
Designed	1939–1941
Manufacturer	Rock Island Arsenal (US)
Produced	1941–1953
No. built	10,300+
Variants	none
	Specifications
Weight	Travel: 5,800 kg (12,800 lb)

For additional analytical, business and investment opportunities information, please contact Global Investment & Business Center, USA at (703) 370-8082. Fax: (703) 370-8083. E-mail: ibpusa3@gmail.com Global Business and Investment Info Databank - www.ibpus.com

	Combat: 5,600 kg (12,300 lb)
Length	Travel: 7.315 m (20 ft)
Barrel length	Bore: 3.564 m (11 ft 8 in) L/23 Overall: 3.79 m (12 ft 5 in) L/24.5
Width	Travel: 2.438 m (8 ft)
Height	Travel: 1.8 m (5 ft 11 in)
Crew	11

Shell	Separate-loading bagged charge
Caliber	155 mm (6.1 in)
Breech	Slow-cone interrupted screw
Recoil	Hydro-pneumatic
Carriage	Split trail
Elevation	-2°/+63°
Traverse	25° left or right
Rate of fire	burst: 4 rpm sustained: 40 rph
Muzzle velocity	563 m/s (1,847 ft/s)
Maximum firing range	14,600 m (16,000 yd)

122MM HM 40

Type	Howitzer
Place of origin	Soviet Union
	Service history
In service	1960–present
Used by	Soviet Union and allies as well as nonaligned and post-Soviet states.
Wars	Soviet–Afghan War Iran–Iraq War Lebanese Civil War

For additional analytical, business and investment opportunities information, please contact Global Investment & Business Center, USA at (703) 370-8082. Fax: (703) 370-8083. E-mail: ibpusa3@gmail.com Global Business and Investment Info Databank - www.ibpus.com

	Western Sahara War Uganda–Tanzania War Gulf War Somali Civil War Yugoslav War Syrian Civil War Iraqi Civil War (2014–present) Yemeni Civil War (2015–present) Saudi-led intervention in Yemen Conflict in Najran, Jizan and Asir, many regional conflicts.
Production history	
Designer	F.F. Petrov
Designed	1950s
Manufacturer	PJSC «Plant № 9»
Produced	1960–present
Variants	See variants
Specifications	
Weight	Combat: 3,210 kg (7,080 lb)
Length	Transport: 5.4 m (17 ft 9 in)
Barrel length	Bore: 4.8 m (15 ft 9 in) 38 calibres
Width	Transport: 1.9 m (6 ft 3 in)
Height	Transport: 1.6 m (5 ft 3 in)
Crew	1+7
Shell	Separate loading charge and projectile
Caliber	122 mm (4.8 in)
Breech	Semi-automatic vertical sliding-wedge
Recoil	Hydro-pneumatic
Carriage	tripod
Elevation	−7° to 70°
Traverse	360°
Rate of fire	Maximum: 10–12 rpm Sustained: 5–6 rpm
Effective firing range	15.4 km (9.6 mi) 21.9 km (13.6 mi) (with rocket-assisted projectile)

The **122-mm howitzer D-30** (GRAU index 2A18) is a Soviet howitzer that first entered service in the 1960. It is a robust piece that focuses on the essential features of a towed field gun suitable for all conditions. The D-30 has a maximum range of 15.4 kilometers, or over 21 km using RAP ammunition.

With its striking three-leg mounting, the D-30 can be rapidly traversed through 360 degrees. Although no longer manufactured in the nations of the former Soviet

For additional analytical, business and investment opportunities information, please contact Global Investment & Business Center, USA at (703) 370-8082. Fax: (703) 370-8083. E-mail: ibpusa3@gmail.com Global Business and Investment Info Databank - www.ibpus.com

Union, the D-30 is still manufactured internationally and is in service in more than 60 countries' armed forces.

The barrel assembly of the 2A18 gun is used by the 2S1self-propelled howitzer. There are also Egyptian, Chinese, Serbian and Syrian self-propelled variants and conversions. The Syrian conversion utilizes the hull of a T-34 tank.

155MM HM 41

Type	Howitzer
Place of origin	Iran
	Service history
Used by	Iran
	Production history
Manufacturer	Defense Industries Organization
	Specifications
Weight	combat: 6,890 kg
Caliber	155 mm
Recoil	Hydro-pneumatic
Carriage	tripod
Elevation	0° to 66°
Traverse	25° right, 23.5° left
Rate of fire	4 round per minute
Effective firing range	22 km
Maximum firing range	30–34 km (with rocket assisted ammunition)

HM-41 is an Iranian howitzer which is claimed to be based on the American M114. In appearance, it is very similar to the South Korean KH179. It has a 155 mm/39 calibre

For additional analytical, business and investment opportunities information, please contact Global Investment & Business Center, USA at (703) 370-8082. Fax: (703) 370-8083. E-mail: ibpusa3@gmail.com Global Business and Investment Info Databank - www.ibpus.com

barrel with a muzzle brake to lessen the recoil.According to Iranian sources, the 155 mm/39 calibre HM41 weighs 6,890 kg and firing a rocket-assisted High-Explosive (HE) projectile, a maximum range of 30,000 m can be achieved. Firing an unassisted HE projectile, a maximum range of 22,000 m can be obtained. This is an improvement as compared to the M114. The Howitzer has been offered for export. But no country is known to be using it except Iran.

A wheeled self-propelled version is reported to be under development. The first prototype was finished in 2011.

In 2012, Iran unveiled laser guided Basir 155 mm artillery shells which were tested by an HM 41 howitzer

FH-77B

Type	Howitzer
Place of origin	Sweden
Service history	
In service	1978 – present
Used by	Swedish Army Indian Army
Production history	
Designer	Bofors
Designed	1978
Manufacturer	Bofors
Unit cost	$3,900,000 (1986)
Produced	1978–1984
No. built	720
Variants	See Variants
Specifications	
Weight	11,500 kg (25,400 lb)

For additional analytical, business and investment opportunities information, please contact Global Investment & Business Center, USA at (703) 370-8082. Fax: (703) 370-8083. E-mail: ibpusa3@gmail.com
Global Business and Investment Info Databank - www.ibpus.com

Length	Combat: 11.60 m (38 ft 1 in)
Barrel length	5.89 m (19 ft 4 in) L/38
Width	Combat: 9.73 m (31 ft 11 in)
Crew	9 to 14
Shell	155 mm NATO
Caliber	155 mm
Action	semi-fixed ammunition, propellant charge is contained in a plastic cartridge case with a steel head
Breech	Vertically sliding breech block, hydraulic ramming
Carriage	split trail with castor wheels
Elevation	-5°/+70°
Traverse	30° left or right from centreline
Rate of fire	4 rounds in 9 seconds, 6 rounds in 25 seconds, sustained 3 rpm for 20 minutes
Muzzle velocity	300 to 770 m/s (980 to 2,530 ft/s)
Effective firing range	21 km (13 mi)
Maximum firing range	24 km (15 mi) (with base bleed-round)
Feed system	hydraulically powered flick rammer assisted loading
Engine	Volvo B20 APU
Speed	6 km/h

Fälthaubits 77 (Swedish "Field Howitzer 77") or **FH77** is a Swedish 155 mm howitzer. It was developed and manufactured by Bofors. It was available in two versions, the original (sometimes referred to as **Haubits 77 A**) with a 38 calibre barrel and sliding block mechanism, and the later **FH77 B** export version with a 39 calibre barrel and an interrupted screw breech.

G-5

Type	Howitzer
Place of origin	South Africa
	Service history
In service	1983–present
Used by	Operators
Wars	South African Border War Iran–Iraq War Gulf War
	Production history
Designer	Lyttelton Engineering Works
Designed	1976–1983
Manufacturer	Denel Land Systems
Produced	1982–present
	Specifications
Weight	13,750 kg (30,314 lbs)
Length	9.5 m (31 ft 2 in)
Barrel length	6.975 m (22 ft 11 in) L/45
Width	3.3 m (10 ft 10 in)
Height	2.1 m (6 ft 11 in)
Crew	8 soldiers
Shell	high explosive
Breech	Semi-automatic interrupted screw
Carriage	Split trail
Elevation	−3° to +75°
Traverse	Up to 15°: 82° Above 15°: 65°
Rate of fire	3 rounds/minute
Muzzle velocity	897 m/s (2,943 ft/s)
Maximum firing range	Standard: 30 km (19 mi) Base bleed: 39 km (24 mi) VLAP: 50 km (31 mi)
Feed system	Breech-loaded

The **G5** is a South African towed howitzer of 155 mm calibre designed and developed in South Africa by Denel Land Systems. The G5 design was based on the Canadian GC-45 155mm gun which was highly modified to suit southern African conditions.

For additional analytical, business and investment opportunities information, please contact Global Investment & Business Center, USA at (703) 370-8082. Fax: (703) 370-8083. E-mail: ibpusa3@gmail.com Global Business and Investment Info Databank - www.ibpus.com

M-115

TYPE 63 MRL/FAJR 1

SELF-PROPELLED ARTILLERY

Model	Type	Quantity	Acquired	Origin	Notes
2S1 Gvozdika	122mm self-propelled howitzer	60		Soviet Union	

Raad 1	122mm self-propelled howitzer	100	1996	Iran	Based on 2S1 Gvozdika
Raad 2	155mm self-propelled howitzer	150	1997	Iran	Based on M109
M-109	155mm self-propelled howitzer	180		United States/ Iran	Remanufactured locally as the Hoveyzeh.
M-1978	170mm self-propelled howitzer	20		North Korea	
M-107	175mm self-propelled howitzer	30		United States	
M-110	203mm self-propelled howitzer	30		United States	
Fajr-3	240mm MRLS	190	1994	Iran	
Fajr-5	330mm MRLS	190	1990	Iran	
Shahin-1	MRLS	+	1990	Iran	
Shahin-2	MRLS	+	1995	Iran	
BM-21 Grad	122mm MRLS	100	1978	Soviet Union	
122mm Hadid/Azrash/Nur	122mm MRLS	55	1994	Iran	Domestic BM-21 developments?

2S1 Gvozdika

Type	Self-propelled artillery
Place of origin	Soviet Union
	Service history
In service	1972–present
Used by	see Operators
Wars	Soviet–Afghan War Iran–Iraq War Gulf War War in Abkhazia (1992–1993) Yugoslav Wars Kosovo War First Chechen War Second Chechen War Iraq War 2008 South Ossetia War Russo-Georgian War First Libyan Civil War Second Libyan Civil War Syrian Civil War War in Donbass
	Production history
Designer	Kharkiv Tractor Plant
Designed	1956-61
Produced	1971–1991
No. built	more than 10,000
Variants	see Variants
	Specifications

Weight	16 tonnes (35,273 lbs)
Length	7.26 m (23 ft 10 in)
Width	2.85 m (9 ft 4 in)
Height	2.73 m (8 ft 11 in)
Crew	4
Shell	separate loading, cased charge
Caliber	122 mm
Breech	Horizontal sliding-wedge, semi-automatic
Elevation	-3 to +70 degrees
Traverse	360 degrees
Rate of fire	Maximum: 5 rpm Sustained: 1-2 rpm
Muzzle velocity	680 m/s (2,200 ft/s)
Maximum firing range	Conventional: 15.3 km (9.5 mi) Extended: 21.9 km (13.6 mi)
Armor	20 mm (.78 in)
Main armament	2A18 122 mm (4.8 in) howitzer
Engine	YaMZ-238N diesel 220 kW (300 hp)
Suspension	torsion bar
Operational range	500 km (310 mi)
Speed	Road: 60 km/h (37 mph) Off-road: 30 km/h (18 mph) Swim: 4.5 km/h (2.8 mph)

The **2S1 *Gvozdika*** is a Soviet self-propelled howitzer based on the MT-LBu multi-purpose chassis, mounting a 122 mm 2A18 howitzer. "2S1" is its GRAU designation. An alternative Russian designation is SAU-122 but in the Russian Army it is commonly known as *Gvozdika*. The 2S1 is fully amphibious with very little preparation, and once afloat is propelled by its tracks. A variety of track widths are available to allow the 2S1 to operate in snow or swamp conditions. It is NBC protected and has infra-red night-vision capability.

For additional analytical, business and investment opportunities information, please contact Global Investment & Business Center, USA at (703) 370-8082. Fax: (703) 370-8083. E-mail: ibpusa3@gmail.com Global Business and Investment Info Databank - www.ibpus.com

RAAD 1

Type	Self-propelled artillery
Place of origin	Iran
	Service history
In service	1996–present
Used by	Iran
Wars	none
	Production history
Designer	Defense Industries Organization
Designed	May 1996
Produced	1996–present
	Specifications
Weight	17.5 tonnes
Length	6.72 m
Width	3.10 m
Height	1.66 m (without the turret)
Crew	4 (Commander, driver, gunner and loader)
Effective firing range	15.2 km
Main armament	122mm 2A18 howitzer
Secondary armament	none
Engine	V-8 diesel 330 hp (246 kW)
Suspension	Torsion bar
Operational range	500 km

For additional analytical, business and investment opportunities information,
please contact Global Investment & Business Center, USA
at (703) 370-8082. Fax: (703) 370-8083. E-mail: ibpusa3@gmail.com
Global Business and Investment Info Databank - www.ibpus.com

Speed	65 km/h

RAAD 2

Type	Self-propelled howitzer
Place of origin	Iran
	Service history
In service	1997 - present
Used by	Iran
Wars	none
	Production history
Designer	Defense Industries Organization
Designed	September 1997
Produced	1997 - Present
Variants	Raad-2M
	Specifications
Weight	36 tons
Length	6.72 m (without the gun)
Width	3.10 m
Height	1.66 m (without the turret)
Crew	3 (commander, driver and gunner)
Rate of fire	5 rounds/min
Effective firing range	30 km (19 mi)
Main	155 mm HM44 howitzer

For additional analytical, business and investment opportunities information, please contact Global Investment & Business Center, USA at (703) 370-8082. Fax: (703) 370-8083. E-mail: ibpusa3@gmail.com Global Business and Investment Info Databank - www.ibpus.com

armament	
Secondary armament	12.7 mm HMG
Engine	V-8 diesel for Raad-2 5TDF for Raad-2M 840 hp for Raad-2 700 hp for Raad-2M
Suspension	Torsion bar
Operational range	500 km
Speed	70 km/h (43 mph)

Raad-2 ("Thunder-2") is an Iranian self-propelled howitzer. In early September 1997 it was reported that Iran had successfully tested a locally built rapid fire mobile field gun known as *Raad*-2 (Thunder-2).

It uses a turret that has a similar layout to the M109A1 155mm/39-cal self-propelled howitzer. The Iranian Defense Industries Organization claimed that the 155 mm HM44 howitzer manufactured by the Hadid facility of the Iranian Defense Industries Organization had a high firing rate and accuracy. It was described as being able to fire five rounds per minute. The gun's range was reported as 30 km (19 mi), and it also includes features such as a laser range-finder and a semi-automatic loading system. The gun looks exactly like 155mm/39-cal M185 gun from M109A1 and is fitted with a double baffle muzzle brake, fume extractor, screw breech mechanism, hydro-pneumatic recuperator and a hydraulic recoil brake. It uses the Iranian-made Boragh APC chassis, a conversion of the either the Russian BMP-1 or Chinese Type 86 (WZ-501) IFV. It was described as being able to move with a speed of 70 km/h (43 mph) on the battlefield.

M-109

ype	Self-propelled gun
Place of origin	United States

	Service history
In service	1963–present
Wars	Vietnam War Yom Kippur War Iran–Iraq War Western Sahara War Persian Gulf War Iraq War 2014 Israel–Gaza conflict Iraqi Civil War (2014–present) Yemeni Civil War (2015–present), Saudi Arabian-led intervention in Yemen Syrian Civil War
	Specifications
Weight	27.5 tons
Length	30 ft (9.1 m)
Width	10 ft 4 in (3.15 m)
Height	10 ft 8 in (3.25 m)
Crew	6 (2 Loaders, Gunner, Assistant Gunner, Commander, Driver)
Shell	separate loading, bagged charge
Caliber	155 mm L/39 caliber
Breech	interrupted screw
Traverse	360°
Rate of fire	Maximum: 4 rpm Sustained: 1 rpm
Effective firing range	Conventional: 18 km (11 mi) RAP: 30 km (19 mi)
Main armament	M126 155 mm Howitzer
Secondary armament	.50 caliber (12.7 mm) M2 machine gun
Engine	Detroit Diesel 8V71T 450 hp (335.56 kW)
Power/weight	18.7 hp/t
Suspension	torsion-bar
Operational range	216 mi (350 km)
Speed	35 mph (56 km/h)

For additional analytical, business and investment opportunities information,
please contact Global Investment & Business Center, USA
at (703) 370-8082. Fax: (703) 370-8083. E-mail: ibpusa3@gmail.com
Global Business and Investment Info Databank - www.ibpus.com

The **M109** is an American 155 mm turreted self-propelled howitzer, first introduced in the early 1960s. It has been upgraded a number of times, most recently to the **M109A7**. The M109 family is the most common western indirect-fire support weapon of maneuver brigades of armored and mechanized infantry divisions.

The M109 has a crew of six: the section chief, the driver, the gunner, the assistant gunner and two ammunition handlers. The gunner aims the cannon left or right (deflection), the assistant gunner aims the cannon up and down (quadrant). The M109A6 Paladin needs only a crew of four: the commander, driver, gunner and an ammunition loader.

The British Army replaced its M109s with the AS-90. Several European armed forces have or are currently replacing older M109s with the German PzH 2000. Upgrades to the M109 were introduced by the U.S. (see variants below) and by Switzerland (KAWEST). With the cancellation of the U.S. Crusader and Non-Line-of-Sight Cannon, the M109A6 ("Paladin") will remain the principal self-propelled howitzer for the U.S. for the foreseeable future.

M-1978

Type	Self-propelled artillery
Place of origin	North Korea
	Service history
In service	1978 - present
Used by	North Korea, Iran
Wars	Iran–Iraq War
	Production history
Manufacturer	Second Machine Industry Bureau, North Korea
Variants	• M-1978 Koksan • M-1989 Koksan
	Specifications

For additional analytical, business and investment opportunities information, please contact Global Investment & Business Center, USA at (703) 370-8082. Fax: (703) 370-8083. E-mail: ibpusa3@gmail.com
Global Business and Investment Info Databank - www.ibpus.com

Crew	8
Caliber	170 mm
Rate of fire	~1-2 rounds per 5 minutes
Effective firing range	~40 km (standard munition), 60 km (booster munition)
Maximum firing range	60 km (with RAP round)
Main armament	170 mm (~6.69") gun
Engine	Diesel
Suspension	Torsion bar
Operational range	~300 km
Speed	~40 km/h

he **M-1978 (Koksan)** is a 170 mm self-propelled (SP) gun of North Korean design and manufacture. Very little information is available due to the secretive nature of the North Korean government. The designations *M-1978* and *Koksan* were given to the type by American military analysts, as they first became aware of it in that year in Koksan, North Korea.

What is known is that it is a 170 mm (~6.69") self-propelled gun of the open turret type. It was first seen publicly during a military parade in 1985. At least one example has been acquired by the United States.

M-107

Type	Self-propelled artillery
Place of origin	United States
	Service history
Wars	Vietnam War Yom Kippur War Iran–Iraq War
	Production history
Manufacturer	FMC Corp., Bowen-McLaughlin-York, General Motors Corp. (transmission)
	Specifications
Weight	Combat: 28.3 metric tons (62,400 lb)
Length	Hull: 6.46 m (21 ft 2 in) Overall: 11.30 m (37 ft 1 in)
Barrel length	L/60
Width	3.15 m (10 ft 4 in)
Height	3.47 m (11 ft 5 in)
Crew	13 (vehicle capacity 5)
Caliber	175 mm (6.9 in)
Elevation	−5° to +65° deg.
Traverse	60°
Rate of fire	Rapid: 1 rpm Regular: 1/2 rpm
Maximum firing range	40 km (25 mi)
Main armament	1 × 175 mm M113 or M113A1 Gun
Engine	General Motors 8V71T; 8 cylinder, 2 cycle, vee, supercharged diesel 405 hp
Suspension	torsion bar
Ground clearance	44 cm (1 ft 5 in)
Operational range	720 km (450 mi)
Speed	80 km/h (50 mph)

The **M107 175 mm self-propelled gun** was used by the U.S. Army from the early 1960s through to the late 1970s. It was part of a family of self-propelled artillery that also included the M110. It was intended to provide long-range fire support in an air-transportable system. It was exported to several other countries including Germany, South Korea, Spain, Greece, Iran, Israel, Italy, the Netherlands, the United Kingdom, and Turkey. The M107's combat history in U.S. service was limited to the Vietnam War;

it also saw extensive combat use in Israeli service. The M107 shared many components with, and in many cases was replaced by, later versions of the M110 8" howitzer. Although withdrawn from U.S. service in the late 1970s, it continues in service with some armies

M-110

Type	Self-propelled artillery
Place of origin	United States
	Service history
Wars	Vietnam War Iran–Iraq War 1982 Lebanon War Gulf War
	Production history
Manufacturer	General Motors Corp. (transmission)
	Specifications
Weight	28.3 metric tons (62,390 lb)
Length	10.8 m (35 ft 5 in)
Width	3.1 m (10 ft 2 in)
Height	3.1 m (10 ft 2 in)
Crew	13 (driver, 2 gunners, 2 loaders, (8 support crew–other vehicle))
Armor	13 mm (.51 in)
Main armament	8" (203 mm) M201A1 howitzer 2 rounds
Secondary armament	none
Engine	Detroit Diesel 8V71T, 8-cylinder, 2-stroke, turbocharged diesel 405 hp (302 kW)

For additional analytical, business and investment opportunities information, please contact Global Investment & Business Center, USA at (703) 370-8082. Fax: (703) 370-8083. E-mail: ibpusa3@gmail.com
Global Business and Investment Info Databank - www.ibpus.com

Suspension	Torsion bar
Operational range	16 km to 23 km
Speed	54.7 km/h (30 mph)

The **8 inch (203 mm) M110 self-propelled howitzer** was the largest available self-propelled howitzer in the United States Army's inventory. Consisting of an M115 203 mm howitzer installed on a purpose built chassis, it was deployed in division artillery in general support battalions and in separate corps- and army-level battalions. Missions include general support, counter-battery fire, and suppression of enemy air defense systems. The M110 was exported to a number of countries.

FAJR-3

Type	Rocket artillery
Place of origin	Iran
	Service history
In service	1996–present
Used by	Iran Syria
Wars	2006 Lebanon War
	Production history
Manufacturer	Shahid Bagheri Industrial Group
Produced	November 6, 1996
	Specifications
Weight	15,000 kg (System) 45 kg (HE Content) 90 kg (Warhead) 407 kg (Rocket)
Length	10.45 m (Launcher) 5,200 mm (Rocket)

Width	2.54 m (Launcher)
Height	3.34 m (Launcher)
Diameter	240mm
Caliber	240 mm
Elevation	0 to 57 degrees
Traverse	90 degrees left/100 degrees right
Rate of fire	4–8 seconds 12 rounds in 48 seconds (est)
Muzzle velocity	?
Maximum firing range	43 km
Engine	280 hp, V-8 liquid-cooled, diesel engine
Speed	60 km/h (road) 25 km/h (off-road)

The **Fajr-3** (rarely **Fadjr-3**) is an Iranian heavy 240 mm intermediate-range multiple-launch artillery rocket (MLRS). The Fajr-3 is a license-built copy, with slight modifications, of a North Korean MLRS called the M-1985. The Fajr-3 was introduced in the 1990s and has since been exported to Syria, Hamas and Hezbollah.

The Fajr-3 launcher fires twelve 5.2 meter long, 240 millimeter-calibre Fajr-3 artillery rockets, with an estimated range of 43 kilometres, weighing 407 kilograms each and carrying 45-kilogram HE warheads. *Fajr* means 'dawn' in Arabic.

FAJR-5

Type	Rocket artillery

For additional analytical, business and investment opportunities information,
please contact Global Investment & Business Center, USA
at (703) 370-8082. Fax: (703) 370-8083. E-mail: ibpusa3@gmail.com
Global Business and Investment Info Databank - www.ibpus.com

Place of origin	Iran
Service history	
Used by	See Operators
Wars	2006 Lebanon War Gaza–Israel conflict Syrian Civil War
Production history	
Specifications	
Weight	1,500 kg (System) 90 kg (HE Content) 175 kg (Warhead) 915 kg (Rocket)
Length	10.45 m (Launcher) 6.485 m (Rocket)
Width	2.54 m (Launcher)
Height	3.34 m (Launcher)
Caliber	333 mm
Elevation	0 to 57 degrees
Traverse	45 degrees left and right
Rate of fire	4–8 seconds
Effective firing range	68–75 km
Speed	1009 m/s

The **Fajr-5** ("Dawn") is an Iranian 333 mm artillery rocket MLRS developed in the 1990s with a range of 75 kilometers (50 mi). Most Fajr-5 rockets are unguided; in 2017 Iran introduced a variant, the **Fajr-5C**, which adds GPS guidance.

SHAHIN-1, SHAHIN-2

- pecifications:
- Shahin-1
- Shahin-2

Type	Artillery rocket
Diameter	0.333 m body
Length	2.9 m
Weight	384 kg
Guidance	Unguided, ballistic flight
Warhead	HE-Frag, 190 kg
Propulsion	Solid propellant rocket motor
Speed	450 m/s max
Range	13 km

For additional analytical, business and investment opportunities information, please contact Global Investment & Business Center, USA at (703) 370-8082. Fax: (703) 370-8083. E-mail: ibpusa3@gmail.com Global Business and Investment Info Databank - www.ibpus.com

The Shaheen 1A Missile is capable of carrying nuclear and conventional warheads to a range of 900 Kms. The missile is an improved version of Shaheen-1 with improvements in range and technical parameters. It is capable of carrying nuclear and conventional warheads. The Shaheen-I missile is a version of China's M-9 missile

. The Shahin is a conventional artillery rocket that follows a ballistic trajectory. The rocket has a long cylindrical body with a cone shaped nose and four fixed wings at the end. The Shahin uses solid propellant and has seven nozzles. The longer range Shahin-2 has a longer body that holds more propellant, but is similar in any other way. The Shahin is launched from a simple triple rail launcher with the missiles seated on top of the launch rail. In Sudanese service the three launch rails are mounted on an Italian Iveco 210-32 truck or its South African license production SAMIL-100 equivalent.

Firepower

The Shahin carries a large 190 kg high explosive warhead. The Shahin-1 has a range of 13 km and the longer range Shahin-2 reaches as far as 20 km. Reloading a launch rail takes several minutes. The accuracy is stated to be limited.

The Shahin is an unarmored system that is vulnerable to any kind of weapon. Therefore the Shahin must be used as a stand-off weapon and operated behind the frontline. The triple rail launch trailer is towed by a standard truck and the SAMIL-100 launch vehicle in Sudanese service is unarmored as well.

The Shahin is a reasonably mobile system since it is not as large and heavy as several other Iranian artillery rocket systems. Its mobility is similar to other truck and trailer combinations.

The Shahin has been acquired in large quantities by Iran and is in use with the army and revolutionary guard. The Shahin has been replaced in production by more capable artillery rocket systems, but remains in active Iranian use. For many years it was thought that the Shahin was never exported but recent videos have indicated that the Shahin-2 is in active use with Sudanese forces and has been used in recent conflicts.

BM-21 Grad

Type	Multiple rocket launcher
Place of origin	Soviet Union
Service history	
In service	1963–present
Used by	See Operators
Wars	Vietnam War Lebanese Civil War Western Sahara War Angolan Civil War Uganda–Tanzania War Cambodian–Vietnamese War Sino-Vietnamese War Iran–Iraq War Soviet–Afghan War Gulf War Nagorno-Karabakh War Yugoslavia War First Chechen War 1995 Cenepa War Second Chechen War Palestinian rocket attacks on Israel Russo-Georgian War Cambodian–Thai border dispute Libyan Civil War (2011)

	Syrian Civil War Operation Serval War in Donbass Yemeni Civil War (2015) Saudi-led intervention in Yemen (2015–present) 2016 Nagorno-Karabakh clashes
	Production history
Designer	Splav State Research and Production Enterprise
Designed	1963
Manufacturer	Splav State Research and Production Enterprise
Produced	1963–present
Variants	See Variants
	Specifications (9K51)
Weight	13.71 tonnes (30,225 lb)
Length	7.35 m (24 ft 1 in)
Barrel length	3.0 m (9 ft 10 in)
Width	2.40 m (7 ft 10 in)
Height	3.09 m (10 ft 2 in)
Crew	3
Barrels	40
Rate of fire	2 rounds/s
Muzzle velocity	690 m/s (2,264 ft/s)
Maximum firing range	20 km (12 mi) (new rockets 30–45 km)
Sights	PG-1M panoramic telescope
Engine	V-8 gasoline ZiL-375 180 hp (130 kW)
Suspension	6×6 wheeled
Operational range	405 km (251 mi)
Speed	75 km/h (47 mph)

The **BM-21 "Grad"**, is a Soviet truck-mounted 122 mm multiple rocket launcher. The weapons system and the M-21OF rocket it fires were developed in the early 1960s, and saw their first combat use in March 1969 during the Sino-Soviet border conflict. *BM* stands for *boyevaya mashina* (combat vehicle), and the nickname *grad* means "hail". The complete system with the BM-21 launch vehicle and the M-21OF rocket is designated as the M-21 field rocket system. The complete system is more commonly known as a Grad multiple rocket launcher system. In NATO countries, the system (either the complete system or the launch vehicle only) was initially known as **M1964**. Several other countries have copied it or developed similar systems.

For additional analytical, business and investment opportunities information, please contact Global Investment & Business Center, USA at (703) 370-8082. Fax: (703) 370-8083. E-mail: ibpusa3@gmail.com Global Business and Investment Info Databank - www.ibpus.com

122MM HADID/AZRASH/NUR

Armament
The Hadid has a total of 40 122 mm diameter rocket launcher tubes with launcher elevation being from -1° to +55° and with a traverse of 102° left and 72° right. Mounted on the rear of the chassis is the turntable with the manually operated elevating and traversing mechanism on the left side of the launcher at the rear.
Rockets
Three types of rocket can be used on the Hadid MRLS vehicle, all unguided, the first, the Noor, sometimes called the Arash 3, is the smallest and has the shortest range. The Arash 1 and Arash 2 provide a boost in the maximum range of the system. All of them can be carried in racks which facilitate quick reloading. Iranian 122mm rockets carry a basic HE warhead as well as AP and AT submunitions, while HE-FRAG, and fuel-air explosives are suspected.
Truck
The HADID HM 20 is based on a older generation Mercedes-Benz 2624 series (6 × 6) truck chassis with the engine and fully enclosed two-door cab at the front. The mercedes-Benz 2624 is motorized with MB OM 355 engine coupled to an gearbox ZF 16S - 130. This truck can run at a maximum speed of 95 km/h.
Accessories
The HADID HM 20 uses the same telescopic and panoramic sights as the BM-21.

The 122 mm HADID HM 20 rocket launcher system is a 40-round launcher assembly system mounted on the rear of a Mercedes-Benz LAK 2624 6 × 6 truck chassis. This vehicle was developed by the Shahid Bagheri Industries division of the Aerospace Industries Organization of Iran.

SURFACE-TO-SURFACE MISSILES

For additional analytical, business and investment opportunities information, please contact Global Investment & Business Center, USA at (703) 370-8082. Fax: (703) 370-8083. E-mail: ibpusa3@gmail.com
Global Business and Investment Info Databank - www.ibpus.com

Model	Type	Quantity	Acquired	Origin	Notes
Kowsar 1/2/3	Anti-ship missile	+		Iran	Light ASCM based on Chinese C-701 and TL-10
Nasr-1	Anti ship missile	+		Iran	Light ASCM based on Chinese C-705 and TL-6
Noor	Anti-ship missile	+		Iran	ASCM based on Chinese C-801 and C-802
Ra'ad	Anti-ship missile	+		Iran	Iranian origin Heavy ASCM similar to Chinese C-401
Qader	Anti ship missile	+		Iran	
Khalij Fars	Anti-ship ballistic missile	+		Iran	Based on Fateh-110
Zafar	Anti-ship missile	+		Iran	Light ASCM for IRGC navy

KOWSAR 1/2/3

Kowsar (or **Kosar**) is a medium-range, land-based anti-ship missile made by Iran. It can defeat electronic jamming systems and "cannot be thrown off course", according to Iranian officials.

The Kowsar designation apparently (Missile Defense Advocacy Alliance 2006) is used to refer to two different missiles: Iranian-produced versions of the PRC C-701 and the TL-10A.

Type	Anti-ship missile
Service history	
In service	2006
Production history	
Manufacturer	Iran
Specifications	
Weight	100 kg
Length	2.507 m
Diameter	0.18 m
Warhead	29 kg time-delayed semi-armour-piercing high-explosive
Engine	Solid rocket engine

Wingspan	0.587 m (unfolded); 0.450 m (folded)
Operational range	15-20 km
Flight altitude	15-20 m (flight)
Speed	Mach 0.8
Guidance system	TV-homing, Infra-red, millimetre radar
Launch platform	Ground-based vehicles and Zolfaghar class fast attack craft

NASR-1

Type	Anti ship missile
	Service history
Used by	Iran
	Production history
Manufacturer	Iran
	Specifications
Weight	350 kg
Length	3.5 m
Diameter	0.28 m
Warhead	150 kg time-delayed semi-armour-piercing high-explosive
Engine	Solid rocket engine
Wingspan	0.9 m (unfolded)
Operational range	35 km
Speed	Mach 0.8 to 0.9
Guidance system	TV-homing, millimetre radar

The **Nasr-1** is an Iranian unlicensed copy of the Chinese C-704 short range anti ship missile. According to its export catalog, it can destroy 1,500-tonne targets such as small frigates. Nasr-1 missile can be launched from both inland bases and offshore military vessels, and is being modified to be fired from helicopters and submarines. The missile has a cigarette shaped body with four large foldable fins attached to the middle part and four smaller ones attached to the end of the missile near the exhaust. In December 2008, an Iranian naval force successfully test-fired the surface-to-surface Nasr-1 during the final stage of "Unity 87" wargames in the Persian Gulf waters. Following the successful test firing, on 7 March 2010, Iran's defence minister announced mass-production of Nasr-1 missiles

NOOR

The **Noor** is a long-range anti-ship cruise missile manufactured by Iran. This missile is in service with Iranian Navy.

Type	Anti-ship cruise missile
Service history	
Used by	Iran Syria
Production history	
Manufacturer	Iran
Specifications	
Engine	turbojet engine
Operational range	30-170 km depending on the model
Flight altitude	Sea-skimming

RA'AD

Type	Anti-ship cruise missile
	Service history
Used by	Iran
	Production history
Manufacturer	Iran
	Specifications
Operational range	360 km
Flight altitude	Sea-skimming

Raad is an Iranian heavy anti-ship missile with the range of 360 km. Development finished in 2004

QADER

The **Qader** is a medium-range anti-ship cruise missile developed by Iran. The missile called "Qader" (Able) is built indigenously by Iranian scientists and has a high destructive ability against coastal targets and warships. The missile, which was unveiled in August 2011, has a range of 300 km and is described by Iranian officials as "the most powerful and precise missile of the Islamic Republic of Iran's Navy" On 10 February

For additional analytical, business and investment opportunities information, please contact Global Investment & Business Center, USA at (703) 370-8082. Fax: (703) 370-8083. E-mail: ibpusa3@gmail.com
Global Business and Investment Info Databank - www.ibpus.com

2013, The head of Iran Aviation Industries Organization announced that an air-launched version of Qader and Nasr-1 will be tested in a week.

KHALIJ FARS

Type	Anti-ship ballistic missile
	Service history
In service	2011–present
Used by	Iran Syria North Korea Vietnam
	Production history
Manufacturer	Iran
	Specifications
Length	8.86 m
Diameter	0.61 m
Warhead	650 kg
Engine	Solid (single stage)
Operational range	300 km
Speed	Mach 3
Accuracy	8.50 m

For additional analytical, business and investment opportunities information, please contact Global Investment & Business Center, USA at (703) 370-8082. Fax: (703) 370-8083. E-mail: ibpusa3@gmail.com Global Business and Investment Info Databank - www.ibpus.com

Khalij Fars ("Persian Gulf") is an Iranian single-stage solid-propellant, supersonic anti-ship quasi ballistic missile with a range of 300 km based on the Fateh-110 missile. It is equipped with a 650 kg explosive warhead and an interception evading guidance system.

The missile was unveiled in February 2011 when the Commander of the Islamic Revolutionary Guards Corps, Major General Mohammad Ali Jafari, announced that it is being mass-produced. The Iranian Fars News agency released a footage of the missile hitting a target ship successfully. The missile was first tested during the Great Prophet 3 naval wargames in 2008. Israeli expert Uzi Rubin describes the missile as a game changer if used against US carriers in the Strait of Hormuz.

There have been two other publicized tests of the missile. One occurred in July 2011 and the other in July 2012. The latter test also showed footage taken by the missile's electro-optical seeker locked onto its target

The missile has an operating range of 300 kilometres (190 mi). It is a single-stage, solid-fuel-propelled vehicle, and is equipped with a 650-kilogram (1,430 lb) explosive warhead that uses a combination of guidance systems to prevent interception. The Persian Gulf has an advanced electronic system that allows the missile to discover and navigate to the target. The missile relies on its own internal navigation system, allowing it to travel without radio interference

ZAFAR

The Zafar (Triumph) cruise missile is the result of those efforts. Built to operate in an active electronic warfare environment, it is placed in box canisters which may be mounted on shore-based missile launchers or the small, high speed craft used by the

navy of Iran. The Defense Ministry developed the missile. It was revealed to be in active duty in February 2012, having its first successful test fire on April 2011.

Iranian television reported that the missile "is a short-range, anti-ship cruise missile capable of destroying small- and medium-sized targets with high precision." It has the maximun range of 25 km

BATTLEFIELD MISSILE SYSTEMS

Model	Type	Quantity	Acquired	Origin
Tondar-69	Rocket artillery	+		Iran
Oghab	Rocket artillery	+	1985–present	Iran
Naze'at	Rocket artillery	+		Iran
Zelzal	Tactical ballistic missile	+		Iran
Fateh-110	Tactical ballistic missile	+	2002–present	Iran

TONDAR-69

Type	Rocket artillery
	Service history
Used by	Iran
	Specifications
Weight	2,650 kg
Length	10.8 m
Diameter	0.65 m (first stage), 0.5 m (second stage)
Warhead	Single warhead
Engine	Two-stage solid-fuel and/or liquid fuel
Operational	150 km

range	
Guidance system	Inertial with command updates

The **Tondar-69** is a short-range ballistic missile (SRBM) originating in China and operated by the armed forces of Iran. It was originally deployed by the Iranian army in 1992. The design is based on the Chinese CSS-8, which itself was designed from the Soviet S-75 surface-to-air missile (SAM).

It is based in transporter erector launchers towed into position. Up to two-hundred CSS-8 missiles were acquired from 1989-1992 and modified to Tondar-69 specifications

OGHAB

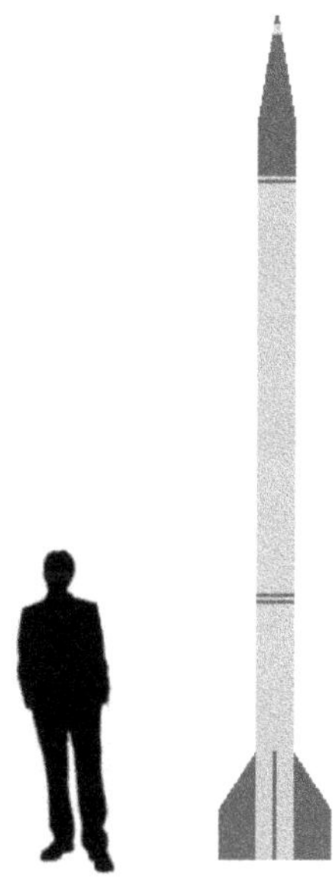

The Iranian **Oghab** (*Eagle*) missile is an unguided 230 mm (9 in) artillery rocket with a range of 34–45 km (20–28 mi). It is spin-stabilized in flight but has a proven circular error probable in excess of 500 m (1,500 ft), making it a highly inaccurate weapon. It carries a 70 kg (150 lb) high explosive fragmentation warhead, though it may also be able to carry chemical warheads. According to US sources, a modified version has been developed that could be carried and fired from Iranian Air Force F-14 Tomcat and F-4 Phantom II aircraft. The launcher is an elevatable triple-rail launcher assembly fitted to a Mercedes-Benz LA 911B 4×4 truck chassis.

The missile was developed from the Chinese Type-83 artillery rocket during the Iran–Iraq War, with the assistance of the People's Republic of China under an agreement signed in 1985. It entered service in 1986 and was immediately used in combat in an

For additional analytical, business and investment opportunities information,
please contact Global Investment & Business Center, USA
at (703) 370-8082. Fax: (703) 370-8083. E-mail: ibpusa3@gmail.com
Global Business and Investment Info Databank - www.ibpus.com

attack on the Iraqi city of Basra in December 1986. Around 260–270 Oghabs were reportedly fired during the war, though their effectiveness was limited. The missile's short range confined its use to attacks on Iraqi border cities and its lack of accuracy meant that Oghab attacks were far less effective than artillery barrages. The Oghab is used by the Iranian Army and the Revolutionary Guards. It is known to have been exported to Hezbollah.

NAZE'AT

aze'at (Persian: نازعات) are a series of Iranian-made artillery rocket with an estimated range of 100 km. There are two known variants, named Naze'at 6-H and Naze'at 10-H, each with different specifications. Like Zelzals, Naze'at rockets don't have a guidance system.

Specifications
Naze'at 6-H rocket
Max. range (km): 100
Min. range (km): 80
Length (mm): 6290
Diameter (mm): 356
Initial weight (kg): 960
Warhead weight (kg): 130
C.E.P (%): <5% Max. range
Average Action Time (s): 9
Specific Impulse (s): 240
Propellant Weight (kg): 420
Type of Propellant: Solid (HTPB)
Service life: 7 years
Naze'at 10-H rocket
Max. range (km): 130

Min. range (km): 110
Length (mm): 8020
Diameter (mm): 457
Initial weight (kg): 1830
Warhead weight (kg): 230
C.E.P (%): <5% Max. range
Average Action Time (s): 10
Specific Impulse (s): 240
Propellant Weight (kg): 865
Type of Propellant: Solid (HTPB)
Service life: 7 years

ZELZAL

Zelzal (meaning "Earthquake") is a series of artillery rockets developed by Iran. The series consists of:
Zelzal-1, with an estimated range of 150 km (93 mi)
Zelzal-2, with an estimated range of 210 km (130 mi)
Zelzal-3, with an estimated range of 200 km (120 mi)
These rockets were developed by SAHID Hassan Tehrani Moghaddam, after developed the Shahab-1 and the Shahab-2.

Zelzal-3 (Persian: زلزال-۳, meaning "earthquake") is an Iranian-made solid propellant unguided artillery rocket with a range of 200 km. It is an upgrade of the Zelzal-2 rocket with slightly improved range and was first shown to the public in 2007. A variant, the **Zelzal-3B**, has a smaller warhead and a range of 250 km. The shape and dimensions of the Zelzal-3 are nearly identical with previous versions except that the nosecone is cone shaped rather than the dome shaped Zelzal-2 and Zelzal-1. The Zelzal-3 has revived little use as the much more accurate Fateh-110 missile was also developed from the Zelzal-2. Firing Zelzal 3 in the Great Prophet VI military exercise by IRGC A number of sources confuse the Zelzal-3 with the Shahab-3 ballistic missile.

**For additional analytical, business and investment opportunities information,
please contact Global Investment & Business Center, USA
at (703) 370-8082. Fax: (703) 370-8083. E-mail: ibpusa3@gmail.com
Global Business and Investment Info Databank - www.ibpus.com**

FATEH-110

Type	Tactical SRBM
	Service history
In service	2002–present
Used by	Iran Syria Hezbollah
Wars	Syrian Civil War
	Production history
Manufacturer	Iran
Unit cost	Unknown
	Specifications
Weight	3,500 kg
Length	8.90 m
Diameter	0.60 m
Warhead	One
Blast yield	Not applicable
Engine	Solid fuel rocket (single stage)
Operational range	300 km
Speed	Mach 3.5
Guidance system	Inertial, global navigation satellite system & electro-optical terminal

The **Fateh-110** ("conqueror") is an Iranian road-mobile single-stage solid-fueled surface-to-surface missile produced by Iran's Aerospace Industries Organization. The first generation of the Fateh-110 was flight tested in September 2002 and began mass production shortly thereafter. The initial range of the missile was 200 km and in September 2004 the second generation of the Fateh-110 increased the range to 250 km. The third generation of the missile, unveiled in 2010, increased the range to 300 km, and the fourth generation (2012) improved the accuracy.

The Fateh-110 was developed from Iran's Zelzal-2 unguided artillery rocket essentially through adding a guidance system. Later versions of the missile modify other aspects of the missile and improve range and payload. The Fateh-110 is also license-built in Syria as the M-600. The missile has been used in the Syrian Civil War by Iran and Syria. In addition to its confirmed use by these two countries, it is widely reported that the Fateh-110 has been exported to Hezbollah of Lebanon.

ANTI-SHIP MISSILES

Model	Type	Quantity	Acquired	Origin	Notes
Kowsar 1/2/3	Anti-ship missile	+		Iran	Light ASCM based on Chinese C-701 and TL-10
Nasr-1	Anti ship missile	+		Iran	Light ASCM based on Chinese C-705 and TL-6
Noor	Anti-ship missile	+		Iran	ASCM based on Chinese C-801 and C-802
Ra'ad	Anti-ship missile	+		Iran	Iranian origin Heavy ASCM similar to Chinese C-401
Qader	Anti ship missile	+		Iran	
Khalij Fars	Anti-ship ballistic missile	+		Iran	Based on Fateh-110
Zafar	Anti-ship missile	+		Iran	Light ASCM for IRGC navy

Anti ship missiles Reference 1: Anti ship missiles Reference 2:

BATTLEFIELD MISSILE SYSTEMS

Model	Type	Quantity	Acquired	Origin
Tondar-69	Rocket artillery	+		Iran
Oghab	Rocket artillery	+	1985–present	Iran

Naze'at	Rocket artillery	+		Iran
Zelzal	Tactical ballistic missile	+		Iran
Fateh-110	Tactical ballistic missile	+	2002–present	Iran

Battlefield missile systems Reference 1: Battlefield missile systems Reference 2

AIR DEFENCE MISSILE SYSTEMS

Model	Type	Quantity
ZPU-4	Anti-air artillery	+
ZU-23	Anti-air artillery	+
Oerlikon 35 mm/Samavat	Anti-air artillery	100+
KS-19/Sa'ir 100mm Anti-Aircraft Guns	Anti-air artillery	+
Mesbah 1	Close-in weapon system	+
ZSU-23-4	Self-propelled anti-aircraft weapon	100+
ZSU-57-2	Self-propelled anti-aircraft weapon	+

AIR-DEFENCE MISSILE SYSTEMS

Model	Type	Quantity	Acquired	Notes
MIM-23 Hawk	Surface-to-air missile	150	1970s-present	Locally manufactured improved version of the original 1960s US Hawk system. The Islamic Republic of Iran Air Force had recently revealed its own version of the MIM-23 Hawk the Shahin which is under production. In 2010 Iran announced that it will be mass-producing its next generation of air defense system called Mersad which would integrate with the Shahin missile.
SM-1	Surface-to-air missile	+		Locally manufactured copy of a c.1970s variant
Shahab Saqeb	Surface-to-air missile	+	2002–present	copy of the Chinese HQ-7 (FM-90) system. This Project was First Joint Winner-Applied Research in 14th Khwarizmi International Award- 2001;Tehran-Iran -The Project Title:Production of Low Range Ground to Air Missile;Shahab Saqeb - Initiator:Iran Aerospace Ind. Org.& Contributor:D.I.O)
SA-2 Dvina/Sayyad-1	Surface-to-air missile	24		Up to 45 Launchers, HQ-2J and indigenous-produced Sayyad-1. Upgraded copy of HQ-2, Sayyad-1A has IR tracking. This Project was First Joint Winner-Applied Research in 14th Khwarizmi International Award- 2001;Tehran-Iran -The Project Title:Manufacture of Sayyad-1 Missile -Initiator: Iran Aerospace Ind. Org.

For additional analytical, business and investment opportunities information, please contact Global Investment & Business Center, USA at (703) 370-8082. Fax: (703) 370-8083. E-mail: ibpusa3@gmail.com Global Business and Investment Info Databank - www.ibpus.com

				Contributor:HESA & Arak Machine Ind. Iran has about 4 sites of Sayyad-1 and HQ-2 which each sites has 6 launchers make it 24
Ghareh	Surface-to-air missile	10		upgraded copy of SA-5 Gammon with 250 km range. Iran has five battalions and each battalion is composed of six launchers and one fire control radar.
SA-6 Gainful	Surface-to-air missile	8	1995–present	Reports of eight SA-6 systems transferred to Iran from Russia in 1995/1996.
SA-5 Gammon	Surface-to-air missile	30		Locally upgraded and improved Iran has about 6 sites of S-200 with each sites 6 launchers and have about 200 missiles
Rapier missile	Surface-to-air missile	30	1971–present	45 towed systems with Blindfire radar delivered before 1979. 72 self-propelled systems and local production of 1,000 missiles cancelled 1979
Tigercat	Surface-to-air missile	15		
SA-22 Greyhound (Pantsyr S1)	Surface-to-air missile	10	2008–present	
Tor missile system	Surface-to-air missile	29	2005–present	
S-300	Surface-to-air missile	8	2016	Iran possess latest S-300 version S-300PMU2 obtained from Russia 4 were received, and also 4 S-300PT from Belarus.Russia has completed the delivery of S-300 air defense missile systems to Iran, RIA news agency quoted Russia's state arms export agency as saying on Thursday Oct 15 2016. Iran announced that it had a "domestically made" system with the same capabilities as the S-300. In 2016 Russia completed delivery all missiles to Iran.
Mersad	Air Defense System	+	2010	Iranian designed Air Defense system using Shahin missiles.
Raad	Air Defense System	8	2012	Iranian air defense system based on Russian Buk.Iran has about 2 sites of it's, each sites has 4 system
Ya Zahra	Air Defense System	+	2013	Mass production began in January 2013.
Herz-9	Air Defense System	42+ estimated	2013	Mass production began in May 2013.
Talaash	Air Defense System	12	2010	Mass production began in November 2013. Iran has about 3 sites of Talaash including Sayyad 2 missile
Bavar-373	Air Defense System	4+	2014	An Iranian long range air defence system whose development began after the Russian refusal to supply the S-300(since 2010 to

				2015). According to Iranian defence minister Hassan Dehghan in an interview, Bavar-373 is a completely indigenous system.

MAN-PORTABLE AIR-DEFENSE SYSTEMS

Model	Type	Quantity
Misagh-1	Man-portable air-defense systems	+
Misagh-2	Man-portable air-defense systems	+
Qaem	Man-portable air-defense systems	+
RBS-70	Man-portable air-defense systems	50
SA-7 Grail	Man-portable air-defense systems	+
SA-14 Gremlin	Man-portable air-defense systems	+
SA-16 Gimlet	Man-portable air-defense systems	700
SA-18 Grouse	Man-portable air-defense systems	+

RADAR SYSTEMS

- Gamma radar (Russian origin)
- Kasta radar (Russian origin)
- 1L13 "Nebo" VHF radar (Russian origin)
- Vostok radar (Belorussian origin)
- Kolchuga (Ukrainian origin)[36]
- JY-14 Radar (Chinese origin)
- Matla-ul-fajr radar (Iranian origin)
- Kashef 1&2 radars (Iranian origin)
- Alim radar (Iranian origin)
- Thamen radar (Iranian origin)
- Ghadir - The Ghadir radar system which covers areas (maximum) 1,100 km in distance and 300 km in altitude (Iranian origin)
- Najm-802 - Phased array radar system (Iranian origin)
- Sepehr - Over-the-horizon radar with a range of 3,000 kilometers (Iranian origin)
- Arash - long range radar (Iranian origin)
- Meraj-4 radar- Phased array radar that has range of 450km-500km,fitted in Bavar 373 missile system (Iranian origin)

For additional analytical, business and investment opportunities information, please contact Global Investment & Business Center, USA at (703) 370-8082. Fax: (703) 370-8083. E-mail: ibpusa3@gmail.com Global Business and Investment Info Databank - www.ibpus.com

TRAVEL TO IRAN

IRAN - US STATE DEPARTMENT SUGGESTIONS

WARNING: The Department of State warns U.S. citizens to defer travel to Iran. Iranian President Khatami has called for a "dialogue of civilizations" and an increase of private exchanges between Iranians and Americans; some limited exchanges have taken place. There is, however, evidence that hostility to the United States remains in some segments of the Iranian population and some elements of the Iranian government. In July 1999, violent anti-government demonstrations took place in Tehran and other cities around the country. There were accusations that the U.S. was behind these demonstrations. Prior to and since that time, some groups of American travelers have encountered harassment by vigilante groups.

The U.S. government does not currently have diplomatic or consular relations with the Islamic Republic of Iran and therefore cannot provide protection or routine consular services to American citizens in Iran. The Swiss government, acting through its embassy in Tehran, serves as protecting power for U.S. interests in Iran. The Iranian government does not recognize dual citizenship and generally does not permit the Swiss to provide protective services for American citizens who are also Iranian nationals. In addition, U.S. citizens of Iranian origin who are considered by Iran to be Iranian citizens have been detained and harassed by Iranian authorities. Former Muslims who have converted to other religions, as well as persons who encourage Muslims to convert, are subject to arrest and possible execution. The Iranian government reportedly has the names of all individuals who filed claims against Iran, and who received awards, at the Iran-U.S. claims tribunal at The Hague pursuant to the 1981 Algerian Accords. There are restrictions on both the import and the export of goods between Iran and the United States. Neither U.S. passports nor visas to the United States are issued in Tehran.

COUNTRY DESCRIPTION: Iran is a constitutional Islamic republic, governed by executive and legislative branches that derive national leadership primarily through the Muslim clergy. Shia Islam is the official religion of Iran, and Islamic law is the basis of the authority by the state. Shia Islamic ideals and beliefs provide the conservative foundation of the country's customs, laws and practices. Iran is a developing country. The workweek in Iran is Sunday through Thursday; however, many government offices and private companies are closed on Thursdays. Friday is a public holiday for all establishments. Offices in Iran are generally open to the public during the morning hours only.

ENTRY AND EXIT REQUIREMENTS: Should you decide to travel to Iran despite the Travel Warning, a passport and visa are required. The Iranian Interests Section of the Embassy of Pakistan is located at 2209 Wisconsin Ave. N.W, Washington, DC. 20007; tel 202-965-4990. U.S. passports are valid for travel to Iran. However, the authorities have often confiscated the U.S. passports of U.S.-Iranian dual nationals upon arrival. U.S.-Iranlan dual nationals have been denied permission to depart Iran documented as U.S. citizens. To prevent the confiscation of U.S. passports, the Department of State suggests that dual nationals leave their U.S. passports at the nearest U.S. embassy or consulate overseas for safekeeping before entering Iran, and to use their Iranian passports to enter the country. To facilitate their travel if their U.S. passports are confiscated, dual nationals may, prior to entering Iran, obtain in their Iranian passports the necessary visas for the country which they will transit on their return to the U.S., and where they may apply for a new U.S. passport.

If dual nationals fail to obtain in advance the necessary transit visas for their return trip to the U.S., the travelers can obtain a "Confirmation of Nationality" from the U.S. Interests Section of the Embassy of Switzerland, which is the U.S. protecting power. This statement, addressed to the relevant foreign embassies in Tehran, enables the travelers to apply for third-country visas in Tehran. Dual nationals finding themselves in this situation should note in advance that the Swiss Embassy will issue this statement only after the traveler's U.S. nationality is confirmed and after some processing delay. Dual nationals must enter and leave the United States on U.S. passports.

DUAL NATIONALITY: U.S. citizens who were born in Iran, who have become naturalized citizens of Iran, or who were at one time citizens of Iran, and the children of such persons, are considered Iranian nationals by Iranian authorities. Therefore, despite the fact that these individuals possess U.S. citizenship, they must enter and exit Iran bearing an Iranian passport. Yet some former Iranian nationals have been issued visas in their U.S. passports. Exit visas are required for dual nationals to depart Iran.

In addition, U.S.-Iranian dual nationals are subject to Iranian laws which impose special obligations upon Iranian nationals, such as military service or taxes. Exit permits for departure from Iran may be denied until such obligations are met. More specific information on Iranian passport and exit visa requirements may be obtained from the Iranian Interests Section of the Embassy of Pakistan.

Dual nationals often have their U.S. passports confiscated and may be denied permission to leave Iran, or encounter other problems with Iranian authorities. Refer also to the above section titled "Entry and Exit Requirements" of this Consular Information Sheet. For additional information on dual nationality, see the Consular Affairs home page on the Internet at http://travel.state.gov for our Dual Nationality flyer.

SAFETY/SECURITY: U.S. citizens should exercise caution throughout the country. In July 1999, foreigners were taken hostage in Kerman and Bam. Travelers should avoid travel to areas bordering Afghanistan and Iraq.

Iranian security personnel may at times place foreign visitors under surveillance. Hotel rooms, telephones and fax machines may be monitored, and personal possessions in hotel rooms may be searched. Taking photographs of anything that could be perceived as being of military or security interest may result in problems with authorities.

CRIME INFORMATION: Major crime is not a problem for travelers in Iran, although foreigners occasionally have been victims of petty street crime. In view of possible thefts, passports and other important valuables should be kept in hotel safes or other secure locations. The loss or theft in Iran of a U.S. passport should be reported immediately to the local police and the U.S. Interests Section at the Swiss Embassy. U.S. citizens can refer to the Department of State's pamphlets *A Safe Trip Abroad* and *Tips for Travel to the Middle East and North Africa* for ways to promote a more trouble-free journey. These pamphlets are available by mail from the Superintendent of Documents, U.S. Government Printing Office, Washington, DC 20402, via the Internet at http://www.access.gpo.gov/su_docs, or via the Bureau of Consular Affairs home page at http://travel.state.gov.

MEDICAL FACILITIES: Basic medical care and medicines are available in the principal cities of Iran, but may not be available in outlying areas. Serious medical problems requiring hospitalization and/or medical evacuation to the United States can cost thousands of dollars or more. Medical facilities do not meet U.S. standards and frequently lack medicines and supplies. Doctors and hospitals often expect immediate cash payment for health services. U.S. medical insurance is not always valid outside the United States. U.S. Medicare and Medicaid programs do not provide payment for medical services outside the United States.

MEDICAL INSURANCE: Uninsured travelers who require medical care overseas may face extreme difficulties. Check with your own insurance company to confirm whether your policy applies overseas, including provision for medical evacuation. Ascertain if payment will be made to the overseas hospital or doctor, or whether you will be reimbursed later for expenses you incur. Some insurance policies also include coverage for psychiatric treatment and for disposition of remains in the event of death. Useful information on medical emergencies abroad, including overseas insurance programs, is provided in the Department of State's Bureau of Consular Affairs brochure, *Medical Information for Americans Traveling Abroad*, available via the Bureau of Consular Affairs home page or autofax: 202-647-3000.

OTHER HEALTH INFORMATION: Information on vaccinations and other health precautions may be obtained from the Centers for Disease Control and Prevention's hotline for international travelers from the United States at 1-877-FYI-TRIP (1-877-394-8747), fax 1-888-CDC-FAXX (1-888-232-3299), or via their Internet site at http://www.cdc.gov.

TRAFFIC SAFETY AND ROAD CONDITIONS: While in a foreign country, U.S. citizens may encounter road conditions that differ significantly from those in the United States. The information below concerning Iran is provided for general reference only, and may not be totally accurate in a particular location or circumstance.

Safety of Public Transportation: Poor
Urban Road Conditions/Maintenance: Good
Rural Road Conditions/Maintenance: Good
Availability of Roadside Assistance: Poor

Drivers all over Iran tend to ignore traffic lights, traffic signs and lane markers. Urban streets are not well lit. Therefore, it is very dangerous to drive around, especially at night. Sidewalks in urban areas only exist on main roads and are usually obstructed by parked

For additional analytical, business and investment opportunities information,
please contact Global Investment & Business Center, USA
at (703) 370-8082. Fax: (703) 370-8083. E-mail: ibpusa3@gmail.com
Global Business and Investment Info Databank - www.ibpus.com

cars. In the residential areas, hardly any sidewalks exist. Drivers almost never yield to pedestrians at crosswalks.

AVIATION SAFETY OVERSIGHT: As there is no direct commercial air service by local carriers at present, nor economic authority to operate such service, between the U.S. and Iran, the U.S. Federal Aviation Administration (FAA) has not assessed Iran's Civil Aviation Authority for compliance with international aviation safety standards for oversight of Iran's air carrier operations. For further information, travelers may contact the U.S. Department of Transportation within the U.S. at 1-800-322-7873, or visit the FAA Internet home page at http://www.faa.gov/avr/iasa/index.htm.

PASSPORT SEIZURES/EXIT BANS: The Iranian government has seized the passports and blocked the departure of foreigners involved in commercial disputes.

CUSTOMS REGULATIONS: Iranian authorities may permit travelers to bring in or to take certain goods out of Iran. However, U.S. travelers should refer to the section of this Consular Information Sheet regarding U.S. Government economic sanctions and the importation and exportation of restricted items in order to avoid any violation of the Iranian transactions regulations.

All luggage is searched upon traveling into and departing from Iran. Tourists can bring in and take out the following non-commercial goods, if they are recorded on the tourist's goods slip upon arrival at customs: personal jewelry, one camera, an amateur video camera, one pair of binoculars, a portable tape recorder, a personal portable computer, first aid box, and a camping tent with its equipment. Iranian authorities allow the departing passenger to take an unlimited amount of Iranian goods and foreign goods up to $160 (US), and their personal non-commercial equipment. Air passengers may also take one carpet up to 6 square meters. However, the U.S. government only allows the importation of up to $100 worth of Iranian-origin goods. Iranian authorities prohibit the export of antique carpets and carpets portraying women not wearing the proper Islamic covering, antiques, original works of art, calligraphic pieces, miniature paintings, different kinds of coins, and precious stones. They likewise prohibit the export and import of alcoholic beverages, weapons, ammunitions, swords and sheaths, military devices, drugs and illegal goods.

CRIMINAL PENALTIES: While in a foreign country, a U.S. citizen is subject to that country's laws and regulations, which sometimes differ significantly from those in the United States and do not afford the protections available to the individual under U.S. law. Penalties for breaking the law can be more severe than in the United States for similar offenses. Persons violating Iranian laws, even unknowingly, may be expelled, arrested or imprisoned. Fines, public floggings, and long prison terms are common. Former Muslims who have converted to other religions, as well as persons who encourage Muslims to convert, are subject to arrest and possible execution. Drinking, possession of alcoholic beverages and drugs, as well as flirting or having sexual contact as an unmarried couple is considered to be crimes. Penalties for possession, use, or trafficking in illegal drugs in Iran are strict. Iran executes scores of persons each year on drug-related charges.

For additional analytical, business and investment opportunities information, please contact Global Investment & Business Center, USA at (703) 370-8082. Fax: (703) 370-8083. E-mail: ibpusa3@gmail.com Global Business and Investment Info Databank - www.ibpus.com

U.S. citizens in Iran who violate Iranian laws, including laws which are unfamiliar to Westerners (such as laws regarding the proper wearing of apparel), may face severe penalties. The Iranian government reportedly has the names of all individuals who filed claims against Iran at the Iran-U.S. Claims Tribunal at The Hague pursuant to the 1981 Algerian Accords. In addition, the Iranian government reportedly has compiled a list of the claimants who were awarded compensation in the Iran Claims Program administered by the Foreign Claims Settlement Commission. The Iranian government is allegedly targeting award-holders who travel to Iran. It is reported that upon some claimants' entry into Iran, Iranian authorities question them as to the status of payment of their respective awards with a view to recouping the award money. It is also reported that the Iranian government has threatened to prevent U.S. claimants visiting Iran from departing the country until they make arrangements to pay part or all of their award money to that government.

SPECIAL CIRCUMSTANCES: In addition to the U.S. government economic sanctions on trade and investment restrictions, travelers should be aware that most hotels and restaurants do not accept credit cards. Cash-dollars (not traveler checks) are accepted as payment. In general, hotel rooms have to be paid with cash-dollars. ATM machines are not available. Foreign currency has to be declared at Customs upon entry into the country, and the amount is entered in the passport. This amount can then be changed at the bank.

U.S. GOVERNMENT ECONOMIC SANCTIONS: On May 6, 1995, President Clinton signed Executive Order 12959, 60 Federal Register 24757 (May 9, 1995), which prohibits exporting goods or services to Iran, re-exporting certain goods to Iran, making new investments in Iran and dealing in property owned or controlled by the government of Iran. The importation of Iranian-origin goods or services into the United States has been prohibited since October 19, 1987. The Office of Foreign Assets Control, Department of Treasury, provides guidance to the public on the interpretation of the order. For additional information, consult the Licensing Division, Office of Foreign Assets Control (OFAC), U.S. Department of Treasury at the OFAC home page on the Internet at http://www.treas.gov/ofac or via OFAC's info-by fax at 202-622-0077 or 202-622-2500. For information regarding banking and compliance, contact OFAC's Compliance Programs Division at 202-622-2490.

FAMILY ISSUES: Children of Iranian citizens, under the age of 18, must have the father's permission to depart Iran, even if the mother has been granted full custody by an Iranian court. Even the non-Iranian wife of an Iranian citizen (who obtains Iranian nationality through marriage and must convert to Islam) requires the consent of her husband to leave Iran. In case of marital problems, women in Iran are often subject to strict family controls. Because of Islamic law, compounded by the lack of diplomatic relationships between the United States and Iran, the U.S. Interests Section in Tehran can provide very limited assistance if an American woman encounters difficulty in leaving Iran.

For information on international adoption of children, international parental child abduction, and international child support enforcement issues, please refer to our Internet site at http://travel.state.gov/children's_issues.html or telephone 202-736-7000.

For additional analytical, business and investment opportunities information, please contact Global Investment & Business Center, USA at (703) 370-8082. Fax: (703) 370-8083. E-mail: ibpusa3@gmail.com Global Business and Investment Info Databank - www.ibpus.com

REGISTRATION/U.S. INTERESTS SECTION LOCATION: There is no U.S. embassy or consulate in Iran. The Embassy of Switzerland serves as the protecting power of U.S. interests in Iran. The U.S. Interests Section at the Swiss Embassy is located at Africa Avenue, West Farzan Street, No. 59, Tehran. The local telephone numbers are 878-2964 and 879-2364, fax 877-3265. The workweek is Sunday through Thursday. The Interests Section does not issue U.S. visas nor accept visa applications. The limited consular services provided to U.S. citizens in Tehran, Iran include:

(a) registering U.S. citizens;
(b) answering inquiries concerning the welfare and whereabouts of U.S. citizens in Iran:
(c) rendering assistance in times of distress or physical danger;
(d) providing U.S. citizens with passport applications and other citizenship forms for approval at the U.S. Embassy in Bern, Switzerland;
(e) performing notarial services on the basis of accommodation; and
(f) taking provisional custody of the personal effects of deceased U.S. citizens.

SURVIVAL INFORMATION

WATER

Tap water is excellent in Tehran and safe for drinking.

ELECTRICITY

220 V AC 50 HZ

LOCAL TIME

GMT +3 1/2

Information: Dial 1 1 9 for exact time, 24 hour service

BUSINESS HOURS:

Government: 7:30 to 14:30 (Saturday - Wednesday) 7:30 to 13:30 (Thursday)

Business: 8:30 to 12:30 to 19:00 (Saturday - Wednesday) 8:30 to 12:30 (Thursday)

Shops: 09:00 to 13:00, 16:00 to 20:00

TIPPING:

Airport: IRR 2,000 3,000 per cart

Hotel: IRR 2,000 3,000 per cart

Restaurant: 1 5% if service charge not included in the bill

CRIME:

Tehran is a very safe city by international standards. However, business travellers should take the normal precautions, as they are often targeted as easy marks.

For additional analytical, business and investment opportunities information, please contact Global Investment & Business Center, USA at (703) 370-8082. Fax: (703) 370-8083. E-mail: ibpusa3@gmail.com Global Business and Investment Info Databank - www.ibpus.com

AIRLINES:

Tehran:

Isfahan:

Alitalia: 871 1889, 871 1512

Iran Air:

57018-19

Austrian Air: 874 5311, 874 5313

Asseman:

55014, 27717

British Airways 205 7483, 204 5477

Gulf Air: 225 3274/5

Ahwaz:

Iran Air: 91 1 1

Iran Air: 22093-7

KLM: 873 2447,873 3973

Aseman: 44041-5

873 7562, 873 7855

Lufthansa: 872 3382-5, 872 3482

Swiss Air: 874 8332-5

Syrian Airline: 889 7584-5

Turkish Airline: 873 7464, 873 7383

TAXIS:

Desks located in major hotel lobbies. Fare for a taxi ride inside Tehran is IRR 8000 to 10,000 per trip depending on distance. Taxis are not equipped with meters, therefore it is advisable to ask for the fare before the ride.

At the airport, take an official taxi from the stand across from the terminal. Avoid the taxi touts at the airport, who will approach you and quote prices in dollars. It takes 30 minutes to an hour to go from the airport to downtown hotels and costs about 25 000 rials in the airport taxi. Other taxi agencies as follows:

Radio Taxis
Tel: 884 0011 to 20

Modern Taxi (Fereshteh)
Tel: 204 1236 & 204 1768Tel:

Daryoush Taxi (Zafaranieh) Tel: 877-1059 & 877-6900

Fereshteh Taxi (Velenjak)
Tel: 876 4864 to 6

Unique Taxi (Mirdamad)
Tel: 222-5504 & 222-7971

Hilton Vanak Taxi (Vanak)
Tel: 877-1059 & 877-6900

Mercuri Taxi (Abbas Abad)
Tel: 876-4864 to 6

HOTELS:

In Tehran payment may be made in either USD bills or USD traveller cheques for which there is a service charge of approximately 3 percent. Outside of Tehran USD bills are required **N.B.** Credit cards (such as Visa & Master) are currently accepted in major hotels in Iran.

Tehran:

Esteghlal Hotel (Ex-Hilton)

Vali-e-Asr Avenue and Chamran Expressway

Tel: 204 0021-5 Fax: 204 7041

Great Azadi Hotel (Ex-Hyatt)

Chamran Expressway,

Tel: 207 3021/9
Fax: 207 3038

Homa Hotel (Ex-Sheraton)

Shahid Khodami Avenue, Vanak Square

Tel: 877 3021-9 Fax: 879 7179

Laleh Hotel (Ex-intercontinental)

Dr. Fatemi Avenue

Tel: 655 021 - 9 Telex: 212300 INCH IR

For additional analytical, business and investment opportunities information, please contact Global Investment & Business Center, USA at (703) 370-8082. Fax: (703) 370-8083. E-mail: ibpusa3@gmail.com Global Business and Investment Info Databank - www.ibpus.com

Isfahan:

Aliqapu Hotel

Char Bagh Avenue

Tel: (031)231282-4

Kowsar Hotel

Mellat Blvd, next to 33 Bridges

Tel: (031)40230-9 Telex: 312408 KIH IR

Abbasi Hotel (Shah Abbas)

Char Bagh-Amadghah

Tel: (031)26008-10 Telex: 312431 ABBASI IR

Ahwaz:

Fajr Hotel (Ex. Austria)

Ayatollah Montazeri Avenue,

Tel: (061)21091-4, 20091-5

Oxyn Hotel

Imam Khomeini Avenue

Tel: (061)2900

RESTUARANTS:

Apart from hotel restaurants, following are recommended (price per person IRR (20,000-30,000):

Papa Restaurant (El-Padrino, continental f ood) Afshar Alley, Shabdiz Street, Fereshteh Avenue,
Tel: 204 0311-204 1075

Japanese Restaurant Shahid Khodami Street, Vanak Square Tel: 877 6301-877 3735

Chinese Restaurant Abdow Alley, in front of Dr. Fatemi Avenue, Vali-e-Asr Avenue, Tel: 890714

Tandoor Indian Restaurant Kutche-ye Ardalan, Opposite Stadium Mofatteh Ave, Tel: 882 5705

Nayeb Restaurant (traditional Iranian food) Aban Street, Karim Khan Zand Avenue Tel: 894643

Nayeb Restaurant (traditional Iranian f ood) In front of Miami Hotel, Vaii-e-Asr Avenue, Tel: 873 3474

Loukse Talaie (traditional Iranian food) Above Moddares Expressway, Cross Road Vali-e-Asr Avenue Tel: 204 9133

For additional analytical, business and investment opportunities information, please contact Global Investment & Business Center, USA at (703) 370-8082. Fax: (703) 370-8083. E-mail: ibpusa3@gmail.com Global Business and Investment Info Databank - www.ibpus.com

Fardis Restaurant (Ex. Swiss Restaurant) Karim Khan ZAnd Avenue, Iranshar St,. Arayeh Alley Tel: 882 8516

Milano Restaurant Dr. Shariati Avenue, Sohail St., No. 6
Tel: 257-9418 & 602-3499

MEDICAL:

Teheran Clinic Ghaem Magham Farahani Avenue
Tel: 873 8113-16

Mehrad Hospital Miremad St, Ostad Motahari Avenue
Tel: 874 7401-9

Arad Hospital Somayeh Street, Bahar Cross Road Dr. Ali Shariati Avenue Tel: 761001 to 6

Iran Mehr Hospital North on Dr. Ali Shariati Avenue near Gholhak Tel: 200 9071 to 8

Burn Treatment Centre Vali-e-Asr Avenue, above Vanak Square, Tel: 877 0031-40

Pharmacies:

Taleghani Pharmacy North on Dr. Ali Shariati Avenue, near Tajrish Square Tel: 223 0588

Alfa Pharmacy Vanak Square Tel: 877 1322

Paskal Pharmacy Dr. Ali Shariati Avenue, at Ostad Motahari Avenue Tel: 840 348-849948

Sizdahe Aban Kheradmand Street, Karimkhan Zand Avenue Tel: 884 488 24 hours service.

*Note: The other pharmacies are opened on a rotating hours basis. Please check with your hotel desk.

SHOPPING:

Big Bazar Ark Square , downtown

Friday Flea Market Seyed Ismail St. (downtown)

Government Handicraft Centre (Downtown Location) Taleghani Avenue, Villa Avenue

North Tehran Centre Valii-e-Asr Avenue, in front of Mellat Park, Tel: 222 0071

BUSINESS TRAVEL TO IRAN

LOCAL CUSTOMS PROFILE

Iran is an ancient and proud civilization with its own customs and traditions. It is also a state where public behavior is strictly governed by laws. And it is an economy where personal relationships are the foundation of business dealings. It is important to bear these facts in mind when doing business there.

ETIQUETTE

Iranians are polite and formal. If offered tea, you should drink it or at least sip it; don't ask for coffee unless offered some initially. You may be served fruit or cakes during the meeting; you should take one after your host has offered. Most meetings will begin with an icebreaking personal conversation; in many instances it is considered rude to get down to business right away -- unless an issue is pressing. While your dealings may sometimes seem slow by Western standards -- both in a given meeting and over the course of the development of the deal you are negotiating -- you are laying the groundwork of personal trust which is very important in Iranian business dealings. Meetings should start on time; punctuality is considered a sign of respect.

GIFTS

The exchanging of gifts is not uncommon is business dealings - which, after all, have a very significant personal element to them in Iran. Usually, pens, pins, books or small souvenirs of either your company or of ypu country are appreciated. The most senior person should always receive the nicest gift.

DRESS

Men should wear conservative business attire, particularly in initial meetings. Iranian men -- particularly government workers -- do not wear ties, as the late Imam Khomeini declared them to be symbols of Western imperialism. After a period of time, more casual attire is acceptable. However, it is not recommended to dress more casually than your interlocutor. Shorts are never worn in public, even to go jogging. Short-sleeved shirts are acceptable in the summer -- as long as Ramadan or the mourning month of Moharram don't fall during the summer. If you cross you legs while sitting, be careful not to show the sole of your shoe.

WOMEN

Women in public must be modestly dressed. Even though standards tend to be less strict for Western visitors than for locals, modest dress is still required by law and by social custom. Women should cover their hair and neck with a scarf and wear a loose-fitting coat that extends below the knee. Shoes should be closed and legs should be covered by pants or stockings.

On the other hand, women can do much of what men do in Iran - go out alone, drive cars, work outside the home. Women can do business with men; however, women and men should not shake hands or have physical contact in public.

SUPPLEMENTS

MILITARY EQUIPMENT AND WEAPON SYSTEMS PRODUCED IN IRAN

AIRCRAFT AND HELICOPTERS

See also: Iran Aviation Industries Organization, Iran Aircraft Manufacturing Industrial Company, and Panha

Azarakhsh - modified copy of U.S. F-5 Freedom Fighter, one-seat fighter aircraft, and combat capable trainer.

Saegheh - fighter aircraft.Second generation Azarakhsh with a twin canted tail configuration.

Shafaq - advanced light fighter/trainer, still in development.

Qaher-313 - Stealth single-seat multi-role combat aircraft.

IR.An-140. - licensed production of Ukrainian Antonov An-140

Parastoo - propeller-driven training aircraft. Reverse engineered Beech F33 Bonanza.

Dorna - training aircraft

JT2-2 Tazarv - third generation of the Dorna mentioned above. Still in prototype stage.

Simorgh (aircraft) - training aircraft.

Fajr F.3 - Indigenous trainer aircraft

Panha 2091 - overhauled U.S. AH-1J SeaCobra refitted with indigenous components.

Toufan I,II - helicopter based on AH-1J and produced by Iran Aviation Industries Organization ,10 Toufan I were delivered to Army in May 2010.Improved Toufan II unveiled in January 2013.

Shabaviz 2061 - overhauled U.S. Bell 206 JetRanger refitted with indigenous components.

Shabaviz 275 - overhauled U.S. Bell 205 JetRanger refitted with indigenous components

Bell 214 - Reverse engineered and built in Iran

HESA Shahed 278 - Developed from Bell 206 & Panha Shabaviz 2061

HESA Shahed 285 - New Iranian Designed Attack Helicopter

Bavar 2 - fixed-wing seaplane capable of patrol and reconnaissance missions.

UNMANNED AERIAL VEHICLES

Ababil - Domestically-manufactured naval surveillance plane. Ababil-5 is for medium-range reconnaissance and surveillance missions and the Ababil-T for short/medium-range attack missions.

Mohajer I/II/III/IV

Rad (with 'offensive' capabilities)

Nazir (surveillance)

Saeghe - Target drone

Sabokbal - First iranian super light-weight drone, capable of recording and dispatching films and can be prepared for flight in less than five minutes.

Zohal - VTOL unmanned aerial vehicle

Talash 1,2 - Iranian training UAV.

Karrar - capable of carrying a military payload of rockets to carry out bombing missions against ground targets. It is also capable of flying long distances at a very high speed.

Sofreh Mahi - Stealth UCAV

A1 - A1 is capable of travelling for at least two hours, and can carry a 5-kilogram payload

Shaparak (Butterfly) - has a maximum operational radius of 50 kilometers (31 miles), and a maximum flight ceiling of 15,000 feet (4,572 meters). This UAV is capable of three and half hours of non-stop flying, and can carry an 8-kilogram (17-pound) payload.

Shahed 129 - UCAV with 24 hour flight capability and armed with Sadid missiles.

Sayeh - Reverse-engineered copies of ScanEagle, made on a domestic production line and put into service by the Iranian armed forces.

Yasir - Modified version of ScanEagle, it has a 19,500 ft service ceiling, an endurance of 24 hours, and an operational radius of about 750 km.

H-110 Sarir - capable of carrying air-to-air missiles.

For additional analytical, business and investment opportunities information, please contact Global Investment & Business Center, USA at (703) 370-8082. Fax: (703) 370-8083. E-mail: ibpusa3@gmail.com Global Business and Investment Info Databank - www.ibpus.com

Hamaseh - A medium range drone, capable of carrying air to ground missiles.

AB-3

Raad 85 - Suicide drone.

Fotros - UCAV with range of 2000 km,flight ceiling of 25000 ft and 16–30 hours flight endurance, armed with missiles.

AIRCRAFT UPGRADES AND COMPONENTS

Iran claims to have upgraded its US-made F-4, F-5, and F-14 fighter jets, and produced spare parts including tires, avionics, and engine components.

Shahed (Observer) flight recorder - able to record flight, image, and sound parameters.

SIMULATORS

F-4 Phantom Simulator

Toufan or AH-1J assault helicopter simulator

Shahed-278 and Bell-206 simulator - Under project Mansour Iran built 27 Bell-206 simulators in 2003.

Bell 214 simulator - it was built under project Qader-3 and it had cost Iran 17 billion and 500 million rials.

Submarine Simulator - Iran's "Tareq-class" submarine.

F-5 Tiger simulator

Misagh rocket launcher simulator

Mig-29 Fulcrum simulator

F-14 Tomcat simulator

RADAR SYSTEMS

Matla-ul-fajr radar system

BSR-1 - VHF radar.

Matla-ul-fajr radar system

For additional analytical, business and investment opportunities information, please contact Global Investment & Business Center, USA at (703) 370-8082. Fax: (703) 370-8083. E-mail: ibpusa3@gmail.com Global Business and Investment Info Databank - www.ibpus.com

Kashef 1&2 radar

Alvand radar

Asr radar - Asr radar is described by Iranian officials as a S band naval three-dimensional phased array radar with a range of 200 km and capable of simultaneously identifying and intercepting 100 targets at water level or above, this radar will be installed on Jamaran frigates.

Alim radar system

RASIT ground-surveillance radar - Iran captured a number of Iraqi radars during the 1980-1988 war, and now manufactures a reverse-engineered version carried aboard a truck

Thamen - radar system

Electro-optical/radar system

E-warfare systems

Sepehr - OTH radar with a range of 3,000 kilometers in radius

Najm-802 - Phased array radar system

Ghadir - The Ghadir radar system which covers areas (maximum) 1,100 km in distance and 300 km in altitude has been designed and built to identify aerial targets, radar-evading aircraft, cruise missiles and ballistic missiles as well as low-altitude satellites.

Arash - long range radar, entered service in December 2013.

MISSILES

MEDIUM RANGE (MRBM)

Ghadr-110 with a range of 2,000 km.

Medium range missiles are considered to have a range between 1000 and 3000 kilometers.

Shahab-3A/B/C - strategic MRBM with a range of 1,200 km to 2,100 km.

Ghadr-110 MRBM with a range of 2000–3000 km.

Ashoura missile 2 stage solid fuel MRBM with a range of 2,000 km.

Sejjil 2-stage solid fuel MRBM with a range of 2000–2500 km.

For additional analytical, business and investment opportunities information, please contact Global Investment & Business Center, USA at (703) 370-8082. Fax: (703) 370-8083. E-mail: ibpusa3@gmail.com Global Business and Investment Info Databank - www.ibpus.com

Fajr-3 MIRV warhead.

SHORT RANGE (SRBM)

Short range missiles are considered to have a range up to 1000 kilometers.

Shahab-1 - Tactical SRBM with a range of 350 km. Copy of Soviet SS-1C/Scud-B

Shahab-2 - Tactical SRBM with a range of 750 km. Copy of Soviet SS-1D/Scud-C

Naze'at - Unguided rocket series.

Fateh-110 - single-stage solid-propellant SRBM with a range of 200 km

Zelzal 1/2/3/3B - Single-stage SRBM with a range of 200 to 400 km

Qiam 1 - Tactical SRBM with a range of 750 km. Uses liquid fuel and has a smart targeting system.

CRUISE MISSILES

Nasr-1 - Iranian made short range missiles.

Meshkat - Iranian cruise missile with range of 2000 kilometers.(under development)

Qader - Iranian anti-ship cruise missile with a range over 200 km.

ANTI-TANK MISSILES

Raad - copy of Soviet AT-3 Sagger

RPG-7 - Copy of Soviet RPG-7. Iran is forecast to manufacture 2.88 percent of the worlds RPG-7's by 2014.

RPG-29

Saegheh - improved version of the RPG-7

Toophan - Copy of American TOW missile

Toophan 2 - Improved Toophan

Toophan 5 - Anti-armor, anti-tank missile with two warheads

Towsan - Iranian version of the 9M113 Konkurs/AT-5 Spandrel

For additional analytical, business and investment opportunities information, please contact Global Investment & Business Center, USA at (703) 370-8082. Fax: (703) 370-8083. E-mail: ibpusa3@gmail.com Global Business and Investment Info Databank - www.ibpus.com

Dehlaviyeh - Locally produced version of the Kornet-E

Tondar - Iranian made version of 9M119 Svir ATGM with max range of 4,000 meters.

RECOILLESS RIFLES

SPG-9 - reverse engineered version of 73mm SPG-9 recoilless rifle

106mm Recoilless rifle - Iranian version of M40 A2 recoilless rifle

AIR DEFENCE WEAPONS

Raad air defense system

Qaem - anti-helicopter, light-weight, laser guided missile

Raad - anti-helicopter system.

Misagh-1 - copy of Chinese QW-1 Vanguard with upgrades

Misagh-2 - copy of Chinese QW-2 Vanguard

23mm Anti-Aircraft Gun - Iranian version of ZU-23 which comes in one or two barrel configurations

Samavat 35mm Anti-Aircraft Guns - Copy of Oerlikon 35 mm twin cannon skyguard

Sa'ir 100mm Anti-Aircraft Guns - Upgraded automatic version of KS-19 100m gun, it can detect and intercept targets automatically through radar or optical systems at low and medium altitude

Shahab Thaqeb - copy of the Chinese HQ-7 (FM-80)

SM-1 copy of RIM-66 Standard.

Sayyad-1 / Sayyad-1A - upgraded copy of Chinese HQ-2,[88] Sayyad-1A has IR tracking.

Sayyad-2 (Hunter II). Upgraded version of the Sayyad-1 system with higher precision, range and defensive power. It is equipped with a 200-kilogram warhead and has a speed of 1,200 meters per second. The Sayyad-1 missile defense system is composed of two-stage missiles that can target all kinds of aircraft, including bombers, at medium and high altitudes.

Fajr-8 - upgrade of S-200

Fajr-27 - advanced sea rapid fire cannon

For additional analytical, business and investment opportunities information, please contact Global Investment & Business Center, USA at (703) 370-8082. Fax: (703) 370-8083. E-mail: ibpusa3@gmail.com Global Business and Investment Info Databank - www.ibpus.com

Fath (victory) - the 40-millimeter naval cannon's range is 12 km and shoots 300 projectiles per minute.

Mersad - Iran's first advanced air defense system based on the US MIM-23 Hawk. It is capable of hitting modern aircraft flying at low and medium altitudes. The Mersad system is equipped with sophisticated radar signal processing technology, an advanced launcher, and electronic equipment for guidance and target acquisition. Mersad uses domestically manufactured Shahin missiles.

Mesbah 1 air defense system - can target and destroy fighters, helicopters, cruise missiles and other objects flying at low altitude. Mesbah 1 is equipped with a three-dimensional interception radar and an optical guidance system. Mesbah 1 can fire four thousand rounds per minute.

Mehrab (altar) - surface-to-air medium-range smart missile. The Mehrab missile is equipped with anti-radar and anti-jamming systems, and if the enemy tries to jam the guidance system of the missile, it immediately identifies the source of the interference and changes its course toward the source and destroys the jammer.

Raad - Air defence system with range of 50 kilometers and engagement altitude of 25 to 27 kilometers

Bavar-373 (under development). Iran's corrected version of Russia's S-300 surface-to-air missile system, which uses two or three types of missiles to confront aerial targets in different layers.

Ya Zahra - Low-altitude mobile air defense system.

Soheil - Quadruped- MANPADS missile launcher, which can detect and intercept aerial targets.

Herz-9 - Passive low-altitude mobile air defense system with operating range of 10 km and operating altitude of 5 km .

Talaash- A mid-range, high altitude missile mobile air defense missile system which uses an upgraded copy of SM-1 (RIM-66) missile called Sayyad-2, on November 2013 Iran launched the production line of Sayyad-2 missile.(The whole system is still under development)

Asefeh - Asefeh is three-barrelled 23 mm Gatling gun that is reportedly capable of firing up to 900 rounds a minute, it is currently under development by IRGC ground force and will be used as a close in weapon system to defend against cruise missiles.

BOMBS

Zoobin electro-optically guided air to surface missile

Qadr - Electro-optically guided 2000 lb glide-bomb

Zoobin - Electro-optically guided 750 lb glide-bomb

Qassed I/II/III - Electro-optically guided 2000 lb bomb. Qassed-2 has a range about 50 km, Qassed-3 has a range of over 100 km

Asre - Laser-guided air-to-ground missile.

Kite - Stand-off sub-munitions dispenser.

Yasser - 750 lb air-to-ground missile.

Air-to-air missiles

Fatter - copy of U.S. AIM-9 Sidewinder

Sedjil - copy of U.S. MIM-23 Hawk converted to be carried by aircraft

Sattar 1/2/3/4 - Medium Range air-to-air missiles developed based on AIM-54 and MIM-23 Hawk

Fakour 90 - Iranian version of AIM-54 Phoenix, it was seccessfuly tested on February 2013.

NAVAL MISSILES

Khalije-Fars anti ship ballistic missile

Ra'ad - Indigenously developed long-range anti-ship missile based on HY-2 Silkworm.

Fajre Darya- copy of Sea Killer II.

Kowsar 1/2/3 - Several versions based on Chinese C-701 TL-10 and C-704

Nasr - Several versions based on TL-6 and C-705

Tondar - upgraded copy of Chinese C-801. Similar to Noor but powered by solid rocket booster and range of 50 km.

Thaqeb - Similar to Noor, modified for submarine launch.

Noor - upgraded copy of Chinese C-802.

Qader - Iranian anti-ship cruise missile with a range over 200 km.

For additional analytical, business and investment opportunities information, please contact Global Investment & Business Center, USA at (703) 370-8082. Fax: (703) 370-8083. E-mail: ibpusa3@gmail.com Global Business and Investment Info Databank - www.ibpus.com

Khalij Fars - Anti ship ballistic missile based on Fateh-110

Zafar - Indigenously developed short range anti ship missile.

Sadid-1 - Ultra light anti ship missile designed for naval version of Shahed 285

TORPEDO

Kuse

Yasin

Hoot - A supercavitation torpedo. Possible copy of the Russian VA-111 Shkval.

Valfajr

ARMORED VEHICLES

Iranian made Zulfiqar tank

Zulfiqar MBT - Developed from U.S. M60 Patton

T-72Z Safir-74 - Indigenously upgraded Soviet T-54/55 and Chinese Type 59

Mobarez - Indigenous upgrade of British Chieftain.

T-72S - Soviet T-72 produced under license in Iran

Sayyad - Quick reaction vehicle for unconventional warfare.

Tosan - Iranian light tank for unconventional warfare, developed from British FV101 Scorpion.

Cobra BMT-2 - Concept vehicle for the Boragh armed with 23 mm anti-aircraft gun for use as a fire support vehicle.

Boragh - Copy of Soviet BMP-1 with indigenous upgrades

Rakhsh - Iranian developed 4x4 armored personnel carrier

Sarir or Tala'iyeh - Newly developed 4x4 armored personnel carrier for IRGC

Hoveizeh - Ultra-light tracked APC.

OTHER VEHICLES

For additional analytical, business and investment opportunities information, please contact Global Investment & Business Center, USA at (703) 370-8082. Fax: (703) 370-8083. E-mail: ibpusa3@gmail.com Global Business and Investment Info Databank - www.ibpus.com

Safir multipurpose vehicle

Sepehr - Iranian tactical vehicle

Ranger tactical car - very light tactical car for using commandos - from this project, other type has built that calls 'Samandar'.

Safir Jeep

Tondar 1.4ton tactical car

Kaviran - 3.4ton tactical car

Neynava - 4x4 military truck of Iran-made

BABR 400 - Heavy military truck(8*8) and modified of Ukrainian MAZ-537

Aras Tactical Vehicle - 3.4ton Tactical Vehicle

Zoljanah heavy truck - 10x10 heavy duty truck

MORTARS

37mm Marsh Mortar - A compact commando mortar developed by the Iranian Army during the Iran-Iraq War

HM 12 - 60mm mortar

HM 13 - 60mm mortar

HM 14 - 60mm mortar

HM 15 - 81mm mortar

HM 16 - 120mm mortar

Razm Mortar - 120mm mortar

Vafa Mortar - 160mm mortar.

120mm mortar shells

130mm mortar shells

ARTILLERY

HM 40 - A 122mm howitzer

HM 41 - A 155mm howitzer

Wheeled 155-mm self-propelled howitzer

Raad 1 - SP gun Chinese Type WZ 501/503 armored infantry fighting vehicle with Russian 122mm gun mounted on top.

Raad 2 - SP gun based on the U.S. M109 howitzer

Basir - Laser guided 155 mm artillery shell capable of engaging moving targets at the range of 20 km.

ROCKET ARTILLERY

HM 20 - Iranian version of the BM-21

Arash - Iranian 122mm unguided artillery rocket

Oghab - Iranian 230mm unguided artillery rocket

Falaq-1 - Iranian 240mm unguided artillery rocket similar to BM-24

Falaq-2 - Iranian 333mm unguided artillery rocket

Fajr-1 - Iranian version of 107mm Type 63 MRS artillery rocket

Fajr-3 - artillery rocket

Fajr-5 - artillery rocket

Fajr 7 - artillery rocket with a range of over 64 km.

SMALL ARMS

MPT-9 - Tondar submachine gun - copy of MP5 (H & K licenced production)

KH-2002 - 5.56mm bullpup conversion kit for the M-16

S-5.56 - copy of Norinco CQ, Chinese clone of the M-16

KL-7.62 - copy of AKM

G3A6 - copy of G3 7.62 mm (H & K licenced production)

For additional analytical, business and investment opportunities information, please contact Global Investment & Business Center, USA at (703) 370-8082. Fax: (703) 370-8083. E-mail: ibpusa3@gmail.com Global Business and Investment Info Databank - www.ibpus.com

MGA3 - copy of MG3 7.62 mm (Rheinmetal licenced production)

PC-9 "Zoaf" - copy of Swiss-German SIG P226 pistol

PKM-T80 - copy of Soviet PKM

MGD-12.7mm - copy of Soviet DShkM

Nakhjir - copy of Soviet SVD

Sayyad - Iranian Steyr HS .50 clone with slightly different muzzle brake and curved pistol grip.

Shaher - Iranian developed caliber 14.5 sniper rifle.

Taktab - Iranian 20 mm sniper rifle under development.

Arash - Indigenous 20 mm sniper rifle.

BOATS AND DESTROYERS

Jamaran frigate

Sina class - heavily upgraded, French Kaman (Combattante II) class missile boats.

Paykan

Joshan

Derafsh

Kalat

Moudge class - upgraded and modified British Alvand (Saam) class (aka Vosper Mk 5 type) frigates.

Jamaran - multi-mission frigate with a displacement of around 1,400 tonnes, can carry 120-140 personnel on board and is armed with a variety of anti-ship and surface-to-air missiles.

Damavand

Zolfaqhar - fast attack craft/missile boat

Seraj - high-speed attack craft

For additional analytical, business and investment opportunities information, please contact Global Investment & Business Center, USA at (703) 370-8082. Fax: (703) 370-8083. E-mail: ibpusa3@gmail.com Global Business and Investment Info Databank - www.ibpus.com

Yunes 6 - six-passenger hovercraft

Tondar - Hovercraft with missile/drone launch capability

Kharg - Helicopter carrier

SELECTED GOVERNMENT AND BUSINESS CONTACTS IN IRAN

British Embassy In Tehran, Ferdossi Ave. Tehran, Iran Tel.: 0098-21-675011-17 Fax: 678 021

Jaam'e Jam TV Network
Through EuTel Sat and with the usage of hot bird 3 Satellite (13 Eastern, FR. 12. 43714 GHZ, H-POL) received in Europe with a dish of 60 cm, North Africa and theMiddle Asia, Western Iran, and the Persian Gulf region with a dish of 150cm.
Jaam'e Jam TV Network, P.O.Box 19395/3754 Tehran - IRAN
Tel.: 0098-21-2047642 - 2042914 Fax: 0098-21-204 3017 Email
The most favorite Programme is **Hamrah** 19:00-20:30 GMT
Tel.: 0098-21-216 2221, 205 4084 Fax: 216 2565

Ministry of Foreign Affairs Tel.: 0098-21-3211
Computer Dept.: 321 2867 - 311 4278
Consulate Dept.: 321 3235 - 40 - 3304
Eco Dept.: 321 3522
Immigration Dept.: 321 3220
Parliament Dept. (Dr. Hadi): 321 3280 - 3420 Fax: 675 447
Passport Dept.: 321 3245 - 47 - 51 - 33
Personnel Status Dept.: 321 3203 - 3346 - 3205 - 3218 - 3209
Publication Dept.: 321 2355 - 3379
Social Affair: 321 3260 - 3262

Red Crescent Society
Tel.: 0098-21-880 3871-8 Fax: 880 6666

TRANSPORTATION COMPANIES

Company Name: PARMAN INT'L TRANSPORT
Managing Director: Mr. FEREYDOUN REZAEI
Address: Iran, Tehran, .3rd Fl., No. 3, Azarshahr St., S. Kheradmand St., Karim Khan-e- Zand Ave
Tel: 8820475
Fax: 8837863 **Telex:** 214455
Company Name:)HAML BAR IRAN (INT`L TRANSPORT
Managing Director: Ms. FIROOZEH SAFFAR ZADEH
Address: Iran, Tehran, .No.41, Molkian Lane, North Iranshahr ave
Tel: 8820843
Fax: 835977 **Telex:** 212853

Company Name:)IRAN CONTARINER (TRANSPORT
Managing Director: Mr. FARSHID GELEH
Address: Iran, Tehran, No.127 (2ng Floor), Sout Kheradmand St., Karim Khan Zand Ave
Tel: 8824177 ,8822507
Fax: 8822507 **Telex:** 215510
Company Name:)IRAN SHETAB (TRANSPORT
Managing Director: Mr. LIDA MOVSESIAN
Address: Iran, Tehran, No.89 (3rd fl) W. Kayhan, S.Sohraverdi Ave
Tel: 8739367 ,8746543
Fax: 8753728
Company Name:)SHENEL (INT`L TRANSPORT
Managing Director: Mr. YOUSEF MOGHADDAMI FAR
Address: Iran, Tehran, No.246 (5th fl) N. Iranshahr st
Tel: 834920
Fax: 8827227
Company Name:)TAKAVAR IRAN (INT`L TRANSPORT
Managing Director: Mr. GHOLAM REZA HASSAN ZADEH GHASABEH
Address: Iran, Tehran, No.135 (3rd fl) N. Iranshahr st
Tel: 8847203-4 ,838837
Fax: 836322 **Telex:** 223402
Company Name:)TIRAN (INT`L TRANSPORT
Managing Director: Mr. HASSAN MIRZA ESMAEILI
Address: Iran, Tehran, No.1884, after Ayatollah Sadre bridge Shariyatee Ave
Tel: 2006497
Fax: 2006225 **Telex:** 226403 TIRA
Company Name:)TOUSHEHBAR (INT`L TRANSPORT
Managing Director: Mr. ANAHID SHAROYAN
Address: Iran, Tehran, No.44 (4th fl) Fajr st, Mottahari Ave
Tel: 8841118-9
Fax: 832673 **Telex:** 213689
Company Name: .BAR SEPID INT`L TRANSPORT CO
Managing Director: Mr. RAFI MOGHARDICHIAN
Address: Iran, Tehran, .No. 33, Delara Alley., Mirzai-e Shirazi Ave
Tel: 8899451
Fax: 8803494
Company Name: BARIRAN (INT`L TRANSPORT
Managing Director: Mr. SEYYED JALALODDIN POUR KHATIBI
Address: Iran, Tehran, No.359, (2 floor), After of 7 Tir Sq, Mofateh Ave
Tel: 8828906 ,8809816 ,8900729
Fax: 8890053

SPACE AGENCIES IN SELECTED COUNTRIES

Space agency	Country	Founded

For additional analytical, business and investment opportunities information, please contact Global Investment & Business Center, USA at (703) 370-8082. Fax: (703) 370-8083. E-mail: ibpusa3@gmail.com Global Business and Investment Info Databank - www.ibpus.com

Name	Initialisms/Acronym		
Belarus Space Agency		Belarus	2010
Aeronautics and Space Research and Diffusion Center (Spanish: Centro de Investigación y Difusión Aeronáutico-Espacial)	CIDA-E	Uruguay	5 August 1975
Mexican Space Agency (Spanish: Agencia Espacial Mexicana)	AEM	Mexico	30 July 2010
Algerian Space Agency French: Agence Spatiale Algérienne Berber: Tafullut Tadzayrit n Tallunt	ASAL	Algeria	16 January 2002
Asia Pacific Multilateral Cooperation in Space Technology and Applications (Chinese: 亚太空间技术应用多边合作会议)	AP-MCSTA	International	February 1992
Asia-Pacific Regional Space Agency Forum (Japanese: アジア太平洋地域宇宙機関会議)	APRSAF	International	1993
Asia-Pacific Space Cooperation Organization (Chinese: 亚太空间合作组织)	APSCO	International	28 October 2005
German: Agentur für Luft- und Raumfahrt (Aeronautics and Space Agency; also Austrian Space Agency; (Austrian Solar and Space Agency 1977–1987)	ALR	Austria	12 July 1972
Azerbaijani: Azərbaycan Milli Aerokosmik Agentliyinin (Azerbaijan National Aerospace Agency)	AMAKA	Azerbaijan	21 February 1974
Dutch: Belgisch Instituut voor Ruimte-Aëronomie French: Institut d'Aéronomie Spatiale de Belgique (Belgian Institute for Space Aeronomy)	BIRA IASB BISA	Belgium	25 November 1964
Spanish: Agencia Bolivariana para Actividades Espaciales (Bolivarian Agency for Space Activities)	ABAE	Venezuela	1 January 2008
Portuguese: Agência Espacial Brasileira (Brazilian Space Agency)	AEB	Brazil	10 February 1994
UK Space Agency	UKSA	United Kingdom	1 April 2010
Bolivian Space Agency	ABE	Bolivia	2012
Bulgarian: Българска академия на науките (Space Research Institute, Solar-Terrestrial Influences Institute) Bulgarian Space Agency	ИКИ-БАН SRI-BAS ИСЗВ-БАН STIL-BAS	Bulgaria	1987
Canadian Space Agency French: Agence spatiale canadienne	CSA ASC	Canada	1 March 1989
China National Space Administration	CNSA	People's Republic of	22 April 1993

For additional analytical, business and investment opportunities information, please contact Global Investment & Business Center, USA at (703) 370-8082. Fax: (703) 370-8083. E-mail: ibpusa3@gmail.com Global Business and Investment Info Databank - www.ibpus.com

(Chinese: 国家航天局)		China	
Spanish: Comisión Colombiana del Espacio (Colombian Space Commission)	CCE	Colombia	18 July 2006
Centre for Remote Imaging, Sensing and Processing	CRISP	Singapore	1995
Commonwealth Scientific and Industrial Research Organisation	CSIRO	Australia	1926
Consultative Committee for Space Data Systems	CCSDS	International	1982
Committee on Space Research	COSPAR	International	1958
Croatian: Hrvatska svemirska agencija (Croatian Space Agency)	HSA CSA	Croatia	October 2002
Czech: Ministerstvo dopravy České republiky (Ministry of Transport of the Czech Republic - Space Technologies and Satellite Systems Department)	Ministry of Transport of the Czech Republic	Czech Republic	2003
Danish National Space Center	DRC DNSC	Denmark	1 January 1968
(Danish Space Research Institute)	DRKI DSRI	Denmark	1 January 2005
Technical University of Denmark – National Space Institute	DTU Space	Denmark	1 January 2006
European Space Agency (French: Agence spatiale européenne) (German: Europäische Weltraumorganisation)	ESA ASE EWO	EU	31 May 1975
Geo-Informatics and Space Technology Development Agency	GISTDA สทอภ	Thailand	3 November 2002
German: Deutsches Zentrum für Luft- und Raumfahrt (German Aerospace Center)	DLR	Germany	1969
Hungarian: Magyar Űrkutatási Iroda (Hungarian Space Office)	MŰI HSO	Hungary	January 1992
Indian Space Research Organization	ISRO इसरो	India	15 August 1969
Greek: Ινστιτούτο Διαστημικών Εφαρμογών και Τηλεπισκόπησης (Institute for Space Applications and Remote Sensing)	ΙΔΕΤ ISARS	Greece	1955
Instituto Nacional de Técnica Aeroespacial	INTA	Spain	1942
Iranian Space Agency	ISA	Iran	2003
Israeli Space Agency	ISA סל"ה	Israel	April 1983
Italian Space Agency (Italian: Agenzia Spaziale Italiana)	ASI	Italy	1988

Japan Aerospace Exploration Agency	JAXA	Japan	1 October 2003
National Space Agency (KazCosmos); Kazakh Space Research Institute	NSA (KazCosmo s); SRI	Kazakhstan	1991
Korean Committee of Space Technology (Korean: 조선우주공간기술위원회)	KCST	North Korea	1980s
Korea Aerospace Research Institute	KARI	South Korea	10 October 1989
Lithuanian Space Association	LSA	Lithuania	2007
Malaysian National Space Agency (Malay: Agensi Angkasa Negara)	ANGKASA	Malaysia	2002
National Aeronautics and Space Administration	NASA	United States	1 October 1958
National Authority for Remote Sensing and Space Sciences	NARSS	Egypt	1994
French: Centre National d'Études Spatiales (National Center of Space Research)	CNES	France	19 December 1961
Spanish: Comisión Nacional de Investigación y Desarrollo Aeroespacial (National Commission for Aerospace Research and Development)	CONIDA	Peru	11 June 1974
Spanish: Comisión Nacional de Investigaciones Espaciales (National Commission for Space Research)	CNIE	Argentina	1961
Spanish: Comisión Nacional de Actividades Espaciales (National Space Activities Commission)	CONAE	Argentina	28 May 1991
Indonesian: Lembaga Antariksa dan Penerbangan Nasional (National Institute of Aeronautics and Space)	LAPAN	Indonesia	27 November 1964
National Remote Sensing Center of Mongolia	NRSC	Mongolia	1987
National Remote Sensing Center of Tunisia)	CNT	Tunisia	1988
Uzbek State Space Research Agency (UzbekCosmos)	USSRA (UzbekCos mos)	Uzbekistan	2001
Ukrainian: Національне космічне агентство України (National Space Agency of Ukraine)	НКАУ NSAU	Ukraine	2 March 1992
National Space Organization	NSPO	Republic of China (Taiwan)	October 1991
National Space Research and Development Agency	NASRDA	Nigeria	1998
Dutch: Stichting Ruimteonderzoek Nederland	SRON	Netherlands	1983

For additional analytical, business and investment opportunities information, please contact Global Investment & Business Center, USA at (703) 370-8082. Fax: (703) 370-8083. E-mail: ibpusa3@gmail.com Global Business and Investment Info Databank - www.ibpus.com

(Netherlands Institute for Space Research)			
Norwegian: Norsk Romsenter (Norwegian Space Centre)	NRS NSC	Norway	1987
Pakistan Space and Upper Atmosphere Research Commission (Urdu: پاکستان خلائی و بالا فضائی تحقیقاتی کمیشن)	SUPARCO سپارکو	Pakistan	16 September 1961
Portuguese: Gabinete do Espaço da FCT (FCT Space Office)	FCT SO	Portugal	2009
Romanian: Agenţia Spaţială Română (Romanian Space Agency)	ASR ROSA	Romania	1991
former Egypt Remote Sensing Center	EASRT-RSC	Egypt	1971
French: Centre Royal de Télédétection Spatiale Berber: Ammas Amrrukan n Tallunt (Royal Centre for Remote Sensing)	CRTS	Morocco	December 1989
Russian: Федеральное космическое агентство (Russian Federal Space Agency)	ROSCOSMOS	Russia	c.1992
	SLSA	Sri Lanka	2010
Turkish: TÜBİTAK Uzay Teknolojileri Araştırma Enstitüsü (TÜBİTAK UZAY) (TUBITAK Space Technologies Research Institute)	TÜBİTAK UZAY	Turkey	1985
Russian: Советская космическая программа (Soviet space program)	СССР	Soviet Union	ca. 1955
Space Research and Remote Sensing Organization	SPARRSO	Bangladesh	1980
Polish: Centrum Badań Kosmicznych PAN (Space Research Centre)	CBK-PAN SRC	Poland	1977
South African National Space Agency	SANSA	South Africa	2011
Space Research Institute of Saudi Arabia	KACST-SRI	Saudi Arabia	—
Vietnamese: Viện Công nghệ vũ trụ (Space Technology Institute)	CNVT VAST-STI	Vietnam	20 November 2006
Swedish: Rymdstyrelsen (Swedish National Space Board)	SNSB	Sweden	1972
Swiss Space Office	SSO	Switzerland	—
Turkmenistan National Space Agency		Turkmenistan	2011
United Nations Office for Outer Space Affairs	UNOOSA	United Nations	13 December 1958
United Nations Committee on the Peaceful Uses of Outer Space	UNCOPUOS	United Nations	12 December 1959
United & Independent Space Agency (in	UISA	Internationa	1 May 2013 (Expected)

For additional analytical, business and investment opportunities information, please contact Global Investment & Business Center, USA at (703) 370-8082. Fax: (703) 370-8083. E-mail: ibpusa3@gmail.com Global Business and Investment Info Databank - www.ibpus.com

formation)			
Space Technology Institute	STI	Vietnam	2006

SPACE AGENCIES WITH LAUNCH CAPABILITY

Space agency		Country	Founded	Capabilities of the space agency			
Name	Acronym			Launch capable	Multiple Satellites Launch capable	Operates Extraterrestrial Probe	Recoverable Satellites capable
China National Space Administration	CNSA	People's Republic of China	22 April 1993	Yes	Yes	Yes	Yes
European Space Agency (French: Agence spatiale européenne) (German: Europäische Weltraumorganisation)	ESA ASE EWO	Austria Belgium Czech Republic Denmark Finland France Germany Greece Ireland Italy Luxembourg Netherlands Norway Portugal Poland Romania Spain Sweden Switzerland United Kingdom	31 May 1975	Yes	Yes	Yes	No
Iranian Space Agency	ISA ISA	Iran	2003	Yes	No	No	No
Israeli Space Agency (Hebrew: סוכנות החלל הישראלית) (Arabic: وكالة الفضاء الإسرائيلية)	ISA סל"ה	Israel	April 1983	Yes	No	No	No
Korea Aerospace Research Institute (Korean: 한국항공우주연구원) (Hanja: 韓國航空宇宙研究院)	KCST	North Korea	1980s	Yes	No	No	No
Korea Aerospace Research Institute (Korean: 한국항공우주연구원) (Hanja: 韓國航空宇宙研究院)	KARI 항우연	South Korea	October 1989	Yes	No	No	No
Indian Space Research Organization (Hindi: भारती य	ISRO इसरो	India	15 August 1969	Yes	Yes	Yes	Yes

For additional analytical, business and investment opportunities information, please contact Global Investment & Business Center, USA at (703) 370-8082. Fax: (703) 370-8083. E-mail: ibpusa3@gmail.com Global Business and Investment Info Databank - www.ibpus.com

अंतरिक्ष अनुसंधान संगठन)							
Japan Aerospace Exploration Agency (Japanese: 宇宙航空研究開発機構)	JAXA	Japan	1 October 2003	Yes	Yes	Yes	Yes
National Aeronautics and Space Administration	NASA	United States	1 October 1958	Yes	Yes	Yes	Yes
French: Centre National d'Études Spatiales (National Center of Space Research)	CNES	France	19 December 1961	Yes	Yes	No	No
Ukrainian: Національне космічне агентство України (National Space Agency of Ukraine)	НКАУ NSAU	Ukraine	2 March 1992	Yes	Yes	No	No
Russian: Федеральное космическое агентство (Russian Federal Space Agency (Roscosmos))	ROSCOSMOS RFSA	Russia	ca. 1992	Yes	Yes	Yes	Yes
Russian: Советская космическая программа (Soviet space program)	СССР	Soviet Union	ca. 1955	Yes	Yes	Yes	Yes

SPACE AGENCIES WITH MANNED SPACEFLIGHT CAPABILITY

Space agency		Country	Founded	Accomplished tasks by the Space Agency				
Name	Acronym			Manned Spaceflight capable	Manned Space launch capable	Spacewalk capable	Space Rendezvous and Docking capable	Operates Space Station
China National Space Administration	CNSA	People's Republic of China	22 April 1993	Yes	Yes	Yes	Yes	Yes
European Space Agency		esa	1975	No	No	Yes	Yes	Yes
National Aeronautics and Space Administration	NASA	United States	1 October 1958	Yes	No (since 2011)	Yes	Yes	Yes
(Russian Federal Space Agency)	ROSCOSMOS RFSA	Russia	ca. 1992	Yes	Yes	Yes	Yes	Yes

ACHIEVEMENTS OF SPACE AGENCIES WITH LUNAR LANDING CAPABILITY

Space agency		Country	Founded	Terminated	Accomplished tasks by the Space Agency				
Name	Acronym				Circumlunar Manned Spaceflight	Unmanned Moon Soft Landing	Unmanned (automated) lunar rover operation	Automated Lunar sample return mission	Manned Moon Landing and sample return
China National Space	CNSA	People's Republic	22 April 1993	—	No	Yes	Yes	No	No

Administration)		**of China**							
National Aeronautics and Space Administration	**NASA**	**United States**	**1 October 1958**	**—**	**Yes**	**Yes**	**No**	**No**	**Yes**
Russian: (Soviet space program)	**CCCP**	**Soviet Union**	**ca. 1955**	**ca. 1991**	**No**	**Yes**	**Yes**	**Yes**	**No**

EXPECTED FUTURE SPACE AGENCIES

Space agency		Country	Possible expected date of foundation	Current status
Name	Acronym			
Pan-Arab Space Agency	PASA	Arab League	—	At proposal stage
African Space Agency	AfriSpace	African Union	—	At proposal stage
Philippine Space Agency	PSA	Philippines		At proposal stage
Sri Lanka Aeronautics and Space Agency	SLASA	Sri Lanka		Immediate goal is to construct and launch two satellites. Sri Lankan Telecommunications Regulatory Commission has signed an agreement with Surrey Satellite Technology Ltd to get relevant help and resources.

TOP COUNTRIES WITH SPACE PROGRAMS

Space exploration makes up a significant chunk in the budgets of some of the world's developed countries today. Read on below to learn more about who's spending the most when it comes to international space spending.

10. Iran – $500 million

The Iran Space Agency runs the country's space exploration programs, and is also a participant in the Asian space race. The Iran Space Agency was created in 2004, with the mandate to support all space-related activities in the country governed by the country's president. Iran was responsible for creating satellite launch vehicle after 2000 when they had the necessary training and preparation to begin production. Iranian satellite launch vehicles include the Shahab 3, Safir SLV, Safir-1B, Simorgh LV, and Qoqnoos SLV.

9. Italy – $1 billion

Italy's space exploration projects are headed by the Italian Space Agency, a government agency created with the mandate to regulate, coordinate, and fund the country's space exploration activities. Early projects were carried out in cooperation with NASA, which eventually led to the conceptualization and development of Italy's first satellite. Since Italy is one of the key countries involved in space exploration early on, it has been a

For additional analytical, business and investment opportunities information, please contact Global Investment & Business Center, USA at (703) 370-8082. Fax: (703) 370-8083. E-mail: ibpusa3@gmail.com Global Business and Investment Info Databank - www.ibpus.com

founder and played an important role in the European Launcher Development Program, as well as the European Space Research Organization. In March of 2013, Italy and the United States signed a bilateral agreement to celebrate both countries' 50 year partnership in working with space exploration projects. The bilateral agreement is poised to lead the way for new opportunities in technological, economical, and scientific sectors.

8. China – $1.3 billion

The China National Space Administration directs the country's space programs, together with the China Aerospace Corporation. China has some ongoing projects in space exploration, including the Tiangong 1 space laboratory module in 2011, and the Change 3 lunar-lander and rover exploration as well as the Shenzhou 10 in 2013.

7. India – $1.3 billion

Space exploration in India is carried out by the Indian Space Research Organization, which is among the largest space agencies in the world. The ISRO works to find developments in space technology for the benefit of the country. Since it was first established in 1969, the ISRO has had significant contributions to space exploration including the development of India's first satellite called the Aryabhatta. In 1980, the ISRO also developed the first satellite in orbit, Rohini. Today, the ISRO is also responsible for the operation of earth observation satellites including the INSAT Series, IRS Series, Radar Imaging Satellites, as well as other satellites.

6. Germany – $2 billion

The German Aerospace Center operates the energy, aerospace, and transport center for Germany. The agency is involved in various space projects, operated both locally and internationally with other alliances abroad and they are also responsible for planning and carrying out German space related programs for the government. The agency is also mandated to explore the earth, solar system, and conduct research that will benefit the environment, while helping develop space technology that is environmentally-friendly. One of the most significant contributions of the German Aerospace Center to the Mars Express Mission of the ESA is the High Resolution Stereo Camera (HRSC), which was the first digital stereo camera which also utilized extremely high resolution lenses.

5. Japan – $ 2.5 billion

The Japan Aerospace Exploration Agency was founded in October 2003, designed to help with the research, development, and technology for space exploration as well as launching satellites into orbit. The agency is also involved in other advanced missions who haven't been partaken by other countries yet, such as asteroid exploration. They are also looking into sending manned expeditions to the moon. Japan has been successful in carrying out various aerospace projects in the past, such as in X-ray astronomy, VLBI (Very Long Base Interferometry), solar observation, and magnetosphere research.

For additional analytical, business and investment opportunities information, please contact Global Investment & Business Center, USA at (703) 370-8082. Fax: (703) 370-8083. E-mail: ibpusa3@gmail.com Global Business and Investment Info Databank - www.ibpus.com

4. France – $2.8 billion

The French space agency Centre national d'études spatiales has been commissioned to work on access to space, sustainable development, security, defense, civil applications of space, and science and technology research. The agency is currently working on projects where they are experimenting with microgravity, and they are also currently collaborating with other international agencies for other projects. France is also the only country with paid UFO investigators, and they have also published their UFO findings on the website and in publications.

3. European Space Agency – $5.3 billion

The European Space Agency is comprised of 20 members states of the European Union. With headquarters in Paris, the ESA is solely dedicated to space exploration. The agency's space flight program also includes human space flight in their participation in the International Space Station program. The ESA is also responsible for unmanned launches to the Moon, and have contributed significantly to science and telecommunications projects. Each of the 20 member states participate in varying degrees to both the agency's mandatory and optional space programs.

2. Russia – $5.6 billion

The Russian Federal Space Agency, also known as Roscosmos, carries out Russia's aerospace programs and research. The Russian space programs are currently focused around the Angara rockets, and development of new tools for communications and navigation. Paying passengers can also avail of the agency's space tourism project, where space tourists pay a fee of $20 million to be flown into space.

1. U.S.A. – $18 billion

The National Aeronautics and Space Administration (NASA) is responsible for developing and operating space programs of the United States. Since the NASA began operations in 1958, they have been at the frontier of many space exploration projects, including the Space Shuttle, the Apollo program, and the Skylab space station. Current programs include the Commercial Crew Program, Beyond Low Earth Orbit Program, and a number of unmanned projects which have been created with the purpose of exploring the earth as well as the solar system. NASA also has existing investigations to learn more about Mars and Saturn. Ongoing spacecraft missions also include the Messenger Program, the first spacecraft to ever orbit Mercury; New Horizons which has been orbiting Jupiter and Pluto; and the Dawn, a space probe designed to explore Vesta and Ceres, two massive objects found within the asteroid belt.

BASIC TITLES ON IRAN

IMPORTANT!

All publications are updated annually!

Please contact IBP, Inc. at ibpusa3@gmail.com for the latest ISBNs and additional information

title

title
Iran A "Spy" Guide - Strategic Information and Developments
Iran A Spy" Guide"
Iran Air Force Handbook
Iran Air Force Handbook
Iran Banking & Financial Market Handbook
Iran Banking & Financial Market Handbook
Iran Business and Investment Opportunities Yearbook
Iran Business and Investment Opportunities Yearbook
Iran Business and Investment Opportunities Yearbook Volume 1 Strategic Information and Opportunities
Iran Business and Investment Opportunities Yearbook Volume 2 Leading Export-Import, Business, Investment Opportunities and Projects
Iran Business Intelligence Report - Practical Information, Opportunities, Contacts
Iran Business Intelligence Report - Practical Information, Opportunities, Contacts
Iran Business Law Handbook - Strategic Information and Basic Laws
Iran Business Law Handbook - Strategic Information and Basic Laws
Iran Business Law Handbook - Strategic Information and Basic Laws
Iran Business Law Handbook - Strategic Information and Basic Laws
Iran Clothing and Textile Industry Handbook
Iran Company Laws and Regulations Handbook
Iran Constitution and Citizenship Laws Handbook - Strategic Information and Basic Laws
Iran Country Study Guide - Strategic Information and Developments
Iran Country Study Guide - Strategic Information and Developments
Iran Country Study Guide - Strategic Information and Developments Volume 1 Strategic Information and Developments
Iran Customs, Trade Regulations and Procedures Handbook
Iran Customs, Trade Regulations and Procedures Handbook
Iran Diplomatic Handbook - Strategic Information and Developments
Iran Diplomatic Handbook - Strategic Information and Developments
Iran Ecology & Nature Protection Handbook
Iran Ecology & Nature Protection Handbook
Iran Ecology & Nature Protection Laws and Regulation Handbook
Iran Economic & Development Strategy Handbook
Iran Economic & Development Strategy Handbook
Iran Energy Policy, Laws and Regulation Handbook
Iran Energy Policy, Laws and Regulations Handbook
Iran Energy Policy, Laws and Regulations Handbook
Iran Energy Sector Handbook
Iran Energy Sector Handbook
Iran Export-Import and Business Directory
Iran Export-Import and Business Directory
Iran Foreign Policy and Government Guide
Iran Foreign Policy and Government Guide
Iran Free Economic Zones Laws and Regulations Handbook
Iran Free Economic Zones Laws and Regulations Handbook
Iran Government and Business Contacts Handbook
Iran Government and Business Contacts Handbook
Iran Immigration Laws and Regulations Handbook - Strategic Information and Basic Laws
Iran Industrial and Business Directory

For additional analytical, business and investment opportunities information, please contact Global Investment & Business Center, USA at (703) 370-8082. Fax: (703) 370-8083. E-mail: ibpusa3@gmail.com
Global Business and Investment Info Databank - www.ibpus.com

title
Iran Insolvency (Bankruptcy) Laws and Regulations Handbook - Strategic Information and Basic Laws
Iran Internet and E-Commerce Investment and Business Guide - Strategic and Practical Information: Regulations and Opportunities
Iran Investment and Business Guide - Strategic and Practical Information
Iran Investment and Business Guide - Strategic and Practical Information
Iran Investment and Business Guide - Strategic and Practical Information
Iran Investment and Business Guide Volume 2 Business, Investment Opportunities and Incentives
Iran Investment and Trade Laws and Regulations Handbook
Iran Labor Laws and Regulations Handbook - Strategic Information and Basic Laws
Iran Land Ownership and Agriculture Laws Handbook
Iran Mineral & Mining Sector Investment and Business Guide - Strategic and Practical Information
Iran Mineral & Mining Sector Investment and Business Guide - Strategic and Practical Information
Iran Mining Laws and Regulations Handbook
Iran Mining Laws and Regulations Handbook
Iran Nuclear Programs and Projects Handbook
Iran Nuclear Programs Handbook
Iran Oil & Gas Sector Business & Investment Opportunities Yearbook
Iran Oil & Gas Sector Business & Investment Opportunities Yearbook
Iran Political and Economic Strategy Handbook
Iran President and Political System Handbook
Iran Recent Economic and Political Developments Yearbook
Iran Starting Business (Incorporating) in....Guide
Iran Tax Guide
Iran Taxation Laws and Regulations Handbook
Iran Telecom Laws and Regulations Handbook
Iran Telecommunication Industry Business Opportunities Handbook
Iran Telecommunication Industry Business Opportunities Handbook
Iran Transportation Policy and Regulations Handbook
Iran: How to Invest, Start and Run Profitable Business in Iran Guide - Practical Information, Opportunities, Contacts

GLOBAL ARMY, DEFENSE, INTELLIGENCE, COUNTERINTELLIGENCE, NATIONAL SECURITY HANDBOOK LIBRARY

(PRICE $149.95 each)

Ultimate handbooks on army, defense policy, intelligence, counterintelligence, national security and related operation, conducted by specific countries. National security and intelligence agencies operations and structure

TITLE
1. Albania Army, National Security and Defense Policy Handbook
2. Argentina Intelligence & Security Activities & Operations Handbook
3. Australia Army, National Security and Defense Policy Handbook
4. Australia Intelligence & Security Activities & Operations Handbook
5. Bangladesh Army, National Security and Defense Policy Handbook
6. Bulgaria and NATO Handbook
7. Bulgaria Department of Defense Handbook
8. Canada Intelligence & Security Activities & Operations Handbook
9. Canadian Security Intelligence Service (CSIS) Handbook
10. China Army, National Security and Defense Policy Handbook
11. Cuba Army, National Security and Defense Policy Handbook
12. Czech Republic Army, National Security and Defense Policy Handbook
13. Estonia Army, National Security and Defense Policy Handbook
14. Estonia Intelligence & Security Activities & Operations Handbook
15. EUROPOL – EUROPEAN POLICE OFFICE Handbook
16. Finland Army, National Security and Defense Policy Handbook
17. Finland Intelligence & Security Activities & Operations Handbook
18. France Army, National Security and Defense Policy Handbook
19. German Intelligence & Security Activities & Operations Handbook
20. Germany Army, National Security and Defense Policy Handbook
21. Global Counter-Terrorism Handbook
22. Global National Intelligence and Security Agencies Handbook
23. Global Terrorism Attacks Encyclopedic Handbook
24. Greece Army, National Security and Defense Policy Handbook

To order and for additional analytical and marketing information, please contacrt
International Business Publications, USA at:
P.O. Box 15343, Washington, DC 20003, USA. Phone: (202) 546-2103. Fax: (202) 546-3275.
E-mail: rusric@erols.com
http://www.ibpus.com

TITLE
25. Greece Intelligence & Security Activities & Operations Handbook
26. Hungary Army, National Security and Defense Policy Handbook
27. Hungary Intelligence & Security Activities & Operations Handbook
28. India Army, National Security and Defense Policy Handbook
29. India Intelligence & Security Activities & Operations Handbook
30. Iraq Economic Sanctions, Customs, Trade Regulations and Procedures Handbook
31. Ireland Army, National Security and Defense Policy Handbook
32. Ireland Intelligence & Security Activities & Operations Handbook
33. Israel Army, National Security and Defense Policy Handbook
34. Israel Intelligence & Security Activities & Operations Handbook
35. Italy Intelligence & Security Activities & Operations Handbook
36. Japan Army, National Security and Defense Policy Handbook
37. Japan Intelligence & Security Activities & Operations Handbook
38. Jordan Intelligence & Security Activities & Operations Handbook
39. Korea North Army, National Security and Defense Policy Handbook
40. Korea South Army, National Security and Defense Policy Handbook
41. Korea South Intelligence & Security Activities & Operations Handbook
42. Latvia Army, National Security and Defense Policy Handbook
43. Lebanon Army, National Security and Defense Policy Handbook
44. Lithuania Army, National Security and Defense Policy Handbook
45. Macedonia National Security, Army and Defense Policy Handbook
46. Malaysia Army, National Security and Defense Policy Handbook
47. Myanmar Army, National Security and Defense Policy Handbook
48. New Zealand Army, National Security and Defense Policy Handbook
49. New Zealand Intelligence & Security Activities & Operations Handbook
50. Norway Army, National Security and Defense Policy Handbook
51. Pakistan Army, National Security and Defense Policy Handbook
52. Pakistan Intelligence & Security Activities & Operations Handbook
53. Philippines Army, National Security and Defense Policy Handbook
54. Poland Army, National Security and Defense Policy Handbook
55. Portugal Intelligence & Security Activities & Operations Handbook
56. Romania Army, National Security and Defense Policy Handbook
57. Romania Intelligence & Security Activities & Operations Handbook
58. Russia Army, National Security and Defense Policy Handbook
59. Russia Intelligence & Security Activities & Operations Handbook
60. Russian KGB Handbook: Past and Present
61. Russian Navy Handbook: History and Modern Situation

To order and for additional analytical and marketing information, please contacrt
International Business Publications, USA at:
P.O. Box 15343, Washington, DC 20003, USA. Phone: (202) 546-2103. Fax: (202) 546-3275.
E-mail: rusric@erols.com
http://www.ibpus.com

TITLE
62. Russia-NATO Cooperation Handbook
63. Singapore Army, National Security and Defense Policy Handbook
64. Slovak Republic Army, National Security and Defense Policy Handbook
65. South Africa Army, National Security and Defense Policy Handbook
66. South Africa Intelligence & Security Activities & Operations Handbook
67. Sri Lanka Army, National Security and Defense Policy Handbook
68. Starting Business (Incorporating) in India Encyclopedic Guide
69. Sweden Intelligence & Security Activities & Operations Handbook
70. Switzerland Army, National Security and Defense Policy Handbook
71. Switzerland Intelligence & Security Activities & Operations Handbook
72. Taiwan Army, National Security and Defense Policy Handbook
73. Taiwan Intelligence & Security Activities & Operations Handbook
74. Thailand Royal Army, National Security and Defense Policy Handbook
75. The French Foreign Legion Handbook
76. The INTERPOL Handbook
77. The United Stated Ambassadors Yearbook
78. Turkey Army, National Security and Defense Policy Handbook
79. Turkey Intelligence & Security Activities & Operations Handbook
80. UK Department of Trade and Industry (DTI) Handbook
81. UK Intelligence & Counterintelligence Handbook
82. UK Intelligence & Security Activities & Operations Handbook
83. UK Intelligence and Security Policy Handbook
84. UK MI5 Security Service Handbook
85. UK Military Intelligence Handbook
86. UK National Intelligence Service Handbook
87. UK National Police Handbook
88. UK Royal Air force Handbook
89. UK Royal Army Handbook
90. UK Royal Navy Handbook
91. Ukraine Army, National Security and Defense Policy Handbook
92. Ukraine Intelligence & Security Activities & Operations Handbook
93. United Kingdom Army, National Security and Defense Policy Handbook
94. US Arms Sales to Foreign Countries Handbook
95. US Business Intelligence Handbook
96. US Counterintelligence Operations against Cuba Handbook
97. US Defense Policy Handbook
98. US Federal Depository Libraries Directory

To order and for additional analytical and marketing information, please contacrt
International Business Publications, USA at:
P.O. Box 15343, Washington, DC 20003, USA. Phone: (202) 546-2103. Fax: (202) 546-3275.
E-mail: rusric@erols.com
http://www.ibpus.com

TITLE
99. US Federal Government Directory
100. US Federal Grant Management Handbook
101. US Military Intelligence Handbook
102. US Ocean Transportation Companies Directory
103. US Political Intelligence Handbook
104. US War Against International Terrorism Handbook
105. US War Against Iraq Handbook: Political Strategy and Operations
106. US-Russia Cooperation Against Terrorism Handbook
107. US-Russia Economic & Financial Cooperation Handbook
108. US-Russia Military Cooperation Handbook
109. US-Russia Political Cooperation Handbook
110. US-Russia Scientific & Technological Cooperation Handbook
111. US-Russia Space Cooperation Handbook

To order and for additional analytical and marketing information, please contacrt
International Business Publications, USA at:
P.O. Box 15343, Washington, DC 20003, USA. Phone: (202) 546-2103. Fax: (202) 546-3275.
E-mail: rusric@erols.com
http://www.ibpus.com

GLOBAL WEAPON SYSTEMS HANDBOOK LIBRARY

(PRICE $149.95)

Ultimate handbooks on army, defense policy, intelligence, counterintelligence, national security and related operation, conducted by specific countries. National security and intelligence agencies

Albania Armed Forced Weapon Systems Handbook
Australia Armed Forced Weapon Systems Handbook
Bangladesh Armed Forced Weapon Systems Handbook
Bulgaria Armed Forced Weapon Systems Handbook
Canada Armed Forced Weapon Systems Handbook
China Armed Forced Weapon Systems Handbook
Cuba Armed Forced Weapon Systems Handbook
Czech Republic Armed Forced Weapon Systems Handbook
Estonia Armed Forced Weapon Systems Handbook
Finland Armed Forced Weapon Systems Handbook
France Armed Forced Weapon Systems Handbook
Germany Armed Forced Weapon Systems Handbook
Greece Armed Forced Weapon Systems Handbook
Hungary Armed Forced Weapon Systems Handbook
India Armed Forced Weapon Systems Handbook
Ireland Armed Forced Weapon Systems Handbook
Israel Armed Forced Weapon Systems Handbook
Italy Armed Forced Weapon Systems Handbook
Japan Armed Forced Weapon Systems Handbook
Jordan Armed Forced Weapon Systems Handbook
Korea North Armed Forced Weapon Systems Handbook
Korea South Armed Forced Weapon Systems Handbook
Latvia Armed Forced Weapon Systems Handbook
Lebanon Armed Forced Weapon Systems Handbook
Lithuania Armed Forced Weapon Systems Handbook
Macedonia Armed Forced Weapon Systems Handbook
Malaysia Armed Forced Weapon Systems Handbook
Myanmar Armed Forced Weapon Systems Handbook
New Zealand Armed Forced Weapon Systems Handbook
Norway Armed Forced Weapon Systems Handbook
Pakistan Armed Forced Weapon Systems Handbook
Philippines Armed Forced Weapon Systems Handbook
Poland Armed Forced Weapon Systems Handbook
Portugal Armed Forced Weapon Systems Handbook
Romania Armed Forced Weapon Systems Handbook
Russia Armed Forced Weapon Systems Handbook
Singapore Armed Forced Weapon Systems Handbook
Slovak Republic Armed Forced Weapon Systems Handbook
South Africa Armed Forced Weapon Systems Handbook
Sri Lanka Armed Forced Weapon Systems Handbook
Switzerland Armed Forced Weapon Systems Handbook
Taiwan Armed Forced Weapon Systems Handbook
Thailand Armed Forced Weapon Systems Handbook
Turkey Armed Forced Weapon Systems Handbook
United Kingdom Armed Forced Weapon Systems Handbook

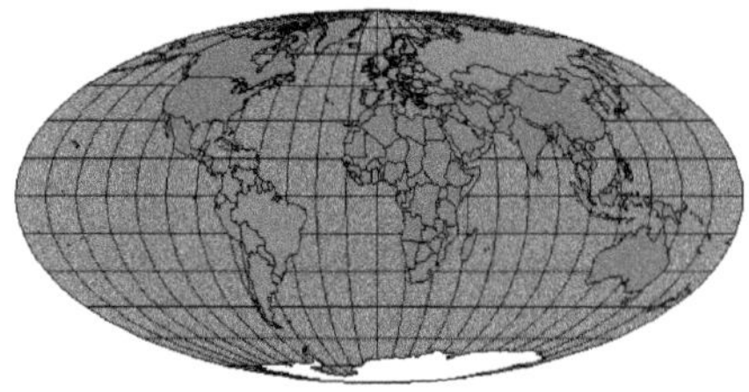

WORLD AIR FORCE HANDBOOKS LIBRARY

Detailed strategic information and contacts on air force of the respected country

Price: $99.95 Each

TITLE
1. Albania Air Force Handbook
2. Algeria Air Force Handbook
3. Argentina Air Force Handbook
4. Australia Air Force Handbook
5. Austria Air Force Handbook
6. Bangladesh Air Force Handbook
7. Belgium Air Force Handbook
8. Bolivia Air Force Handbook
9. Brazil Air Force Handbook
10. Brunei Air Force Handbook
11. Bulgaria Air Force Handbook
12. Canada Air Force Handbook
13. Chile Air Force Handbook
14. China Air Force Handbook
15. Croatia Air Force Handbook
16. Cuba Air Force Handbook
17. Cyprus Air Force Handbook
18. Czech Republic Air Force Handbook
19. Denmark Air Force Handbook
20. Egypt Air Force Handbook
21. El Salvador Air Force Handbook
22. Estonia Air Force Handbook
23. Finland Air Force Handbook
24. France Air Force Handbook
25. Germany Air Force Handbook
26. Greece Air Force Handbook
27. Honduras Air Force Handbook
28. Hong Kong Air Force Handbook
29. Hungary Air Force Handbook
30. Iceland Air Force Handbook
31. India Air Force Handbook
32. Indonesia Air Force Handbook
33. Iran Air Force Handbook
34. Iraq Air Force Handbook
35. Ireland Air Force Handbook
36. Israel Air Force Handbook
37. Italy Air Force Handbook
38. Jamaica Air Force Handbook
39. Japan Air Force Handbook
40. Latvia Air Force Handbook
41. Lithuania Air Force Handbook
42. Macedonia Air Force Handbook

TITLE
43. Malaysia Air Force Handbook
44. Mexico Air Force Handbook
45. Mongolia Air Force Handbook
46. Morocco Air Force Handbook
47. NATO Air Force Handbook
48. Nepal Air Force Handbook
49. The Netherlands Air Force Handbook
50. New Zealand Air Force Handbook
51. North Korea Air Force Handbook
52. Norway Air Force Handbook
53. Oman Air Force Handbook
54. Pakistan Air Force Handbook
55. Panama Air Force Handbook
56. Paraguay Air Force Handbook
57. Peru Air Force Handbook
58. Philippines Air Force Handbook
59. Poland Air Force Handbook
60. Portugal Air Force Handbook
61. Romania Air Force Handbook
62. Russia Air Force Handbook
63. Saudi Arabia Air Force Handbook
64. Serbia Air Force Handbook
65. Singapore Air Force Handbook
66. Slovakia Air Force Handbook
67. Slovenia Air Force Handbook
68. South Africa Air Force Handbook
69. South Korea Air Force Handbook
70. Spain Air Force Handbook
71. Sri Lanka Air Force Handbook
72. Sweden Air Force Handbook
73. Switzerland Air Force Handbook
74. Syria Air Force Handbook
75. Taiwan Air Force Handbook
76. Thailand Air Force Handbook
77. Tunisia Air Force Handbook
78. Turkey Air Force Handbook
79. Ukraine Air Force Handbook
80. Uruguay Air Force Handbook
81. Venezuela Air Force Handbook
82. Yugoslavia Air Force Handbook

For additional analytical, business and investment opportunities information,
Please contact Global Investment & Business Center, USA
at (202) 546-2103. Fax: (202) 546-3275. E-mail: rusric@erols.com
http://www.ibpus.com

www.ingramcontent.com/pod-product-compliance
Ingram Content Group UK Ltd.
Pitfield, Milton Keynes, MK11 3LW, UK
UKHW051459290926
15471UKWH00008B/1305

9 781438 723839